RETAILING
SHOPPING, SOCIETY, SPACE

LARRY O'BRIEN

Special Needs Information
Research Unit
Department of Geography
University of Newcastle upon Tyne

FRANK HARRIS

Department of Geography and Geology
Cheltenham and Gloucester College
of Higher Education, Cheltenham

David Fulton Publishers
London

David Fulton Publishers Ltd
2 Barbon Close, London WC1N 3JX

First published in Great Britain by
David Fulton Publishers, 1991

Note: The right of L. G. O'Brien and F. W. Harris to be identified as authors of
this work has been asserted by them in accordance with the Copyright, Designs
and Patents Act 1988.

British Library Cataloguing in Publication Data

O'Brien, L. G.
  Retailing: shopping, society, space.
  1. Great Britain. Retail trades
  I. Title   II. Harris, F. W.
  381.10941

  ISBN 1-85346-122-9

Typeset by Chapterhouse, Formby

Printed in Great Britain by BPCC Wheatons Ltd, Exeter

Contents

List of Figures

List of Tables

Preface

This is a book about the retailing industry and its various spatial expressions in Britain. Retailing is an industry; indeed it is one of Britain's largest industries, but it is so familiar to the general public that we tend to take it for granted. Most of us buy things in shops at one time or another but, unless we happen to work there, very few of us visit factories, shipyards or working farms. We therefore tend to assume that shops will be with us just as they have been in the past. But they have not always been with us in the past, and it is debatable that the shops of the next century will look very much like the ones we have now.

The purpose of this book is to describe the factors which influence British retailing. As economic geographers we have emphasised factors which have a spatial dimension. However the spatial structure of society does not exist independently of economic, social and historical factors whose influences range from the local to international scales. Space simply adds the experience of 'real places' to abstract theory.

A large number of people have contributed to this work by providing examples of retailing change in specific parts of Britain and abroad, or by reviewing and commenting on the perspective we have adopted. We owe the following our particular thanks: Ewan Anderson, Peter Atkins, Bill Brown, Martin Charlton, Peter Dicken, Cliff Guy, Elizabeth Howard, Ray Hudson, Peter Lloyd, Mark McFetridge, Malcolm Newson, Donald Nisbet, Mark Overton, Peter Taylor, Nigel Thrift, Neil Wrigley and two anonymous referees who helped clarify the debate at an early stage. Sheila Taylor, Anne Hedison and Erica Breuning made valuable contributions to the production of early drafts. We would particularly like to thank Richard Hookway for his transformation of our cryptic sketches into the illustrations, and our publisher, David Fulton, for his patience. Most importantly however, we would like to thank our families (Ottie, Matthew, Julia, John and David) who not only provided space for our work, but also contributed an enormous quantity of practical information on contemporary retailing. The usual limitations on responsibility apply.

Introduction

Themes

This book is about shops and shopping in Britain and the retailing industry which supports them. Its purpose is threefold:

(1) To describe the contemporary retailing system and to show why it exists and how it seeks to meet consumer needs.
(2) To describe the relationships between these needs and the built environment, concentrating on those factors which lead to spatial patterns in shopping provision (for example, in high streets, shopping centres of various types, and edge-of-town developments such as retail parks).
(3) To describe the dynamic nature of retailing, emphasising the relationships between retailers, consumers, developers and land use managers (such as local authority planners), whose combined influences affect the visible character, style and ambience of British townscapes.

The principal thrust of the text is geographical, focusing on the types of retailing which can be found in towns and cities around Britain. This perspective provides retailing with its 'spatial face', which is the visible expression in local economies of underlying social, historical, economic and political processes. These may be idiosyncratic to the area concerned or reflect national and international pressures affecting the tempo and direction of capitalist western economies. The differences in scale associated with these processes can lead to highly variable space economies which cannot be fully described, let alone understood, if geography is excluded.

The location of a retailing outlet and its relationships with its local, regional, national and international environments are important issues for geographers, whose work can rarely, if ever, be scale-free. However, location and scale are not concepts which are devoid of social, historical, economic or political meaning. 'Real' places affect 'real' people. A 'sense of place' can help in understanding the geographies of needs, opportunity and enterprise. To study place we need to accommodate many factors such as the prevailing attitudes to work, the home and leisure, demographic factors such

1

as falling birth rates and the drift of professional populations from the cores of British cities, the development of a global economy and culture, and the proclivities of business. These are interests shared by a wide audience of academics, researchers and business analysts. We hope, therefore, that our geography-centred approach will also be of value to them.

The need for analysis

An analysis of retailing is particularly relevant as we move into the 1990s given the importance of the industry to the British economy. Retailing is a major employer, it is the single largest employer of women and contributes well over £50 billion to the national economy each year. In spite of this, studies of shopping and the retailing system have tended in the past to be considered the poor relations of studies of agriculture and manufacturing (see for example, the critique of economic geography in Applebaum 1954). The main reason for this relative lack of interest is that retailing has been seen as a reactive (non-productive) sector of the economy whose behaviour responds to consumer needs, tastes and fashions rather then helps form them in the first place. This implies that retailing cannot identify the key social and economic processes which underlie capitalism and so it is not a priority for analysis. From this perspective, retailing is a 'non-basic' sector of the economy whose health largely depends on the effective workings of manufacturing and agriculture.

Today, many social scientists interested in retailing and the mechanisms of national and international distribution consider this to be an extremely dated argument (see, for example, the series of articles edited by Enis and Cox 1988). There is now much greater acceptance that retailing is both reactive and proactive, is able to generate wealth in its own right, and so can influence and create tastes and fashions which subsequently affect other parts of the economy. The distinction between 'basic' and 'non-basic' sectors – a product of traditional economic thinking – has been replaced by a perspective dominated by post-industrialism and the information society (Bell 1973). The growth in texts during the 1980s (see, for example, Davies and Rogers 1984; Dawson and Lord 1985; Wilkie 1986; Jones and Simmons 1987; Kay 1987; Wrigley 1988; Gardner and Sheppard 1989; Couch 1989 and Dale 1989) testifies to the increasingly central position of retailing in social science research.

The following four reasons may be advanced to justify the present study of retailing:

(1) It is a sector of the economy which is very visible to the general public, being located throughout urban areas in physical developments such as high streets, shopping centres, speciality zones and retail parks.

(2) It is a highly dynamic sector which undergoes changes which can radically alter the character of towns and cities.
(3) It reflects social attitudes and aspirations more readily and topically than the faceless and less familiar industries of the mines, factories or the City.
(4) It is evident that retailers are among the most active in redeveloping and restructuring urban spaces. They are among the most effective of modern property speculators and developers, yet they are also interested by developments in consumer psychology, buying behaviour, computer systems and information technology.

Retailing thus offers a means of studying many aspects of contemporary society, for example, individual and group behaviour in real places, changing public attitudes and preferences, the workings of multinational corporations, land use changes, and the politics of the built environment. In effect, it offers a useful and pertinent route to a study of modern capitalism, allowing the sectoral shifts which are now taking place in the economies of the developed western world to be described at local, national and international levels.

The need for a geographical perspective

The motivation for a geographical perspective is the belief that geography provides the acid test of the adequacy of social or economic theorising. Real environments are the proper test bed of theory and the addition of space to economic, social and political theories helps to clarify what they mean. This is in contrast to the idealised picture of homogeneous landscapes and economic man which often underlies theoretical work on retailing (see Chapter 4). While it may seem simplistic to note that all retailing activity has to take place somewhere, a failure to recognise this truth significantly reduces the value of so much social science work.

This 'reductionism' tends to be the case with descriptions of retailing in the financial, business and economics literatures (see, for example, Bamfield 1980, 1988; Johnson 1987; Stern and Stanworth 1988 and Couch 1989). Though extensive in their content, they underplay the importance of local and regional influences. From these studies one might begin to suspect that retailing is identical around the country and is subject to all the same processes and pressures. It is not, though there are aspects which seem to be general. Though the national and international forces affecting retailing may apply across the country, their spatial expression in terms of what is built and where, cannot be understood without acknowledging the specific circumstances of the areas concerned (Cadman and Austin-Crowe 1978).

In Britain, as in most modern western societies, the construction of a system of retailing illustrates the interplay of retailers, consumers, developers and the various managers of land who compete for position in a largely urban setting. Most British people live in towns and cities dividing their time between domestic duties, paid jobs and leisure. In return for 'work' they receive 'income' which they can then 'exchange' for goods and services. This is taken to be the 'natural' way of doing things today and conditions all aspects of modern British life. There are very few fully self-sufficient Britons living exclusively off the fruits of their labours on the land. Instead, the great majority of us have come to rely on retailing to meet our needs. Food comes from supermarkets (for example, Sainsburys, Tesco), market stalls and allotments; clothes come from chain stores (Marks and Spencer, Littlewoods) and fashion boutiques (Benetton, Monsoon); shelter comes from builders (Wimpey, Bovis, Barratt), building societies (Halifax, Cheltenham and Gloucester) and estate agents (Cornerstone), and warmth comes from the newly privatised gas and electricity companies. Meeting modern needs requires a sophisticated mix of general and specialist retailers.

What is built in these urban landscapes depends on which protagonists are most active and powerful. Urban development is driven by the desire to make money or to provide public services, is restricted by history and existing land use, is welcomed by some, hated by others and is framed by legal opinion which often may be years out of date. The interplay of these factors leads to highly variable townscapes in which competing and opposite forces may be at work. For example, demands for the development of edge-of-town hypermarkets may compete with the preservation of the green belt; retail parks may clash with powerful conservation schemes developing 'appropriate' retailing in historic areas; and the call for the pedestrianisation of city centres may conflict with demands for increased car access, especially for the elderly and the disabled. In all these things, retailing epitomises the tensions in urban environments and their many often incompatible modes of relief.

Some recent trends in retailing in Britain

In the last twenty or thirty years British retailing has undergone major changes in both its commercial and economic organisation and in its geographical character. Three factors stand out as being particularly significant. First, there were changes in ownership patterns which led to the growth of large national and international corporate retailers at the expense of smaller, more local operations. Second, there were changes in the way retailing is delivered to the public. Self-service and the removal of the shop counter opened the way for supermarketing, which was initially a form of marketing but is now more generally understood as a form of shop. In turn, this has spawned a variety of styles of selling, each requiring different types of location. The commercial success of these different styles of selling depends increasingly upon their ability to offer consumers shopping environments which are comfortable, convenient and convivial. Third, there was a decentralisation in the location of consumer demand away from the centres and inner areas of cities to their suburban fringes and beyond. Though this trend is showing some signs of being reversed as increasing transport costs combined with traffic congestion make commuting less glamorous than in the past, many key developments in shopping provision are now focused on the edge rather than the centre of British towns and cities.

These changes have to be placed in context. At the national and inter-national levels there has been a restructuring of the global economy with the power to direct international markets moving away from Europe to the USA and South East Asia (particularly Japan). The sovereignty of nation states in the fields of domestic economic and social policy has declined alongside this globalisation of capital (Wallerstein 1979, 1984; Knox and Agnew 1989). Major restructuring has also taken place within western economies with the relative decline of manufacturing and the expansion of services and informa-tion-processing (Gershuny and Miles 1983; Massey 1984; Hudson and Williams 1986). These have led to new forms of work and working practices and have not benefited equally either all occupations or all parts of the country (see Chapter 4).

These are not the only factors which need to be considered in setting the scene for contemporary retailing. Also important is the growing feminisa-tion of the workforce which has altered the economic base of society; the expansion in leisure time aided by the growth in real disposable income and credit; increased personal mobility associated with rising levels of car owner-ship, and changing social and political attitudes towards the quality of products, the state of the environment and the use of time. All of these have brought their influence to bear on what is demanded of retailing by the general public and on how these demands should be met.

Perhaps the most marked effect in contemporary retailing has been the breakdown in mass markets and the growing importance of specialist retailing for clearly-defined client groups. Such 'market segmentation' has radically altered the ways in which many retailing organisations operate. Instead of attempting to cater for all tastes, attention is focused on the needs of specialist groups such as working women, teenagers, and children (see Chapter 6). By subdividing the market into distinct groups along these and other lines, retailers have sought to develop new markets (often termed 'niche' markets) or increase the size of existing markets by introducing competition where none was previously thought necessary. Such activity represents a major response by retailers to the intense competition affecting retail profit margins in recent years.

Organisation of this book

A rough definition of retailing is that it is an economic system for distributing the products and services of industries to meet consumer wants, needs and desires in a context of scarcity. Leaving aside the debate about what is or is not scarce (see Kohn 1986 for a critical discussion of this topic), it is clear that retailing is in some sense concerned with matching production decisions with consumer demand. At one level, needs are fairly easy to define because all people, whoever they are, need 'basics' such as food, clothing, warmth and shelter. However, the fact that western societies have largely overcome the problems of supplying these and yet acquisition of material goods still remains important, means that a wider, more sophisticated definition is required. This is difficult to provide as needs are relative to the societies concerned, and subgroups within them. It can also be argued that needs are dictated by capitalism to maintain some form of productive *status quo* and so are not an intrinsic property of free-thinking individuals. This is a thorny issue and one which cannot be studied without reference to key economic changes occurring over the last 150 years or so, for example, the growth of urbanisation and the creation of a world economy. Some of the issues involved are considered in Chapter 1.

Chapter 2 is concerned with the supply of retailing through the development of trade and commerce. Both represent attempts by societies to meet the needs of their populations. Simple societies may perhaps meet their needs from their immediate environment; the needs of more complex societies may require the movement of goods and services from all around the world. The ability to move such goods and services over space is not haphazard but is organised by a variety of specialist institutions, for example, manufacturers, brokers, shippers, wholesalers, haulage companies. These and others collectively form a 'marketing channel' which varies in character and complexity depending on cultural context and what is being marketed.

In many areas of retailing, control over marketing channels has tended to shift in favour of the retailer and away from both producer and 'middlemen' such as wholesalers. Two factors help to explain this. First, the growth of corporate multiple retailers has significantly increased their commercial power and has often allowed them to dictate their precise product requirements to manufacturers and farmers (so-called 'specification buying'). Companies such as Marks and Spencer have been able to preserve their image of quality by only selecting suppliers who meet their stringent requirements. Those chosen gain access to a well-defined and potentially lucrative market, but are constrained in what they can produce and in how they operate. Second, most retail markets are today dominated by companies who do not specialise in any single product or service. Modern grocers such as Sainsburys now sell electrical goods, cooking utensils and pot plants as well as food. This 'scrambled merchandising' ensures that retailers are the only institutions in marketing channels who have access to comprehensive information on sales and trends in consumer behaviour. They are thus able to manipulate channels to their advantage by feeding back selected information which maintains or improves their competitive edge.

Chapter 3 is concerned with the character of the modern British retailer. It notes that the conventional image consisting solely of corner shops and high streets is truly out of date. Instead, modern British retailing is actually dominated by national and international business organisations which have interests in many types of economic activity besides distribution, for example, property development, information technology and consumer research. This chapter considers the commercial pedigree of typical British high streets or shopping centres, and notes that the wide variety of shops to be found there may actually be component companies within one or two larger businesses.

Chapter 4 presents an introduction to some of the theoretical approaches to retailing developed by geographers, economists and planners. Most British towns and cities display a hierarchical pattern to their retailing provision which is evident at both the inter-urban and intra-urban levels. Research suggests that these patterns may be linked to specific types of spatial economic behaviour reflecting the interplay of retailers and consumers. However, recent developments have called the primacy of the hierarchy into question.

Chapter 5 looks more specifically at the built environment for retailing services and at contemporary trends such as the development of shopping areas, centres and retail parks. The movement from craftsman-retailer to international business over the last 150 years has radically changed the British townscape and the position of retailing within it. However, the commercial re-definition of retailing, a process which is consistent with all types of capitalist production and reproduction, is likely to lead to pressures for even greater changes in the future. Some of these may be thought desirable (the redevelopment of dilapidated historic buildings), others irresponsible (expansion of retail developments into the Green Belt). The planning profession has a key role to play in this. Some of its functions are introduced here.

Chapter 6 is concerned with the modern British consumer and attempts to describe the processes which have led retailers to turn away from mass marketing for a 'general' public to segmented marketing for a specific client group. This is an important practical and conceptual change by retailers, which is based on their own, more comprehensive perception of their role in society and on their commercial aims. Niche marketing, which flows from market segmentation, has grown in commercial importance as retailers have become more accustomed to describing the economic process they are part of as a 'series of transformations from meaningless to meaningful heterogeneity' (Alderson 1958). Retailing plays a key part in defining this heterogeneity and working towards its commercial exploitation.

Chapter 7 is concerned with the industry's demand for and use of information on shopping habits and practices. Today, this is needed more than ever because of the tight profit margins available to most retailing businesses. Competition for customers and sites for new shopping developments increasingly demands coherent and well-considered business plans. New developments in technology and money-management offer unrivalled opportunities to the retailer to obtain crucial commercial information. Though expensive, and requiring specialist staff to make the most of them, they are likely to influence future marketing initiatives and the development of new styles of retailing. This chapter also considers how retailing and consumer behaviour information is used by retailers to tailor their businesses more closely to market segments. Techniques based on geographical information systems, demographic profiles and psychographics are presented.

Chapter 8 considers a key type of retailing for the 1990s and beyond: green retailing. This is a form which has evolved to meet the demands of the increasingly-political environmental consumer: one who sees simple daily consumption decisions as having a direct influence on the health of the planet. This chapter reviews some of the arguments involved in this important area and assesses how far a conventional retailing system based on capitalist principles can meet this demand. It notes that while the spirit of green retailing may involve a shift in emphasis from the 'self' to a broader social and environmental awareness, green consumers come in many shades. The potential for market segmentation and niche retailing is just as real here as for the rest of the industry, and may give it a way of coping with what might otherwise be a catastrophic change in consumption.

Finally, Chapter 9 draws together some of the principal themes presented in the text. It provides an overview of retailing developments in the recent past and suggests some of the factors which are likely to be important in the future. Future retailing will be faced by some major qualitative differences in British society. The population continues to live longer with many old people surviving well beyond retirement age. As a group, the elderly are major consumers of welfare and healthcare. Their treatment will be a testament to the type of society we have become. Conversely, the number of people available for employment will fall as a result of the 'demographic dip'. There will be fewer workers available and the skills shortage coupled to the costs of providing education and training may make many of the available workers unemployable. Traffic congestion in cities and environmental degradation will grow in importance and are set to become strategic issues. If towns are closed to the car, what happens to the massive retailing investment in the city centres?

The future may not be all doom. Leisure time and life quality are expected to increase for those in work and with the sensitivities to know how to enjoy themselves and the incomes to achieve it. The development of the integrated European Market after 1992 may open opportunities not yet anticipated. There may be a new deal for working females, as 'women's work' is redefined to attract the career professional (Evans 1990). These are the sorts of questions British retailers will have to face in the future.

CHAPTER 1

Retailing: Economy and Society

Introduction

The function of a retailing system is to supply goods and services to meet the needs, wants and desires of the public. In Britain, this public lives mainly in towns and cities and exchanges its labour for work in shops, offices and factories. Very few people live an entirely self-sufficient life out in the country (Hudson and Williams 1986, Cater and Jones 1989). Britain has been a predominantly urban-industrial country for well over one hundred years but the character of its towns and cities and the employment they offer has changed dramatically since the Second World War. Work in agriculture and manufacturing has declined rapidly, deepening existing structural difficulties for those regions relying on them. At the same time the supply of work in service industries such as retailing has been steadily increasing, so that today, services and new information-processing industries based on the use of computers and telecommunications account for well over half of the working population (Hepworth 1989).

This restructuring of the British economy has been accompanied by a restructuring in the world economy. The Second World War crippled Europe – the traditional heartland of international capitalism – and allowed the mantle of authority over world markets to pass to the USA. They, in turn, have allowed it to pass to Japan, though competition from other countries in South East Asia, a rejuvenated European Community and a potential US-Canada-Mexico free trade zone (Charles 1989) may make it difficult for them to hold it for long. As a subsidiary member of an increasingly global economy, 1990s Britain is much less capable of looking after her own affairs than in the past. The tempo of the economy is dictated both from within and without. Britain's manufacturers now rely heavily on global sourcing of goods and materials (Dicken 1986). Britain's retailers increasingly sell products made both at home and abroad, bought from multinational corporations whose production bases can be footloose and whose commercial visions are global in extent (Frobel *et al* 1980). This is the commercial context in which Britain's retailers operate and which underpins the sorts of retailing they provide.

The aim of this chapter is to describe contemporary British needs, wants and desires and to show that they are related to the state of the national and international economies. It begins with a brief resume of the state of 1990s Britain, focusing on work, society and changing patterns of consumption. Some attention is then given to defining the term 'needs' and discussing how they are created by societies. As British needs are mainly urban needs, this means considering some of the relationships which exist between urbanisation, production and consumption. The chapter concludes with a discussion of Abraham Maslow's model of psychological needs. This suggests that in 'advanced' societies, personality and motivational needs ('learning to live to my full potential') become paramount for the individual. This has important implications for the processes of market segmentation which are crucial to a contemporary description of British retailing.

The state of contemporary Britain

Work

The term 'work' is formally used to refer to that process where individuals exchange their time and labour for a weekly pay packet or a monthly salary cheque. Going to work involves the movement of people from their homes to workplaces and has considerable implications for land use, transport and the quality of life. People who exchange their time and labour are 'workers', those providing work are 'employers', and the purpose of the whole exchange is the 'production' of goods and services. These goods and services are produced to be 'consumed'. Consumers may include government, commercial organisations, public services, foreign companies and house-holds. Frequently, goods and services are consumed by those workers whose purpose is to produce them in the first place. The whole process is circular with workers as consumers relying on workers as producers to meet their everyday needs.

This type of system can be an enormously powerful arrangement which significantly increases the number and diversity of goods and services available to the public. However, it depends on the workers accepting their roles and playing their parts. Such a system is not natural or 'god-given' but is one created to meet specific economic ends by particular organisational means. Key among these has been the extensive division of labour which has led to an intense specialisation in types of work and in the creation of designated places of work such as factories and business districts. Such specialisation implies that no individual or firm is entirely self-sufficient, but is locked into a complex web of economic interrelationships with other individuals or firms to meet their needs. The resulting process of exchange between individuals and firms provides the motivation for the creation of a system of retailing.

The system described above is based on formal relationships between employer, worker, government and other interested parties such as employers' and workers' organisations. The present employment structure of Britain (Table 1.1) has evolved over time from one based predominantly on the primary sector (agriculture, quarrying, mining, fishing and forestry). This was followed by an industrial period when the bulk of the workforce was involved in manufacturing.

In the postwar period, Britain has seen some major changes in its industrial and occupational structure. De-industrialisation has led to employment decline in manufacturing, initially in industries such as clothing, textiles, leather goods and shipbuilding, but thereafter, more widely. Accompanying this have been changes in government policies which have moved away from the post-war preoccupation with full employment to the contemporary concerns for the management of inflation. A significant restructuring of the economy has followed from this which has favoured the growth and development of service industries covering public consumption (health and education), private consumption (retailing) and producer services (business and financial services). Figures published in the *Labour Market Quarterly Report* (May 1990, p. 2) show that in the year to December 1989 the number of service employees increased by 534,000 compared with

Economic activity	1954–71			1971–81			1981–87			1987–95*		
	Total	Male	Female	Total	Male	Female	Total	Male	Female	Total	Male	Female
Primary and Utilities	−972	−949	−23	−195	−190	−5	−268	−244	−24	−97	−82	−15
Manufacturing	+46	+251	−205	−1852	−1229	−623	−1014	−744	−270	−231	−220	−11
Construction	+124	+88	+36	−39	−75	+36	+41	+36	+5	+202	+194	+8
Production Industries	−802	−610	−192	−2086	−1494	−592	−1241	−952	−289	−126	−108	−18
Distribution, transport etc.	+216	−77	+293	+378	+13	+365	+350	+179	+171	+433	+241	+192
Business and miscellaneous services	+739	+393	+346	+880	+346	+534	+1297	+759	+538	+1218	+667	+551
Non–marketed services	+805	−127	+932	+640	+30	+610	+224	+48	+176	+198	+15	+183
Service industries	+1760	+189	+1571	+1898	+389	+1509	+1871	+986	+885	+1849	+923	+926
Whole economy	+958	−421	+1379	−188	−1105	+917	+630	+34	+596	+1723	+815	+908

Note *Projected values

Table 1.1 Change in employment by broad economic activity in the United Kingdom 1954–95. (Figures in thousands)

(Source: Compiled from Table 4, Review of the Economy and Employment, Institute for Employment Research, 1988–89. Vol. 1)

the 490,000 increase in all other industries. Banking and financial service employment grew by nearly 8% over the same period compared with the nearly 6% decline in agriculture. These changes have been associated with a growth in real disposable income. Between 1981 and 1988, real disposable income rose by 25%. Median gross weekly earnings for full-time male employees have risen considerably since the 1960s. Figures reported in the *New Earnings Survey* were £188 for manual workers and £260 for non-manual workers. The equivalent figures for 1971 were £28 and £34 respectively. Figures for full-time female employees were £116 and £157 in 1988 compared with £15 and £18 in 1971.

Formal employment is not, however, the only form of work arrangement one can find in contemporary Britain. Gershuny (1978), and Pahl (1984) draw attention to the workings of an 'informal' economy in which the nature of work and the jobs which go with it are defined not by government classifications but by social groups themselves. Frequently such work is conducted outside the formal arrangements of legal contracts and VAT, with 'payment' being either in cash or in kind.

The figures listed in Table 1.1 show that among those in formal employment the lion's share is increasingly being taken by the services sectors – what have been termed the 'post-industrial' sectors of an economy (Bell 1973, 1980). Bell suggests that developments in information technology – computer-controlled telecommunications – lie at the core of the modern economy and society and that this is

> decisive for the way economic and social exchanges are conducted, the way knowledge is created and retrieved, and the character of work and occupations in which men (*sic*) are engaged. (Bell 1980, p. 532)

In Bell's model, the traditional sectors of the economy – primary, secondary, and tertiary – are replaced by three alternative foci defined to show the penetration of information-craft throughout all economic activity: extraction, fabrication and information activities.

The key elements of information technology are computers, telephones, facsimile transfer systems, cable and satellite television, and video disks. Increasingly the machinery operating these services is becoming more integrated, leading Bell to suggest that there will be

> a vast reorganisation in the modes of communication between persons; the transmission of data; the reduction if not the elimination of paper in trans-actions and exchanges; new modes of transmitting news, entertainment and knowledge. (Bell 1980, p. 533)

He anticipates that all these developments will open the way for mankind to pursue individuality while benefiting from a vastly increased supply of goods and services. The key to this good society is the ability to produce for increasingly diverse consumption patterns while freeing many of the workers from the need to work. David Bolter (1984) goes even further: he sees computers as 'defining technologies' which bring about transformations in the human sense of self. Humans come to see themselves as 'information processors' and nature as 'information to be processed'. With humankind redefined in terms of machinery, our social needs are likely to be redefined too.

The problem with both the post-industrial and the information societies is that they are 'chaotic conceptions' – rag-bag classifications which cut through social relationships with little concern for meaning. As Lyon (1988) correctly points out, the statistics which note that 60% or more of the population work in information related jobs do not place these people in social contexts. Information jobs are variable, including data analysts and information consultants at one end to data preparation staff (glorified typists) at the other. The output from information work may vary from financial reports to lectures, or from computer bulletin boards to free newspapers. There is no clearly-defined account of how information work differs from other type of work. The range may also conceal significant gender differences with female employment in informatics being ghettoised towards the lower end. This is a point also taken up by Miles and Gershuny (1986) who suggest that information work has a multitude of different meanings. The future of the post-industrial and information societies will not be led by technology, they argue, but by political decisions made by people who may have come to rely on technology. The two are not the same.

Retailing is noted for its reliance on information, particularly on changing tastes and patterns of consumer behaviour. Commercial pressure has forced the major retailers to invest heavily in information technology, both in-store (for example, in computer-controlled check-outs) and for stock control in their warehouses. Information technology has created new employment opportunities in retailing with the growth of the career professional whose job is information management and forecasting. Few of these work on the shop floor. The majority of shop workers who are in regular contact with the public are women, many of whom are employed part-time. Their jobs frequently require them to use advanced computer-controlled equipment such as laser-scanner check-outs, which can be used successfully after minimal training. The levels of skills needed in shop-floor workers has fallen as a result with significant deskilling in some areas. Some of the issues associated with retailing and the post-industrial society are taken up in more detail in Chapter 7.

Society

Britain has undergone many changes in its social structure since the Second World War which are reflected in the ways social needs and desires are created. A major factor has been the considerable increase in public consumption allied to the development of the Welfare State. Not only has this provided opportunities for new types of work in health care, social services and education, many of which have been taken up by women, but it has also changed attitudes towards the domestic division of labour and family life.

Of particular significance has been the growing acceptance among young people of new forms of family formation. Whereas previously, the traditional model of the British family was of a household consisting of two parents and dependent children, recent figures from the *General Household Survey* for 1988 show this to be only one of a number of competing alternatives for the 1990s (OPCS Monitor 5th December 1989). Today, only 26% of households fall into this traditional model. The largest grouping at 36% is married or cohabiting couples without children or with non-dependent children (frequently multi-income households). Indeed, cohabitation for women aged 18–49 doubled between 1981 and 1988. Single person households make up 26% of British households and lone parents a further 12% of all households surveyed. Britain currently has the highest marriage and divorce rates in the European Community.

One of the key changes which underwrites many of the developments in British retailing is female employment in paid work outside the home. Opportunities for female employment have increased considerably since the Second World War and this had led to financial independence for many women and the desire to place a career before child-bearing. Of the 26.5 million workers in Britain in December 1989, nearly 12 million are women of whom 5 million work part-time. Labour force projections to 2001 suggest that the number of female workers will increase to approximately 13 million, whereas the numbers of males in employment will remain much the same. Self-employment among female workers (6.6%) is however considerably less than among their male counterparts (16.8%). The implications for domestic life are considerable in that many jobs previously thought to be unpaid 'women's work' (domestic cleaning, child care) are now seen as personal services which can form the basis for new types of employment.

Other data reported in the preliminary results from the *General Household Survey* for 1988 and in *Social Trends* indicate other important social changes. The pattern of tenure is particularly interesting with an increasing proportion of personal income being spent on housing. The survey results show that the level of owner occupation continues to rise from 49% in 1971, 52% in 1981, to 63% today. At the same time, the percentage of households renting privately or from local authorities has continued to fall (26% in 1988).

The ability to buy a house depends on employment status, the demand for mortgages and the present and assumed future economic health of the economy. There are considerable regional differences in these variables.

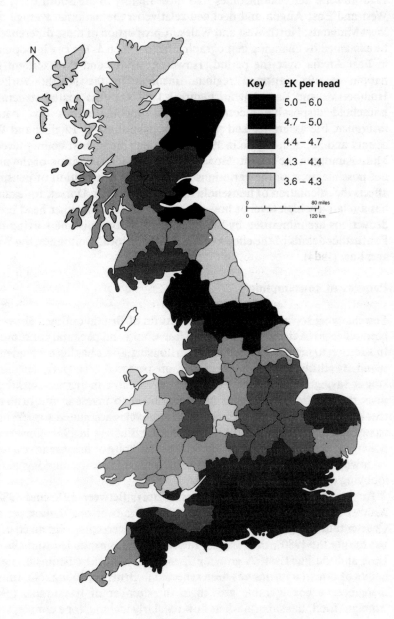

Figure 1.1 Household Disposable Income per head by County/Region (1987)

(Source: Central Statistical Office)

Data published in *Economic Trends* (April 1990) suggest that the regional differences in the levels of disposable household income are increasing. From 1978–88 total personal incomes rose most rapidly in the South East, South West and East Anglia and declined relative to the national average in the West Midlands, North West and Wales. A proportion of these differences can be explained by changing demographic factors such as the rise in population in East Anglia over the period. However, strikes and the excellent grain harvest in 1983 affected regional incomes in the North, Yorkshire-Humberside and East Anglia. Figure 1.1 displays the spatial structure of household disposable income per head (income minus tax, national insurance, life assurance and pension contributions) by English and Welsh county and Scottish region in 1987. Surrey has the highest county level and Mid-Glamorgan the lowest. However, a simple interpretation of the map is not possible because the variations in the spatial distribution of pensioners affects the calculation of household disposable income. Dorset, for example, has a relatively high level of household disposable income per head because deductions are minimised by the large numbers of pensioners living there. For further details of the effects of the elderly on local economies, see Warnes and Law (1984).

Patterns of consumption

The changing social and economic structures of Britain outlined above have been reflected in changing patterns of household and personal consumption. In addition to increased expenditure on housing, there has been a tendency to spend increasing amounts of money on personal transport, leisure and labour-saving devices. Car ownership levels have increased considerably since the war as governments have continued to invest in motorway and trunk routes. In 1988, cars, taxis and motorcycles accounted for 80% of all passenger movements in Britain compared with 50% in 1961. Government policy is still in favour of personal transport in spite of increasing congestion in towns and cities, the proven inefficiency of the technology and the lobbying of environmentalists.

Air transport has also grown considerably. Between 1976 and 1988 the number of flights increased by 75% to stand at over one million per year. Charter tourist flights to the Mediterranean have accounted for much of this, but during the 1980s, the range of destinations has expanded to include the USA and the Far East. A growing familiarity with the customs and eating habits of other countries has been reflected in British retailing. Not only has there been a considerable growth in the number of restaurants offering 'foreign' food, but supermarkets now regularly include, for example, Greek, Italian, Spanish, Chinese and Indian items as basic lines.

With women increasingly working outside the home, the traditional domestic division of labour has changed radically since the war. In particular, it has led to the demand for labour-saving devices to minimise housework. Figures from the *General Household Survey* 1988 show that 83% of households have washing machines, 83% telephones, 74% deep freezers, 73% central heating, but only 8% have dishwashers. The high levels of penetration for some of these products reflects the fact that they have been available for some time and have become accepted as offering useful services which reduce effort. However, the low figure for dish washers indicates that the demarcation in domestic duties has not yet been eradicated. New products such as videos and microwaves have shown rapid increases in penetration in recent years. In 1986 only 38% of households had a video. Today, the figure is 46%. Similarly, 30% of households in 1987 had microwave ovens compared with 23% a year earlier.

A particularly significant change in domestic consumption has been the advent and almost universal acceptance of the television. In 1988 more than 50% of British households had two or more TVs with the average person aged over 5 watching between 16 and 20 hours a week (nearly 50% of the average working week). The development of a TV 'three minute' culture has been blamed for declining attention spans noted in children and for their almost insatiable appetites for TV advertising. A TV culture which brings images and ideas into every living room in the country is a very powerful medium for manipulating tastes and fashions.

The power of TV, video and, increasingly, satellite broadcasting is evident from the decline in the numbers attending public entertainment in theatres and cinemas. The 1988 figures show that in the 4 weeks preceding the survey only 11% of households made use of arts or public entertainment services, 7% saw a play, 8% went to art galleries and 26% visited a library. All of these indicate a replacement of public services by private services which can be enjoyed in the home.

Patterns of substitution are also evident in aggregate consumption. Of the £284 billion of household expenditure in 1988 (measured at 1988 prices), food accounted for £37 billion (13%), housing £43 billion (15%) and transport £50 billion (18%). This compares with 1976 when food was the largest component at 19%, transport was second with 15% and housing contributed 14%. Over the same period, expenditure on tobacco and alcohol has fallen from 4% and 8% respectively to 3% and 7%. The substitution effects are particularly marked between households on different levels of income. In general, poorer households spend considerably more on food and considerably less on transport than richer households (26% and 7% compared with 16% and 17%). Fuel and lighting expenditure is also much higher for poorer households (12% compared with 4%).

Substitution within the market for food and groceries is also evident. Since 1961, expenditure on milk, cream, red meat and butter has fallen, by 60% in the case of butter. Conversely, expenditure on cheese, poultry, fish and fish products, vegetables and vegetable products, fresh fruit, fruit and fruit products, non-white bread and instant coffee have all increased. Expenditure on wholemeal bread has increased by five times over the same period as white bread has declined by 50%. These changes have had marked effects on the supply of groceries. Today, the demand for organic and environment-friendly foodstuffs is considerable and has outstripped the ability of British domestic suppliers to meet demand. Supermarket chain Safeway has responded to this by sponsoring a major campaign in Scotland to increase significantly the number of organic farms. (The implications of green consumption on British retailing are considered in Chapter 8.)

Britain's destiny

Williams (1981) notes that three major historical developments are associated with the advent of capitalism: first, the move towards a universal 'popular' culture; second, the development of an international market (perhaps even a world market), and third, the growing importance given to the production and distribution of ideas and information. The combined effect of these has been to eliminate many of the traditional boundaries between states which previously accorded places a degree of sovereignty. The production and distribution of needs, wants and desires thus takes on new meaning as the convergence of time and space has created a global economy with production centres which are liable to shift temporally and spatially. The main implication of this is that Britain is not in control of her own destiny.

There is little doubt that Britain's economic, social and political affairs are not entirely within her own control. Membership of international organisations such as the European Community imposes commitments on Britain which sometimes seem restrictive (witness, for example, the furore over the Common Agriculture Policy and the Social Charter), leading to heated political debates in Westminster about sovereignty and the future of Britain's style of democracy. These commitments arise because of treaty obligations which require the government to discuss policy matters with other countries. These may be to achieve some desired purpose such as minimising the risk of another European war or establishing a common foreign policy stance towards South Africa.

These commitments pale into insignificance when compared with the economic interrelationships of western economies. Britain is a trading nation whose rise to commercial prominence during the 19th century was due to its creation and commercial exploitation of a large, international empire. This provided Britain with its own miniature world economy, offering both raw materials and controlled markets for British industry. So long as Britain could dominate in this, its need to compete more extensively was limited. The breakup of the Empire in the 20th century, and increasing competition from new trading areas in Europe, North America and South East Asia has resulted in Britain being drawn more closely into trading arrangements which she cannot dominate or hope to control (Hudson and Williams 1986). The evidence for this is visible in the markets for chemicals and cars, and most recently in the 'invisible' markets for financial services which are global in scope and wholly beyond the control of any single national government (Wilkinson and Lomax 1989).

The latter is particularly important because it provides for the first time a global market in investment securities and information. Stock exchanges around the world are now linked together by telecommunications and computer networks to the extent that differences in space and time have been largely eliminated. 'Round-the-clock' trading is a feature of the 1990s securities markets with large volumes of international trade being dominated by Japanese companies such as Nomura, Daiwa and Yamaichi. While the status of financial trading in London seems to have benefitted from the presence of the Japanese (Lomax 1988), the financial stability of British companies does appear to be under threat from the globalisation of investment possibilities. The most notorious modern development is the 'junk bond' – publicly-traded debt obligations – which may be used for a wide variety of types of trading, including general purpose financings and leveraged-buyouts. These financial strategies suggest that no company operating anywhere in the world and requiring investment income to survive is safe from a predator who feels, for whatever reason, that an improved trading performance would result after a takeover and re-alignment of its trading pattern (Molyneux 1990). As retailers are frequently component companies in larger national and multinational business groups, such developments are of relevance to them. Recent examples of retailing takeovers involving the use of leveraged buy-outs are Magnet and Lowndes-Queensway (*The Guardian* July 6th 1990).

The fact that retailers operating in Britain sell goods produced both at home and abroad means that they too are affected by the processes of globalisation and internationalisation of production and sourcing. These affect British companies in different ways. Some expand and become predators abroad, others become prey in their own backyard. A simple example of expansion is provided by companies such as Marks and Spencer, Laura Ashley and Habitat, which trade in North America and several European countries under their familiar British logos. Marks and Spencer also trade in the USA under the Brooks Brothers logo, having acquired this prestigious company in 1988. Other British companies trading in this way in the USA are Ratners (acquired Sterling in 1987), Dixons (trading as Silo and Tiptons) and Sainsburys (acquired Shaws supermarkets in 1987 and Landoli supermarkets in 1988).

The most obvious recent example of a British retailer falling victim to a foreign takeover is the acquisition of House of Fraser (which includes the world-famous Harrods department store in Knightsbridge) by the Egyptian

Al-Fayed brothers. While this story was headline news, it is perhaps of less significance than the penetration of foreign retailers into the British domestic market. For years, Britons have bought products in C & A without perhaps realising that this is a Dutch company. More recently, companies such as Benetton (Italy), Ikea (Sweden), and Makro (Netherlands) have been operating successfully in Britain and extending their business interests. A

Rank	Company Name	Country	Core Retail Activity	Sales £m*	Year End
1	Albrecht	Germany	Discount Food	6,802	12.87
2	Carrefour	France	Hypermarkets	5,742	12.87
3	Tengelmann	Germany	Supermarkets	5,555	6.88
4	Casino	France	Supermarkets	5,222	12.87
5	Gateway Corporation	UK	Supermarkets	5,144	4.88
6	Auchan	France	Hypermarkets	5,081	12.87
7	Vendex International	Netherlands	Multi-sector	5,076	1.88
8	Co-op Societies	UK	Co-operative	5,048	12.86
9	Rewe-Leibbrand	Germany	Supermarkets	5,007	12.87
10	J Sainsbury	UK	Supermarkets	4,792	3.88
11	Marks & Spencer	UK	Variety Stores	4,578	3.88
12	Otto Versand	Germany	Mail Order	4,184	2.88
13	Tesco	UK	Supermarkets	4,119	2.88
14	Karstadt	Germany	Dept. stores	4,057	12.87
15	Promodes	France	Hypermarkets	3,538	12.87
16	Ahold	Netherlands	Supermarkets	3,531	12.87
=17	Co-op Unternehmen	Germany	Co-operative	3.522	12.87
=17	Edeka	Germany	Supermarkets	3,522	12.86
19	Asko Deutsche Kaufhaus	Germany	Hypermarkets	3,435	12.87
20	GB Inno BM	Belgium	Multi-sector	3,424	1.88
21	Kaufhof	Germany	Dept. stores	3,387	12.87
22	Argyll	UK	Supermarkets	3,236	3.88
23	Schickedanz/Quelle	Germany	Mail order	3,133	1.88
24	Asda	UK	Multi-sector	2,729	3.88
25	Boots	UK	Chemists	2,697	3.88
26	C & A Brenninkmeyer	Netherlands	Clothing	2,548	12.87
27	Cora-Revillon	France	Hypermarkets	2,382	12.86
28	Great Universal Stores	UK	Mail order	2,366	3.87
29	Sears	UK	Multi-sector	2,360	1.88
30	Galeries Lafayette-Monoprix	France	Dept. stores	2,337	12.87

Note. *Exchange rates used are the average for the calendar year.*

Table 1.2   The top 30 retailers in the European Community

(Source: Extracted from The Retail Pocketbook 1989)

report published in *The Independent* (May 15th 1990) notes that there is a gap in the market for discount food chains (companies selling groceries at significantly reduced prices) and that this is likely to be increasingly targeted by German discounter, Aldi, who have plans to open 200 stores in Britain. This is a trend which is likely to increase after the completion of the single European market in 1992 because, as Table 1.2, shows, few British retailers are among the largest currently operating in the European Community (Retail Pocketbook 1989).

Needs, wants and desires: The demand for retailing

'Basic' needs

All individuals are faced with a 'basic set' of needs which must be satisfied to ensure survival. These include things like food, drink, warmth, shelter, and clothing. Without these, the individual would not survive for long as *homo sapiens* is ill-equipped physically to endure major changes in climate. However, not all of this 'basic set' is basic to every human being. For example, clothing is really only important in climates where protection from the elements is an essential factor in survival (for example, in the heat of the desert or the cold of the Arctic). For peoples living in less extreme climates, the need for clothing is more social than physical: it reflects an aesthetic or ceremonial convention of a society, perhaps even a taboo.

However, most 'advanced' countries would regard the above list as only a subset of basic needs. In his preface to the *North-South* report (ICIDI 1980), Brandt suggests that health, literacy, and equality of opportunities are also basics, without which countries cannot hope to develop their own productive capabilities and lift themselves out of poverty. Geographical inequalities in literacy, health and poverty are often used as indicators of 'economic health'. These operate at both an international and national scale and are used to guide investment strategies and to decompose mass markets into consumer segments, some of which have only a limited geographical extent. Given that retailing is privately financed and motivated by the pursuit of profit, investments will be channelled to where they can reap the greatest return. On the whole, this will result in retail development being attracted to the most lucrative markets, compounding the problem of geographical inequality. However, and perhaps paradoxically, many of the largest and most innovative developments in retailing are taking place in the peripheral North and Midlands (for example, the Metro Centre in Gateshead, Meadowhall in Sheffield, Merry Hill in Dudley). There are specific local reasons for these developments, most importantly, the availability of extensive areas of derelict, former industrial land. These issues are considered in greater detail in Chapters 4 and 5.

There is no reason why a definition of 'basic' should be restricted to material things. Peter Palumbo, writing in the preface to the 1989 Arts Council Annual Report makes the following point:

> A prosperous society in economic terms will create a cultural climate in direct proportion and importance to that economic prosperity. Food for the body in material terms must have the counter-balancing factor of cultural prosperity – food for the soul – if society is not to become philistine and sterile. (Arts Council 1989, p. 3)

To Palumbo, works of art and artistic experiences have as much right to be seen as basic as food production and the provision of health care. Retailers and developers have come to realise this too and are now concerned that shopping centres, shop frontages and internal layout should not be considered as merely functional but as important components in creating a successful retail environment which appeals to increasingly sophisticated consumers.

'Relative' needs

Whereas some needs are basic to all people, many more reflect the societies producing them. Dicken and Lloyd (1981) argue that needs may only really be understood in terms of the domestic and power relationships which have been created to link individuals and groups within a society. They note:

> behaviour at the individual level needs to be seen within its broader context: the prevailing social, economic and political structure and the inherited culture. In order to understand how and why human activities are arranged spatially we need to understand the way in which society operates. (Dicken and Lloyd 1981, p. 12)

This task is rather harder than it may sound because 'society' is both difficult to define adequately and is itself a social construction which varies spatially (Williams 1976, 1981). Reporting observed or even intended behaviour probably will not do, because similar behaviour even within a single society may arise for a variety of reasons.

The cornerstone of the Dicken and Lloyd argument is unambiguous: most needs are relative rather than absolute. Once a society is capable of reproducing itself (that is, ensuring its survival from one generation to the next), the predominance of 'basic' needs diminishes or changes qualitatively to reflect the aspirations of the society. They note:

> Hunger may be removed by a bowl of rice or maize, by a beefsteak or by a dish of caviar. Similarly, shelter may be a mud hut, a four-bedroom detached house or a penthouse suite. Each, in its own way, provides food or shelter yet not all would be universally acceptable. Thus, what is regarded as basic in one society

may be an undreamt of luxury in another. What is standard diet in one society may be unacceptable to others. (Dicken and Lloyd 1981, p. 13)

In order to understand this relativity it is necessary to consider how needs are created in the first place.

Society and the creation of needs

It is useful to distinguish between needs which are essential for survival and those which are social and merely add to the 'quality' of life. Clearly food and drink, shelter and perhaps clothing fall into the former. Almost everything else falls into the latter. What is considered important or even basic depends on the society concerned and, perhaps, even on particular subgroups of it. The relationship between the status of social groups and the types of consumption they are prepared to make varies within society. Weber notes that:

> classes are stratified according to their relations to the production and acquisition of goods; whereas 'status groups' are stratified according to the principles of the consumption of goods as represented by special 'styles of life'. (Weber 1948, p. 193)

Retailing as an industry therefore has to consider both the ability of people to buy its goods and services and the types of consumption that may be associated with particular groups of consumers.

In an advanced economy such as Britain we have come to rely heavily on the workings of commerce to meet our basic needs. Like all peoples we require food, clothing, warmth and shelter, but these are now so regularly provided by our economic system that most of us (though not all) take them for granted. We worry about these only when the gas or electricity is turned off, or when bread, tea, sugar and other 'essentials' suddenly become scarce on the supermarket shelves. For most of us, our needs are more likely to be for employment and status, personal security, good health or happiness. These become issues in the West as our emphasis changes from the means of sustaining life to the quality of life. Today, consumer groups as well as many members of the general public are concerned about the quality of their food and water, atmospheric pollution, endemic unemployment in peripheral areas, standards of health and education. These become issues because their presence is seen to challenge perceived needs for decent standards of living.

Needs and production

The economist, JK Galbraith argues that in western societies the problem of meeting basic needs has been largely resolved. The nature of the capitalist economic system which has been created over the last two hundred years sees to this. However, this does not mean that wants and needs have been eliminated. Like Weber, he argues that the medium for articulating needs lies in the status groupings and classes which exist in western societies. However, going further than Weber, he suggests that the real source of needs lies in the structural mechanisms within economies which seek to preserve the existing economic order. For example, he notes:

> As a society becomes increasingly affluent, wants are increasingly created by the process by which they are satisfied. This may operate passively. Increases in consumption, the counterpart of increases in production, act by suggestion or emulation to create wants. Or producers may proceed actively to create wants through advertising and salemanship. Wants thus come to depend on output. (Galbraith 1969, pp. 152–3)

He terms this the 'dependence effect', to show that the production of goods and services satisfies the wants that the consumption of these goods creates or which producers can create for them artificially. Production creates the impetus for more production through its relationship with consumption.

For the most part in western societies, wants and needs are contrived by the economic system in, so Galbraith claims, its attempt to achieve economic security. But the economic system is not an asocial concept, it is a series of power relationships between vested interests (people, groups, companies) both within a country and increasingly between countries. Status and power relationships within and between these groups form the keys to understanding the creation and maintenance of needs in western societies.

Needs and urban living

The processes associated with the reproduction of an economy cannot be described without acknowledging the spatial manifestation of western societies. Britain, like most western countries, is a predominantly urban society engaged in non-agricultural tasks. The chief characteristic of an urban society is that basic needs are purchased either from private business or are provided by the state. Houses are built by local authorities and by private developers, clothing is supplied by clothing retailers and food is bought from supermarkets. In order to survive, an urban population must be able to obtain these basic requirements without expending unnecessary effort. Agglomeration into a relatively small number of areas allows business to tap into a large existing demand and provides it with an opportunity to develop new markets. This is possible because urban populations have changed qualitatively from their ancestors who depended on their own agricultural efforts for sustenance. Today, a system of economic production and distribution exists to provide sustenance, but at the same time, maintains a level of dependence designed to ensure its own survival. It is thus clear that for most people, the benefits of urban living can only be had if they are prepared to risk their being dependent on this system and on the proclivities of those who manage and maintain it. The function of urban life in the West is thus the reproduction of the capitalist economic system (for details of these arguments see, for example, Harvey 1982).

Psychological needs and market segmentation

There are many potential classifications of needs. One which has received some attention in the geographical and retailing literature is that of the humanistic psychologist, Abraham Maslow (see Dicken and Lloyd 1981, p. 13; Couch 1989, pp. 74–75). Underlying Maslow's approach is a philosophical position that individuals are constantly making choices which collectively determine the sort of people they become. By making such choices in the face of personal and social limitations, individuals, according to Maslow, are seeking to discover a satisfying sense of their personal identities and thus give their lives some meaning. He terms this process 'self-actualisation' (Maslow 1968, 1970).

His model of psychological development includes an hierarchical arrangement of needs which develops from basic or lower needs to self-actualisation. The base of the system is termed physiological, and refers to the need for food, warmth and shelter discussed above. Next comes safety, principally the need for protection from wild animals and other hostile humans. Above this are the needs for love and belongingness, personal esteem and self-actualisation. Figure 1.2 illustrates the basic idea. It is useful to note that the physiological needs are essentially individual, but as we move to the right, become communal and social.

The horizontal axis of Figure 1.2 describes some form of measurement which Maslow terms 'psychological development'. To the left are the basic needs. These are assumed to predominate among the needs of societies which are in some (unspecified) sense 'primitive'. As these societies begin to exert greater control and influence over their environment, the immediate needs of physiology and safety diminish and other, less tangible, psychological needs become increasingly important. Thus in an 'advanced' society (again unspecified), the need for personal 'self-actualisation' becomes particularly important. People begin to see themselves as individuals rather more than as members of groups and respond to activities which claim to help them develop as people. The desires to 'come to terms with oneself' or to 'get to know oneself as a person' are particularly popular in western societies though it has to be noted that the pursuit of individuality is itself probably the result of social or peer-group pressure (Kohn 1986, Lyon 1988).

While Maslow's model is intuitively attractive it does have its deficiencies.

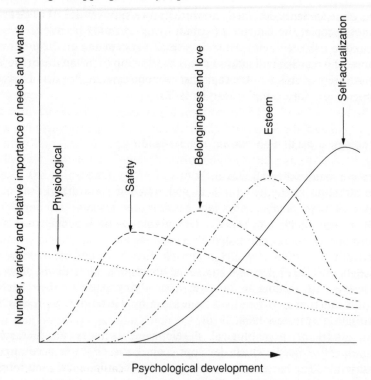

Figure 1.2   Diagrammatic representation of Maslow's hierarchy of needs and wants

(Source: Based upon Dicken and Lloyd 1981)

The expression of the horizontal axis in a relative rather than an absolute metric means that it is impossible to locate any specific society (or any group within a society) to any part of it. Even in so-called 'developed' countries such as Britain, one can find evidence for all five levels in the hierarchy. The growth of underclasses in the West, leading to increased homelessness, low morale, disease and destitution, juxtapose uneasily with the materialism of the 1990s. While house prices in the south east of England have rocketed, the numbers of people sleeping rough in the streets of London and relying on soup kitchens and charity for their basic needs has also risen sharply. To attach any single country to Maslow's model misses the essential point of modern western society: it is segmented from within and the differences between the 'haves' and the 'have nots' are growing rapidly. In other words, while Maslow emphasises the potential of choice albeit within a system of constraints, it is possible to argue that many people have few or no choices open to them.

Another deficiency of the model is that it implies that increasing psychological development necessarily means a progression through the five levels. There is no facility in Figure 1.2 to jump a stage or to jump backwards in the journey from left to right. While few would argue about the importance of physiological needs at the base of the classification, there is no reason to believe that the curves interweave as portrayed in the figure. Love and belongingness may be a prerequisite to gaining the self-esteem which encourages people to feel safe. As wealth increases and people acquire more and more material possessions, the need for safety may re-emerge in a new and qualitatively different form, perhaps leading on to the security state in which developments such as neighbourhood watch and personal surveillance are seen as essential public needs.

This is the key difficulty with the model; it fails to show that the manner in which needs can be articulated and satisfied can vary both temporally and spatially. For students in a bed-sitter living on a tight budget, meals will usually be basic, filling and cheap. Occasionally, there may be the possibility for some luxury. When qualified and employed however, their improved financial position enables them to increase their ability to consume. This may lead to them buying a wider range of foodstuffs, taking on a mortgage, and buying a wider range of products such as washing machines, videos or cars. At the height of their economic success, their status and position may mean they 'need' an executive office, a company car, two foreign holidays a year, and visits to prestigious restaurants for expensive cuisine. Even the language required to describe these needs changes, indicating that consciousness changes with status (Williams 1976).

Conclusions

There is little disagreement about what constitutes a 'basic set' of needs. Humankind requires food, drink, clothing, warmth and shelter to survive in the many hostile environments found on the planet. However, the quality of the products and services which meet these needs may vary enormously, suggesting that even in a single place and time, different people may be experiencing lives which are 'worlds apart'.

Needs are relative; they reflect the aspirations and motivations of those who seek to satisfy them. Needs are also manufactured to maintain existing social and economic conditions. For Britain, as for other western societies, needs are essentially urban needs. Our population lives predominantly in built-up areas – towns, cities and rural commuting belts whose rural ambience may be due more to 'horsiculture' than agriculture. Very few people live self-sufficiently in rural bliss. Urban dwellers, by their very nature, are not self-sufficient. Left to their own devices they would soon reach destitution in a world whose international distribution system had broken down. They thus have a vested interest in ensuring that it does not break down, and that what does exist works in ways that make meeting needs easy and satisfying.

The way in which such needs are met in a modern western society is by having a well-developed, integrated retailing system. Today, British retailing is concerned to supply goods and services which may be globally sourced to meet needs and wants which are part of an international culture. Some of the ways in which it does this are described in the next chapter.

CHAPTER 2

Marketing and Retailing

Introduction

Getting the right goods to the right markets in response to or anticipation of consumer demand is the key function of marketing. Unlike selling which is primarily concerned with the needs of the seller, marketing is primarily concerned with the needs of the buyer. The relationship between buyer and seller is not, however, an entirely random process. Consumers are able to exert a degree of sovereignty over what they buy but producers and sellers can help to fashion that demand by monitoring consumption patterns through time and over space, and in focusing demand on images, lifestyles and products through advertising and special promotions. The processes which link the investigation of the characteristics of the market with production, distribution, sales and after-sales service is termed the 'marketing channel'.

The demand for retailing services in Britain is widely distributed geographically and reflects the major patterns of population. However, the shops and factories supplying them are much more focused spatially. There is thus a practical problem in moving goods over space from producers via shops to consumers. The high cost of this process requires careful coordination and planning. To meet a high level of consumer demand the industry needs to ensure the production of goods in bulk, as well as their storage, packaging and transport to the shops. Once produced, bulk has to be broken into quantities which consumers, predominantly households, will be prepared to buy. Each stage in the sequence from raw materials to final product incurs costs which cannot always be passed directly to the consumer. The ability to introduce procedures to save money depends on the goods being handled and the nature of the channel.

Marketing considered

Marketing is a discipline in its own right with a considerable literature. For the purposes of this book, we have selected only those aspects which we felt

31

necessary to support our discussion of the development and geographical expression of retailing markets in Britain. The books by, for example, Enis and Cox (1988), Cannon (1986) and Kotler (1980) provide a much more comprehensive treatment of the subject.

Some definitions

There are numerous definitions of marketing. The Marketing Staff at Ohio State Univesity (quoted in Dawson 1979, p. 19) suggest the following:

> Marketing is the process in a society by which the demand structure for economic goods and services is anticipated or enlarged and satisfied through the conception, promotion, exchange and physical distribution of such goods and services.

Alternatively, Enis and Cox suggest (1988, p. xi):

> Marketing is that phase of human activity that produces economic want-satisfaction by matching consumers' needs and the resources of business firms. From the firm's point of view, consumer satisfaction is the result of its marketing strategy. Strategy is based in marketing philosophy and is derived from the analysis of consumers and their functional inter-relationships with such market forces as economic conditions, competitors' actions, institutional change, and other environmental factors.

Thirdly, Levitt (1960) suggests that:

> Marketing (is pre-occupied) with the idea of satisfying the needs of the customer by means of the product and the whole cluster of things associated with creating, delivering and finally consuming it. (Levitt 1960, reproduced in Enis and Cox 1988, p. 10)

These definitions indicate that marketing is primarily concerned with meeting consumer needs, both in terms of products and services and in the ways they are delivered by companies. The emphasis of a marketing strategy in the Enis and Cox quotation is particularly important because it suggests that companies may approach the problem in different ways. One may attempt to emphasise price, another the quality of the service it offers, while a third may trade on its image. This is a theme taken up more specifically by Levitt who suggests that a product is rather more than a material entity. It can, for example, be indicative of social standing and status. Creating and delivering a product to the market thus involves understanding how it will be viewed by certain types of consumer. However, before dealing with this, it is necessary to consider how retail markets are created in the first place.

Creating retail markets

According to Beaujeu-Garnier and Delobez (1979), exchange is not an original and inescapable part of human activity. Consequently, neither are markets. Both are products of social and economic relationships which may vary from systems which are based largely on subsistence to those which are complex and can be global in extent.

The development of markets presupposes the existence of goods and services to be traded. These may be surpluses which were unexpected by producers (for example, harvest gluts), or they may have been planned for explicitly. At one extreme, in the isolated, closed system typified by castaways and hermits, surpluses have no particular value. Survival merely requires obtaining an adequate supply of necessities. A glut of production is not necessarily an advantage as problems of storage and perishability can significantly increase an already arduous workload. A surplus can be of value if it can be used for trading with others to obtain goods or services which can materially improve the quality of life.

Modern Britain is, of course, not a society based on castaways and hermits. It is a particularly complex and sophisticated society based on a global system of trade and exchange (see Dicken and Lloyd 1981). The production of surpluses to trade underlies this system and depends upon the tacit acceptance of large-scale production with all its economic, social and environmental implications. As was noted in Chapter 1 very few Britons rely on self-sufficiency. Instead, each individual exists within a finely-stratified, complex division of labour, contributing only a very small, specialised part to the overall production process. Such a system survives because individuals come to accept their economic roles as workers, exchanging their time and labour for wages or salaries which they in turn spend on the products of other specialists. A feature distinguishing modern western societies is that this specialisation applies to the production of both necessities and luxuries, and to the types of consumption associated with them. The mechanism which brings together the surpluses of these different specialists (firms, institutions, individuals) is the market. In modern Britain, this refers to a specialised form of commercial activity rather than to a particular place or building.

The nature of products

When retailers market products, what are they actually providing? Kotler and Levy (1969) suggest that there are at least five distinct types of product, each of which has a different function. These are: physical products (tangible items such as clothes, soap, and food); services (intangible items such as insurance, consultation, banking); persons (marketing the image of individuals such as filmstars or politicians); organisations (marketing the images of companies and institutions using logos), and ideas (disseminating information to change public attitudes, for example, on the use of seat belts in cars or the dangers of passive smoking). These five types are not mutually exclusive. Personal and image marketing can be used with a physical product in the hope that it will be purchased by association. Instead of merely being soap or perfume the product is marketed as aiding cleanliness or beauty. A recent important example is 'green retailing' (see Chapter 8), in which marketing efforts are aimed at saving the planet and popularising products which are environmentally-friendly. Products should thus not be seen merely as functional; they may have a much wider appeal. Marketers can use this to develop positive images for their physical products suggesting that in addition to their function (cleaning, providing a convenience breakfast) they offer health, beauty and status.

A classification of products

The fact that products are more than merely functional means that it is rather complex to classify them into distinct types. The American Marketing Association (1948) suggested the following classification: convenience goods, shopping goods and speciality goods. Convenience goods were defined as those which the consumer buys frequently, immediately and with little effort. Shopping goods were those which customers take more trouble over, comparing different products according to price, quality, style and suitability. Finally, speciality goods were those for which significant groups of consumers were prepared to make special purchasing efforts, for example, travelling considerable distances to make comparisons. The key to this classification was the amount of effort which customers are prepared to put into making a purchase.

Bucklin (1963) suggests that this classification is flawed in a number of ways, principally because it ignores past consumption experience and treats the decision to buy a product and the search for it as independent functions. Bucklin suggested that by recognising past experience, a classification based on a product-patronage matrix could be produced (Table 2.1). The nine categories of this classification are based on assumptions about consumer behaviour which concern both the product being purchased (including specific branded items and undifferentiated items) and the store being patronised. It recognises that for certain types of good, for example, bread, consumers are unlikely to be prepared to worry too much about its manufacturer or where it is bought. Any shop selling bread is thus a likely candidate. However, the combination of speciality good and store indicates the opposite. For these purchases both the producer and supplier are important, perhaps for social status reasons. Both aspects are important influences in the purchasing decision.

Store type	Good type	Purchasing Behaviour
Convenience	Convenience	Buys most readily available product at most accessible store
Convenience	Shopping	Buys best alternative from most accessible store
Convenience	Speciality	Buys favourite brand from most accessible store stocking it
Shopping	Convenience	Indifferent to brand but buys from store which provides best service or price
Shopping	Shopping	Chooses from among goods and shops available
Shopping	Speciality	Chooses preferred brand from store offering best service or price for it
Speciality	Convenience	Buys at specific store but is indifferent as to brand
Speciality	Shopping	Buys at specific store but looks for best product
Speciality	Speciality	Buys preferred brand at preferred store

Table 2.1 Bucklin's classification of goods

While the Bucklin strategy is an improvement on the earlier classification it still fails to capture the complexity of modern shopping. It assumes that the goods being purchased and the choice of stores available are known in some detail and that the shopping trip is predominantly for a single purchase. Both aspects are unlikely to be true on all occasions. Frequently, shopping trips are exploratory or done for fun; a great number of trips are multi-purpose (Williams 1979, Jansen 1989). Furthermore, it says nothing about the types and styles of shopping that are available. In grocery retailing the types of shops found in particular locations are frequently synonymous with styles of shopping. O'Brien and Guy (1985), for example, showed that in Cardiff, studies of organisational differences in retailing could not be separated adequately from locational differences. Large supermarkets operated by national chains tended to predominate in district centres while smaller superettes (frequently independents or members of voluntary chains) predominated in local centres. Increasingly, different types of location offer different types of shopping experience. This topic is considered in more detail in Chapter 5.

Marketing channels

Definition

Marketing channels are collections of institutions which exist to link the productive activities of specialists operating at different spatial scales to consumption patterns in a global economy. The channels assemble, transport, package and distribute the products from source to point of consumption and need to be sensitive to changing consumption practices. Some hypothetical channels are described in Figure 2.1.

The nature of marketing channels varies from product to product and from culture to culture and reflects characteristics of the product such as perishability, standardisation, bulk, unit value, and service requirements (including after-sales service). They also reflect the organisation of modern retailing and its tendency for scrambled merchandising. Firms retailing a variety of products are clearly going to need a different form of channel to those specialising in only one type of product. Dawson (1979) distinguishes two types of channel: product channels and title channels. The former is concerned with the logistics of getting the right products to the right markets. The latter is concerned with the rights of ownership, organisation and exchange. Difficulties can exist if the interests of any one part of the channel conflict with any other.

Channel institutions

Producers and consumers lie at either end of a marketing channel. Between them can be found a variety of different institutions such as wholesalers and transport companies. The efficiency of the channel depends on how the various institutions co-operate. In the last century the channel leaders – those institutions which tended to dominate the performance of the channel – were the producers, especially if they were selling a strongly branded item. They could determine how much was put onto the market in the first place and

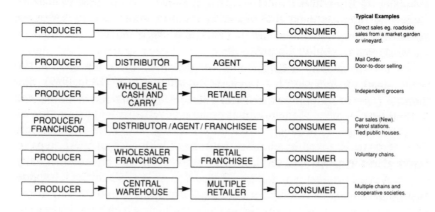

Figure 2.1   Some examples of Marketing Channels

could play retailers off against each other. During the inter-war period, control began to pass from the producer up the channel to intermediaries such as wholesalers, or on to the retailers. Today, the size and national coverage of multiple chain retailers means that they can use specification buying to determine exactly what they want to sell and what they expect from manufacturers. Moreover, some chains have adopted strategies of vertical integration so that they themselves control the production process. Some of the issues involved are discussed in Chapter 3.

Company growth and the marketing mix

According to Levitt:

> There is no such thing as a growth industry . . . There are only companies organised and operated to create and capitalise on growth opportunities. (Levitt 1960, reproduced in Enis and Cox 1988, p. 6)

From the perspective of the retailer, this means searching for consumer characteristics which relate significantly to spending practices and developing products most capable of exploiting them. As discussed in Chapter 1, new trends in work, society and consumption have created considerable growth opportunities for those companies best placed to accommodate them. Successful companies are those which can make the best use of their available information and turn it into products which significant market segments actually want to purchase. Most companies have extensive data holdings on their customers which they can place in context by accessing central and local government reports and statistics, or the publications of property consultants and specialist retail and marketing consultancies such as URPI, Pinpoint Market Research, CACI, the Oxford Institute of Retail Management and Hillier Parker. These data sources may be used to identify the location and characteristics of customers, providing companies with the marketing information they need. (This is a complicated issue which is treated in more detail in Chapter 7.)

The process of anticipating consumer demand to the delivery of the product and its after-care is termed the 'marketing mix' (Dale 1989). She suggests that seven separate steps are involved in this: research on the market; development of the product; pricing; advertising and promotion of the store, image or product; distribution; selling; and after-sales service. Care needs to be taken by channel institutions with each of these steps to ensure that the goods and services being offered for sale are commercially viable. A good product may fail to sell even if there is a market for it because of poor packaging or display, or because it has been offered for sale at the wrong price. This does not simply apply to products which are over-priced. A product which is thought by its intended market to be too cheap will also fail to sell adequately. This is because some products impart social status rather than function and are bought for the image they convey of the purchaser (for example, Porsche cars, designer jeans, vintage champagne).

In general, marketing involves delivering aspects of a way of life (see the discussion on needs and society in Chapter 1). These ways of life vary in their character geographically, reflecting the many local expressions of broader social, economic, and historical processes. It follows therefore, that products and services may need to be marketed differently in different places, and that products which sell particularly well in one part of the country may not sell at all in another.

Researching the market

Who is buying what, where and when are the crucial questions which retailers need to answer. Much of the information needed to answer these can be provided by analysing the retailer's own till receipts and customer files. However, bare quantitative information is not entirely satisfactory as it is always retrospective; it tells the retailer what happened in the past. Information on shopping trends in the near to middle future is rather more useful for exploiting growth opportunities.

One of the most important pieces of information needed by retailers about modern markets is whether they are mass markets – open to the total population – or segmented – really only associated with particular ages, sexes, places, occupations and income groups. A key feature of retailing developments in the post-war period is that mass markets have been breaking down, fragmenting into a plethora of market segments, and retailers have been forced to develop merchandising techniques for specific customer groups. Segmentation is essentially a form of merchandising which creates a specific image for a company or product. The Next group is particularly associated with one form of this type of trading – edited retailing – which involves offering for sale a limited range of coordinated products for a specific client group. The initial target was 'women who care about fashion first and price second' (Ody 1984), but this was soon followed up by Next for Men, Next Interiors and Next Jewellery. Market segmentation is perhaps most obvious in the fashion business, but is evident throughout the whole industry. The processes involved in identifying segments and analysing retailing data are considered in Chapter 7.

Development of products

In the past many retailers were noted for their specialisms in particular types of retailing, for example, butchers, bakers, drapers. However, many of the most important of today's retailers are 'scrambled merchandisers', that is, they sell a wide range of products though they may still have a core business. Grocers such as Sainsbury and Tesco have expanded their product ranges from grocery items to include goods such as electrical equipment, home furnishings and pot plants.

The responsibility for getting the right goods into the shops lies with the retail firms' buyers (not to be confused with customers). In small shops the owner or manager may do the buying based on his/her experience of local market tastes. In larger companies however, buying is likely to be done centrally by professional specialists using a sourcing network which may be national or international. The information they use may be gathered from previous contacts with suppliers, or from trade magazines, sales literature and trade conferences. Many of the latter are major events bringing together buyers and producers from all over the world (for example, the fashion shows in Paris, the Book Fair in Frankfurt, and the Toy Fair in Harrogate).

Large companies can also use their size and commercial muscle to ensure that the products they sell are tailored for their needs. Whereas smaller retailers have to rely on what they can get from producers or wholesalers, larger companies can operate a form of 'specification buying' where manufacturers produce to meet their specific needs. This is a key feature of modern retailing in that the balance of power in marketing channels has shifted in favour of the retailer. Scrambled merchandising allows retailers to gather comprehensive information on a wide range of different goods produced by many different manufacturers who are competing for their trade. They are the only institution in the marketing channel to have this strategic information and are increasingly exploiting it to their commercial advantage.

Pricing

The price of a product or service is the amount of money required to purchase it. This sounds simple enough, but it can be difficult to calculate. Retailers have to set their prices sufficiently high to cover the costs of buying, storing, transporting and displaying the products. They must also pay their staff, many of whom are not actively involved in selling, pay their local and national taxes, and have sufficient money available to reinvest in the company. In recent years, the refurbishment of many stores and the relocation of others to new sites has added a significant level of expense to British retailers. Bamfield (1988) suggests that £500m and £1000m are being spent per year on refurbishment and relocation respectively (see Chapter 5). Fixing the right price therefore depends on assessing what the customer is willing to pay in the context of stock turnover, costs, government legislation, royalties and risk (Dale 1989).

Many companies use price as only a component in developing their corporate image. Marks and Spencer, for example, emphasise the quality of their merchandise as their principal marketing feature. Food discounter Kwiksave, on the other hand have trimmed virtually all design features from their stores in an effort to minimise their prices. Low pricing is part of the corporate image, quality of store design is not. *The Independent* (15th May 1990) notes that the market for low-cost grocery retailing served by Kwiksave and being targetted by German discounter, Aldi, is bound to increase, especially from the pool of captive buyers who live on peripheral housing estates and rely on public transport.

Companies can offer goods under a variety of different pricing strategies depending on the goods they sell and the market they are trying to build. New products which are likely to be novelties and of interest to innovators and enthusiasts can initially be priced expensively but later reduced as they become more widely popular. This 'market skimming' was used with most of the major electrical products offered for sale since the 1960s, for examples, hi-fis, home computers, compact disc players, and video recorders. Alternative pricing policies include: loss leaders (usually routine shopping items); odd pricing (pricing to 99 pence or £99 in an effort to suggest cheapness), and quality pricing (charging significantly above-cost prices to suggest the item is a quality product).

Advertising

The principal purpose of advertising is to encourage sales by creating a positive attitude to a product or company. Lavidge and Steiner (1961) note that advertisers should not expect to see an immediate increase in sales as a result of an advertising campaign. They suggest that:

> consumers normally do not switch from disinterested individuals to convinced purchasers in one instantaneous step. Rather they approach the ultimate purchase through a process or series of steps in which the actual purchase is but the final threshold. (Lavidge and Steiner 1961, p. 59)

The purpose of advertising is to produce awareness, then turn that into emotions favouring the product, and finally produce a motive for purchasing. Large sales can be expected if the right customer groups can be turned from unaware consumers into motivated consumers whose attention is focused on the particular product.

To attain this, advertisers need to know something about why people purchase products and where they live. Adverts on television or on commercial radio can reach a huge audience but this will not necessarily produce sales if the groups most likely to be interested to do not see or hear them. A better strategy might be to advertise in particular newspapers or on particular radio stations. Adverts for specialist products or services can be placed in their special interest literature such as gardening, hi-fi and photography magazines.

Donaldson (1973), echoing Galbraith (1969), notes that all advertising provides some information on products and services and that this may lead to an increase in consumer choice. Conversely, advertising campaigns may be almost devoid of information, seeking instead to emphasise the name of a company or to extol the virtues of a product only in the most general terms. In so far as such advertising seeks to persuade customers to change their purchasing behaviour, it may be thought to limit consumer sovereignty. These issues are considered in more detail in Chapter 6.

Distribution

Distribution is concerned with getting the goods into the store and onto the sales floor. Many goods are produced in bulk and cannot possibly be offered for sale unless repackaged into consumable bundles. At the same time as the goods are broken in bulk, they can be prepared for display with labels and prices attached. However, all this takes time and costs money. It is also enormously difficult to administer. Sparks (1986) notes that the largest component cost in retailers' distribution channels is administration. Attaining economies of scale in administration as well as storage, transport and inventory can reduce product handling time and costs, making scrambled merchandising possible. Without these being achieved, it is unlikely that many of the modern forms of trading could occur as the handling costs of different types of product serving different markets would be prohibitive.

The breaking of bulk can take place either at the retail store, at the place of manufacture, or at some intermediate point in the marketing channel such as at the premises of a wholesaler. Many retailers have invested in their own warehousing facilities, creating regional or local distribution networks which only forward goods to the point of sale when they are actually required. These systems are controlled centrally and are designed to keep stock in storage for as little time as possible. Such 'just-in-time' systems are immensely efficient at reducing distribution costs and increasing selling space in shops, and are now considered a vital component in policies to maintain or increase market share.

Selling

There are numerous ways of selling products. Three approaches which involve the customer being present in a shop are: counter service, self-service and assisted self-selection. Counter selling is most widely adopted today to sell expensive high-status products such as perfumes, jewellery and fashion goods. Frequently, these will be sophisticated products which attract premium prices and which cannot be sold effectively without an element of personal service. The sales skills required for this form of selling may be considerable, involving, for example, technical knowledge about the product. A typical example might be helping an undecided purchaser of a camera or home computer select the product which is most appropriate to his/her needs. As the purchaser to some extent 'depends' on this advice, the company's reputation can suffer dramatically if the advice is incorrect or given in a curt or undiplomatic way. Clearly, this method of selling is relatively expensive to operate and, although it is traditionally important in British retailing, most companies have limited its use wherever possible.

For products which do not carry status connotations, cheaper methods of selling may be adopted. In self-service selling goods are collected from around the store by the shoppers themselves and interaction with staff is severely limited. The only member of staff involved in the purchasing process may be the check-out operator, whose level of knowledge about particular products may be limited in the extreme. Self-service allows the customers to pick and choose from the available goods on offer without feeling intimidated by sales staff. This may make the goods seem rather more attractive as more time can be spent comparing them with other brands and items on sale. The grocery industry has pioneered the development of self-service, but in recent years, has mixed this procedure with some counter service where particular products merit this attention (in-store delicatessens, bakeries, fish counters).

The third form of selling – assisted self-selection – falls somewhere between counter service and self-service. It is predominantly a form of self-service in that customers are allowed to browse and select goods at will but in the knowledge that help is available should it be required. Garden centres tend to offer this type of selling by providing specialist horticultural and landscape design staff who may be consulted should advice be required.

A form of selling which does not require the customer to be present in the store is direct mail selling. This is a process by which companies sell their products and services directly to the public using the post or parcel delivery systems. The company produces a catalogue or series of seasonal or special-interest catalogues and distributes these to potential customers whose names and addresses have been selected from company or public records (see Chapter 7). The catalogue provides information on prices and delivery and frequently some form of credit or budget arrangement is available. There is nothing new in catalogue shopping; the Sears Roebuck catalogue has been available in the USA since the late 19th century, bringing big town shopping to people located anywhere in the country. In Britain, a major direct mail retailer is Great Universal Stores (GUS) who trade using a variety of names, of names, and who operate their own nationwide van delivery system, White Arrow.

A hybrid of all four types of selling listed above is illustrated by stores such as Argos and Index. These make use of catalogues to publicise their stock, but also employ counter staff for products such as jewellery. Sales are made by the customer filling in a sales slip and handing this to till operators. They in turn call the goods from a warehouse, handing them to customers over the counter after a short delay. Such a system has been designed to minimise costs by reducing 'evaporation' (a euphemism for shoplifting).

After-sales service

Product reliability is a major element in assessing its quality. If a product is expensive and relatively novel, it is unlikely to develop mass appeal unless some additional support is offered to the customer should it break down. Government legislation offers protection against the sale of defective goods or goods which do not perform as described. However, claiming one's rights can involve going to court which can be expensive and is in any case a deterrent to many people. After-sales service and retailer guarantees provide one way of reducing the risks associated with consuming potentially defective products. They can also be used as a form of marketing device in that stores can be differentiated in terms of the help they provide customers who are dissatisfied with purchases. Clearly a company which is helpful and willing to listen is likely to do better than one which is not.

Marketing trends

The growth of merchandising for market segments is the key development for the 1990s. Bamfield (1988) suggests that many of the most successful multiples trading today are using new marketing techniques to develop trade. Some are focusing their attention on niche markets specialising in particular products (for example, Tie Rack, The Body Shop, Knickerbox), or are concentrating their efforts on key merchandising areas (Woolworths). Others are trading upmarket, developing images of quality, comfort and convenience to attract customers. Cooperation, corporate acquisitions and relocation are also being adopted by the bigger operators. Many of these are considered in more detail in Chapter 3.

Much of the motivation for these developments comes from recent retailing experiences abroad. An article in *The Times* (17 June 1989) noted that retailers are flocking to Japan to get new ideas about retailing. It claimed that Japan has the best department stores in the world offering customer services which are unrivalled anywhere. For example, Seibu's Yurakucho branch has an interactive video system with information available in four languages, and a dozen in-house restaurants. These have been designed to make shopping attractive and enjoyable as well as informative for both the consumer and the retailer. The Japanese have been particularly innovative concerning retailing with a list of developments including in-store computer systems, curved escalators, in-shops (small companies trading as departments within department stores), galleria (vertical shopping malls with shops and cafes), and in-store credit cards. The article concluded:

> What makes the Japanese so influential is not just the range of merchandise that they have to offer, although that is certainly important. It is the way things are sold that really counts. (*The Times* 17 June 1989, p. 43).

This does not mean that all new retailing developments will have to be large corporate developments. Indeed, there is already evidence to suggest that corporatism is too readily associated by discerning consumers with sameness. Up and down the country one can find stores operated by single companies which look and feel very much like each other. The store design and layout are manipulated to create a market image which will be immediately recognisable to shoppers wherever they come from. However, this can lead to very dull shopping with the particular attractions of locations being ignored in pursuit of a national image. Increasingly, even the larger companies have come to recognise the importance of being distinctive.

Conclusions

Marketing is a process which attempts to meet public demands for goods and services by establishing their supply. The nature of the demand, its frequency, magnitude and spatial extent all influence the type of marketing decisions which can be made. These may vary from the periodic market in which trade only takes place when products become available, to the commonplace shopping systems of Britain and most western capitalist economies in which goods always seem to be available, even 'out of season'. In these, marketing is an established business in its own right which attempts to iron-out the imbalances in demand and supply by manipulating both. It may do this in a number of ways. First, by contributing to the decisions of producers about what to produce and when, and so influencing the channel of supply. Second, by affecting the types of outlet that are available and so influencing the channel of demand. Third, by affecting qualitative changes in the market, both in terms of what is demanded and by whom. This type of manipulation affects the very nature of demand which, in turn, influences supply. These are important issues for contemporary British retailing.

CHAPTER 3

British Retailing

Introduction

The purpose of this chapter is to describe some of the more significant characteristics of modern British retailing. Britain has something of a reputation for being a nation of small shopkeepers. However, data on the organisational structure of British retailing show that it is far removed from this image. Many British retailers are large national and international business conglomerates whose activities tend to require large shops suitably sited with respect to their markets. They are often powerful businesses with commercial interests outside retailing, whose entry into a local economy can have major implications for the existing provision. In addition, they are also major employers, particularly of women, providing jobs for approximately 10% of the workforce. However, retail employment is very variable in its nature and character, ranging from part-time shelf-filling to fully-developed business careers. The educational and gender differences between these two extremes are considerable.

Throughout the twentieth century the trends in British retailing have been towards concentrating commercial power in the hands of a relatively small number of corporations, each adopting some form of scrambled merchandising from specially selected sites. This does not mean that all retailers fit this pattern, merely that the key forces underlying British retailing change have been like this. There are still many opportunities for small operators to exploit niche markets and niche locations. The corporations have not as yet cornered the whole of the market. This chapter looks at the character of the British retailer and emphasises the importance of ownership, organisation and location.

The development of retailing in Britain

The marketing processes leading to the contemporary retailing system can be traced back historically for little more than 150 years. What types of shopping are available to us today are the results of capitalist, industrial, economic processes operating and developing over that period.

A classic account of the historical development of British retailing is Jeffreys (1954). This is largely an economic analysis of retailing change in the period 1850–1950. Several distinct phases are identified. First, the period before 1850 when Britain was still largely an agricultural country with a predominantly rural population. Second, the period 1850–1914, which corresponded with increasing urban growth and industrialisation. Third, the period from 1914–1950, which saw a consolidation of the previous trends in large-scale retailing, but with the introduction of a degree of rigidity in certain retailing markets.

Pre-industrial retailing

Before 1850 there were essentially four distinct ways of buying finished consumer goods. First, from trade shops associated with particular guilds (for example, grocers, hosiers, haberdashers, and mercers of various kinds). Second, from producer-retailers, such as blacksmiths, cobblers and cabinet-makers, who would make the produce they sold. Third, from markets and the occasional fair (for example, the St Giles' fair in Oxford) in which local agricultural products could be bought alongside imported items. Fourth, from itinerant traders, peddlers and bagmen who carried whatever items they considered saleable. This system, however spartan compared with today's retailing system, was already a development on practices common before 1800 which emphasised self-sufficiency and the use of fairs and periodic markets. However, though

> the changes of the previous hundred years had ended the practice of the family unit growing and making an important proportion of the essential goods it required . . . dependence of the whole population on the market for the supplies of necessities was not yet complete. (Jeffreys 1954, p. 3)

By 1850, there were few seeds of the modern system as retailing was still largely a series of skilled trades requiring formal training or an apprenticeship. Retailers were almost invariably working for themselves from small premises and few would have more than one shop. In the towns and cities, one might find all four types of retailing, but with types one and two probably catering for the needs of a more well-to-do clientele whose interests and demands could dictate what was produced. Though this has an element of modern niche marketing about it, its overall effect was minimal at this time. As Jeffreys notes:

> The basic structure and character of the distributive trades, the small-scale of the units engaged in the trade, the emphasis on skill and experience in retailing, the higgling as to price, and the important role played by open markets, had not been changed fundamentally. (Jeffreys 1954, p. 5)

Pre-1914 retailing

The period after 1850 and before the First World War was a time of significant economic change in Britain. The 1851 Population Census showed, for the first time, that Britain was no longer an agricultural country with a largely rural population. Instead, more Britons lived in towns and cities than on the land, and had consequently come to rely on the products of industrial capitalism for their sustenance. During this period, Britain's imperial power reached its height, with a world-wide marketplace leading to major structural changes in the nature of the domestic economy. An increasing (urban) population, a buoyant economy and low levels of unemployment led to new demands for goods and services. The Empire allowed new sources of supply to be tapped, and industrialisation made new methods of production possible. A developing transport system, both within Britain (railways), and overseas (steam ships and refrigeration), also made new channels of distribution inevitable. The economic shift occurring at this time, opened new opportunities for retailing, and laid the ground for our modern system.

These changes affected retailing in a number of ways. First, the importance of skill and tradition gradually diminished as more emphasis was placed on salesmanship and commerce. Products could now be marketed, especially by price, and customers attracted to buy merchandise by advertising (billboards, sandwich-board salesmen etc). Second, there was a growth in the number of 'lock-up' shops. These were premises used exclusively for business and contrasted with the shops of the previous period which also functioned as family homes for the shopkeeper. Third, entirely new forms of retailing began to emerge during this period. Large-scale retailing began to assume importance in a number of trades, and led to new forms of shop, for example, the multiple, the co-op and the department store. Fourth, haggling was superseded in most trades to be replaced by 'shop prices' set by the retailer. Between 1875 and 1900 there was a period of severe price competition as a result, and this led to demands by the public and smaller retailers for the introduction of a system of resale price maintenance The advantage of such a system was that the responsibility for setting prices was shared by retailers and manufacturers, with the latter's influence restricting extreme price variability.

The key development of this period was the emergence of large-scale retailing, that is, commercial practices which benefit from some of the economies of scale typically associated with manufacturing. The development of the co-operative system (especially in the North and Scotland), multiple retailing (mostly nationwide) and department store trading owed much to the presence of several desirable circumstances. The concentration of the population in urban, industrial areas provided retailers with a large, steady and consistent demand for products. Industrial productivity made it possible to produce a large, steady and consistent supply of these products, and the exploitation of the Empire and overseas trade increased the volume of trade and changed the character of other established trades. There were now markets for entirely new products such as factory-made footwear and clothing, patent medicines and margarine. Traditional markets for dairy produce and meat were transformed by the introduction of refrigeration and bulk trading.

These factors made it possible for retailers to think of regional and even national markets for their products instead of restricting themselves to local markets. The introduction of limited liability made the task easier because the funds for expansion could now be raised from shareholders on the Stock Exchange and not merely from the use of retained profits. While the use of profits might allow limited expansion from local to regional scale, few companies could possibly afford the financing of national operations solely from their own resources. By 1914 a number of giant firms existed which had successfully established national distribution networks and operated from many hundreds of branches. Among these were WH Smith, The Singer Sewing Machine Company, Eastmans and James Nelson (both butchers), Home and Colonial Stores, Maypole Dairy, Liptons Ltd., Freeman, Hardy and Willis (shoes), and Boots. Such developments were made possible by their achieving scale economies in buying, specialisation economies in administration and standardisation economies in selling. All these companies were multiple traders, operating from many branches around the country, but offering a similar range of standard products at reasonable prices.

Multiple trading grew steadily from the middle of the nineteenth century. In 1875, Jeffreys notes that there were some 29 multiple firms in Britain controlling nearly 1000 branches. Most of these were in the footwear and grocery trades. By 1895, the figure had risen to 201 firms and 8000 branches, and by 1915, 433 firms and 23,000 branches, and many more trades were involved (for example, men's outfitting and chemists). Between 8% and 10% of all retail trade passed through the hands of the multiple retailer, compared with 9% for co-ops and 3% for department stores.

Pre-1950s retailing

By 1920 the three principal forms of large retailer – the multiple trader, the co-op movement and the department stores – accounted for more than 20% of the retail trade in Britain, a figure which had grown from about 3% in 1875. Between 1914 and 1950, the relative importance of the large retailer continued to grow. A number of important differences distinguish this period from the past. Of particular significance was the relationship between large-scale distribution and large-scale manufacturing. By introducing resale price maintenance, the government had given manufacturers a particularly strong hand in the distribution and sale of their products. Retailers carrying these products were obliged to work within guidelines laid down in consultation with manufacturers. These affected the ways the products were presented, displayed, advertised and sold (with restrictions on price levels particularly important). A distinction needs to be drawn between products which had strong brand and market images and those which were generic. Manufacturers with a particular intention to promote and develop their own branded items exerted a strong influence over retailers during this period compared with manufacturers whose trade did not depend on branded products.

The relationships between manufacturer and retailer were affected by other factors too. New systems of credit, purchasing agreements and sales strategies were developed between them. Deliveries from manufacturers to retailers became more frequent and better organised, and a whole new type of work was created to support them, for example, the company representative, the order clerk, delivery men, etc. These arrangements ensured that both retailers and manufacturers obtained information on what was required in advance of time and so could prepare adequately for it.

The relationship between retailers and consumers also changed during this period. The high street became the centre of retailing and greater attention was paid by retailers to getting an appropriate site (see Chapter 4). More care was also paid by retailers to ensure that their shops were attractive and elaborately fitted, encouraging consumers to regard shopping as a pleasurable activity rather than a routine chore. Home delivery was encouraged, small orders were accepted and a wide assortment of credit arrangements (both formal and informal) were possible.

Since 1950 there have been major changes in British retailing which have radically altered this traditional pattern. Resale price maintenance was abolished in 1964 leading to price competition between the major firms and the development of 'discounters' in the grocery trade. Price cutting and the introduction of trading stamps were all attempted in the effort to retain market share. The emphasis of counter service was replaced by self-service, initially in grocery retailing, but later throughout much of the industry allowing consumers the opportunity to handle products themselves. In the 1980s, competition by price became relatively less important, and many retailers became more concerned with factors such as competition by quality, image, and store location.

Britain's contemporary retailing industry

Table 3.1 presents a description of the industrial structure of the British economy in 1987 based on the Department of Employment's Standard Industrial Classification (1980 definition). This classification attempts to

Industry	Class (1980 SIC)	Number of employees (in 000s)	%of total workforce
Banking, finance insurance	81 – 85	2,306	11
Retail Distribution	64 – 65	2,074	10
Public Administration	91 – 92	1,974*	9
Education	93	1,645	8
'Other' services	94, 96 – 99	1,610	7
Medical, Health and veterinary services	95	1,267	6
Wholesale distribution and repair	61 – 63, 67	1,218	6
Hotel and catering	66	1,095	5
Construction	50	988	5
Transport	71 – 77	895	4

*Note: Figures for Public Administration exclude those employed in building, education, health etc.

Table 3.1   Employees in employment in Britain's top ten industries – June 1987

(Source: Extracted from Tables 1.1 and 1.2, Employment Gazette, November 1987)

provide a fair and consistent picture of the character of the British economy by identifying what work is being performed and aggregating it into categories which are as similar as possible. The aggregation used in Table 3.1 is based on industrial classes. Retailing, or retail distribution to give it its full name, covers classes 64 and 65.

From Table 3.1, which shows only the top ten industries in 1987, we can see that more than 2 million people rely on retailing for work. It is the second largest industrial grouping behind banking, finance and insurance, and is roughly twice as large as the hotel and catering industry and the construction industry. Manufacturing, extractive industries and agriculture – the old core of industrial Britain – do not appear in the top ten. As these core industries have declined, retailing has been growing in importance, both relatively and absolutely. The proportion employed has risen by 7% between 1978 and 1988. Employment in manufacturing fell by 26% over the same period.

Like all classification schemes, the label 'retailing' subsumes a wide variety of different types of work. To see how the overall total is composed, the industrial classes forming retail distribution (classes 64–5) can be disaggregated into their component industrial groups. This shows that more than 300 different occupations contribute to the industry as a whole, with many people employed behind the scenes at different points in a range of

Group	No. of employees in thousands		% of workforce employed part-time	
	Female	Male	Female	Male
641 Food	377	218	69	27
653 – 656 'Other' retail distribution	366	161	54	18
645 – 646 clothing, footwear, leather goods	196	53	60	17
642 Confectioners, Tobacconists etc.	99	35	74	43
648 Household goods, hardware and Ironmongery	97	107	53	NA
643 Dispensing and other chemists	95	17	56	29
651 – 652 Motor vehicles and parts, filling stations	64	161	39	18
All retailing groups	1,304	771	63	37
Notes: NA = Not Available				

Table 3.2 Employment in retail distribution in June 1987 by industrial group (1980 SIC)

(Source: Based on figures published in Table 1.4, Employment Gazette, November 1987)

marketing channels. Table 3.2 shows some of the key areas of retail employment in June 1987.

The largest contributing group is the food industry with roughly 30% of the industry total, followed by non-food retailing which contributes almost another quarter. Though women make up two-thirds of all retailing employees, in almost every contributing group they are employed in predominantly part-time jobs. Only in groups 651–2 (motor vehicles and parts, filling stations) is the percentage of female part-time workers less than 50% of the female workforce. Compared with all industries and services, we can see that part-time female employment is relatively over-represented in retailing, and full-time male employment is relatively under-represented (Table 3.3). This leads to a bimodal labour force, with repetitive tasks such as cleaning, shelf-filling and operating cash registers being performed

	Female		Male	
	% full-time	% part-time	% full-time	% part-time
Retail Distribution	24	38	31	7
All industries and services	25	20	51	4

Table 3.3   Percentage distribution of part-time/full-time workforce (June 1987)

(Source: Based on data from Employment Gazette)

predominantly by women and management tasks – buying, advertising, stock control, site location – by men. This bimodality is particularly striking in the retail grocery industry (Wrigley 1988).

The combined effect of retailing activity on the economy is summarised in Table 3.4. This shows the volume of retail sales produced by the industry since 1950. Accompanying this growth in volume have been major restructurings of the industry, with trends towards fewer, larger stores and the concentration of retailing in a smaller number of companies. Some of the largest of these are household names, for example, Marks and Spencer, Burton, House of Fraser. What is perhaps not always realised is the scale and success of these companies. Dale (1989) notes that Marks and Spencer has a turnover of £4 billion, while the Sears group, which includes Selfridges department store, Dolcis footwear, Mappin and Webb jewellers, as well as a host of other high street names in clothing and fashion, has a turnover of £2 billion. Wrigley (1988), focusing exclusively on grocery retailing, notes that the major actors – Sainsburys, Tesco, Asda, the Dee Corporation (including Gateway), and the Argyll Group (including Safeway) – all have annual levels of turnover between £2 billion and £4 billion. If the overall total is barely £60 billion, the relative importance of these large companies is considerable.

Wrigley (1988) suggests six technological changes which have helped retailing reach this position of strength: the introduction of self-service in many areas of business; the search for economies of scale by merchandising and substituting labour; the development of automated or mechanised warehousing; the use of pallets or cages to remove distribution difficulties on the sales floor; computerised stock control, and enhanced distribution

Date	Number of outlets	Volume (£bn)
1950	583,000	40.6
1982	342,000	57.2
Note: Constant 1980 prices.		

Table 3.4   Volume of retail sales

(Source: Institute of Fiscal Studies 1984)

networks and marketing channels. Although these changes are perhaps most evident in grocery retailing, other areas of the industry have benefited from them too.

A classification of British retailing

One feasible classification of modern British retailing has already been introduced earlier in this chapter: multiple chain stores, co-operatives, department stores. These tend to be the 'big' retailers with many shops, large workforces and high levels of turnover. A fourth major type of retailer not considered in any detail earlier – the independent – is normally defined as having fewer than ten shops. These are perhaps the major organisational classes currently extant. However, there are a number of specialist subtypes and hybrids: voluntary chains, franchises, mail order firms, door-to-door selling, mobile shops, and periodic markets. Finally, there is the informal sector, consisting of things as diverse as hospital shops and flea markets. These distinctions are not necessarily mutually exclusive.

Multiple chain retailing

The multiple chain retailer was first defined by the 1961 Census of Distribution as a company operating from 10 or more outlets. The purpose of multiple trading is to offer consumers a wide range of standardised products at competitive prices, achieving these by bulk purchasing and other scale economies. Each store in the chain is deliberately designed to look like any other so that customers become familiar with the company's corporate image. Each store will typically stock the same products and use the same sorts of advertising and window display to attract customers. The major retailing groups mentioned above are all multiple chain retailers. This is by far the most important sector of the industry. Dawson (1979, p. 155) notes that using the 1961 definition:

> it would be estimated that well over half retail sales in Britain pass through the multiple retail organisations who are fewer than 2 percent of all retail firms.

The top ten retailers in the UK in 1988 as measured by sales were all corporate multiples. Each had sales figures exceeding £1 billion. Sainsbury topped the list with sales of £4.3 billion, followed by Marks and Spencer and Tesco with sales of just over £4 billion. The other members of the top ten were: Gateway, the Argyll Group, Asda, Woolworth Holdings, Boots, Sears and the John Lewis Partnership. A particular feature of corporate multiples in retailing is that they are frequently larger than their suppliers. This has meant that they can often dictate the pace of change in retail markets and compete with producers directly by the use of 'own-brand' products. In 1988, 37% of packaged goods sales in Safeways (a member of the Argyll Group) was of own-brand items.

Co-operative retailing

The co-operative movement is a particular form of multiple chain retailing developed originally during the early and middle nineteenth century to provide working class shoppers with a form of 'honest trading' to counter the abuses associated with the truck or company shop system. Unlike other types of multiple chain, the co-operative system is not designed primarily to make profit. In the original model, said to have been developed in Rochdale in 1844 (but see Purvis 1986 for an alternative interpretation), shoppers formed their own societies to buy groceries and household items at preferential prices. Any profits generated as a result of trading were passed back to members in the form of annual dividends. The underlying philosophy of the movement was fairness and consumer control rather than creating a new form of commercial activity. The movement was particularly strong in the north of England and in Scotland. Jeffreys (1954) notes that in 1919, 45% of the residents of Northumberland and Durham were members of co-operatives. This contrasts with the 5% of London residents who made use of this form of retailing.

Since the Second World War, competition from multiples and independents has squeezed the co-ops whose share of the retail market has fallen from 11% in 1961 to 5% in 1984 (Bamfield 1988). There are several reasons for this decline. First, in spite of increased co-operation between societies and the creation of a single brand name and advertising symbol, the co-operative movement has failed to achieve the levels of co-ordination necessary to compete successfully with multiple retailers (Davies 1976). Second, the process of dispersing profits by an annual dividend has reduced the resources available for re-investment in new stores and locations. Many co-ops are today poorly located with respect to their markets. Third, there has been a conflict of interest between those who see co-operatives as commercial enterprises and those who see them in their original terms. This has led to an inadequate marketing focus and a poor market image in many parts of the country.

Department Stores

The department store emerged in the mid-nineteenth century as a development of the drapery trade. Its purpose was to sell a wide variety of products under the same roof – in many ways the original scrambled merchandiser – focusing attention on the emerging middle classes. Originally, they traded on price, but after 1900, more attention was paid to the range of products available, their quality and the attractiveness of the premises. Jeffreys (1954, p. 20) notes:

> special lines were advertised at low prices from time to time, but the main sales emphasis had moved (by 1900) almost imperceptibly from price appeal to selection, amenity, comfort and service appeal.

Today, many well-known department stores are parts of chains of stores. The House of Fraser chain for example controls stores all over the country, including Harrods (Knightsbridge), Rackhams (Birmingham), Kendals (Manchester), Dingles (Bristol), Binns (Newcastle), and Cavendish House (Cheltenham). Each store trades under its local name (though it does trade as House of Fraser in major edge-of-town developments such as the Gateshead Metro Centre and Sheffield's Meadowhall) capitalising on an image which may have taken decades to create. The type of shopping environment offered varies depending on the size and shape of the stores, but efforts have been made to standardise facilities as far as possible. Customer services are identical, and each store sells products under the chain's own brand – Allander. In contrast, department stores such as British Home Stores, Selfridges and Debenhams are part of more diverse groups (Storehouse, Sears and the Burton Group respectively). Products on sale in other members of the group are likely to be different from the department stores, but in-house credit and budgeting facilities for use at some if not all members offers some degree of standardisation.

Independents

The independent sector of retailing corresponds to all those businesses which have fewer than ten outlets. In many cases they are sole proprietorships or partnerships which operate usually from one or two small shops, but it is useful to distinguish between 'large' and 'small' independents, the latter being single outlet retailers.

Since the Second World War there has been a major decline in shop numbers (Table 3.5). Much of the loss has been felt in the independent sector which was either financially incapable of responding to change or was too conservative to try. Dale (1989) notes that independents have largely disappeared from many of their original trades and now can only function if they offer a special service (for example, ethnic retailing) or are prepared to open at unsocial hours. However, the development of corporate retailing has not eliminated specialist independents who trade in products such as gifts, musical equipment, hobbies and models, and antiques. For these retailers the nature of the personal service they can provide means that they trade differently from the multiples and so have not been devastated by their growth. Because the cost of entering the independent market is relatively small, independent traders are still common in typical high street trades such as meat, greengrocery and hardware.

Voluntary chains

One of the more interesting strategies adopted by the independents to compete against the multiple traders has been to form voluntary chains. These may be organised either by the retailers themselves or by wholesalers and are designed to obtain for members the benefits of bulk purchasing and a corporate image. Voluntary chains are best known in the grocery industry through companies such as Spar, Mace, VG and Londis. Each of these companies has over 1000 outlets which provide a similar range of products and style of retailing. Corporate logos and standardised shop design have been attempted to create public awareness of the shops.

Voluntary chains and buying groups also exist in other areas of retailing. Examples include the Unichem, Vantage and Numark 'chains' of chemists. Unichem is the largest of these with over 5000 outlets compared to the 2000 or so outlets in each of the others. The sheer size of these groups makes them candidates for development into corporate multiples. Similarly, Interflora (florists), Intersport (sports goods) and Spectrum (computers) are also voluntary chains.

Franchises

A franchise is a form of semi-independent retailing which occurs throughout the industry but is perhaps most widely associated with fast food, toiletries and fashion clothes. It has developed very quickly in Britain during the 1980s with support from the four major clearing banks. In the USA where franchising is more widely established, it accounts for roughly 34% of all retail sales and 10% of gross national product. Stern and Southworth (1988) note that there are essentially four distinct types of franchises. The classification, based on the work of Charles Vaughn is: manufacturer-retailer franchises; manufacturer-wholesaler franchises; wholesaler-retailer franchises; and business format franchises. The business format franchise is the type most commonly recognised by the public though it is the most recent of the four.

The idea behind business format franchising is that independent shopkeepers purchase the right to market a well-known, tried and tested product which has a strong market image. Examples include Kentucky Fried Chicken, Pizza Hut, Prontaprint, Benetton and The Body Shop. These businesses started from small roots but have proven to be commercially successful. Therefore, rather than the originator continuing to develop the business in the conventional way by opening more stores and taking on greater commercial risks, he/she trades in the market image of the business as a franchisor, allowing others (franchisees) to take the risk of operating the new stores in return for a continuing service fee. The franchisor agrees to provide training, marketing skills and management advice. The franchisee agrees to market the product along the lines required by the franchisor, retaining for a period, a small spatial monopoly in the product. This is not a bad deal for either party as the high-profile image of the business probably removes much of the risk anyway. A study funded by the National Westminster Bank and cited in Stern and Stanworth (1988) notes that there are currently about 15,000 franchised business format outlets operating in Britain, providing employment for 145,000 people and generating an annual turnover of £3 billion.

The three alternative types of franchise defined in the Vaughn classification are examples of marketing channels set up by producers and wholesalers to control the distribution of a product. Car-lorry dealerships and petrol service stations fit the first category, accounting for 32% of all US franchises in 1986; the soft drinks bottling industry controlled by manufacturers such as Coca-Cola, Pepsi and Seven-Up fits the second, and the voluntary chains described above fit the third.

Door-to-door selling

Door-to-door selling is used with a wide variety of different types of product. At one extreme, there are latter-day 'pedlars'; at the other, there are the trained sales staff of major companies selling products such as cosmetics (Avon) or cleaning equipment (Betterware). A variant of the basic approach is the Tupperware party where householders are effectively commissioned to sell products to their friends and neighbours. This party planning idea has been extended successfully to other product lines such as childrens' clothes, books and china. 'Cold calling' by telephone is another modification which is useful where door-to-door selling is thought to be commercially viable but the products being offered are expensive (double glazing, time-share holidays, life assurance).

Mail order

Mail order trading was described as a form of selling in Chapter 2. It involves producing catalogues of goods and services which are marketed directly to named consumers or are provided for customers to take from retail stores.

Companies such as Grattan, Kays, and Family Album trade entirely by mail order, while others, such as Habitat, provide a mail order service to supplement their high street operations. Most of the key operators in the business are members of multiples. However, charities and voluntary organisations also make use of mail order, using their subscription lists for direct selling. Mail order trading has grown throughout the 1980s with annual spurts of over 11% in 1985 and 1988. Its penetration has been greatest in the clothing and footwear trades where it now accounts for over 10% of trade.

Mail order trading is dominated by two groups – Great Universal Stores and Littlewoods – who have 40% and 25% of the market respectively. These groups trade under a variety of different names producing catalogues for closely targeted markets. The companies trading under the Great Universal Stores banner include Great Universal, John England, Family Album, Marshall Ward, Kays, and John Myers. Companies trading under the Littlewoods banner include John Moores, Brian Mills, Janet Frazer and Imagination. Other groups with 10% of the market are Freemans (Together, SW5) and Grattan (Grattan, Kaleidoscope, Scotcade, Streets of London).

Mobile shops

One of the earliest forms of trading to be developed in Britain involved the sales of products by itinerant craftsmen and bagmen (Alexander 1970). In spite of the concentration of retailing in stores and shopping centres, there is still room for mobile shops, whether they be for the sale of ice-creams, fish, fruit, vegetables, or tea. The most important form of mobile shop currently to be found in Britain is the milk float. Increasingly milk floats provide a wide variety of products in addition to milk, for example, eggs, butter, soft drinks, yoghurt, potatoes, and bottled water. They, perhaps more than any other form of retailing, are taken for granted. Mobile shops are also important in rural areas where access to stores and shopping centres is often difficult for the dispersed population.

Periodic markets

Historically, the principal form of retailing in Britain was in the periodic market. These could occur two or three times a week or less frequently, in specially-designated areas within towns and cities. The types of product available for sale might vary with location; for example, some might specialise in fruit and vegetables while others would sell meat or dairy products. This pattern persists today in many parts of the country, with markets being held both in special-purpose market halls (for example, Leeds,

Cork) or in open-spaces where the produce is sold from temporary stalls (for example, Moreton-in-Marsh). Although they are visually significant elements of the townscape, their contribution to total retail sales is thought to be very small. Davies (1976) suggests a figure of no more than 1%, but with many markets being relatively informal, there are great difficulties in quantifying this sector. A recent development in this form of selling is the growth of craft and antique markets especially in attractive freestanding 'market' towns in popular tourist areas (for example, Cirencester).

Informal retailing

Informal retailing includes those types of shopping facility which develop in an *ad hoc* fashion. An example might include hospital shops which can sell a variety of items for patients though they are not specifically designed to function as retailers. Similarly, car-boot sales and Women's Institute weekly markets which sell home baking, pot plants and knitwear may also be thought of as informal retailing. However, these must be distinguished from many of the Charity Shops found in the country. Oxfam, for example, has over 830 shops in Britain, and Dr Barnado's, Save the Children, The Spastics Society and Imperial Cancer Research all have over 200 shops.

Farm shops may also be a part of the informal sector, where surplus products can be sold at the farm gate to a passing trade. However, not all forms of farm shopping can be considered informal. With the diversification of farming activities due to the tightening of farm profit margins under the Common Agricultural Policy, a great number of hitherto peripheral activities have become commercially important to farmers. Farm-house holidays, 'pick-your-own' fruit and vegetables, 'dig your own' Christmas trees, farm trails and adventure playgrounds, have all been successful in boosting farm incomes. Initiatives which are specific to retailing include the specialisation by farmers in producing organic meat and vegetables, ice-cream, and cheese for sale directly from the farm.

Retailing for the 1990s

In an important contribution to the recent retailing literature, Joshua Bamfield suggests that:

> The most significant changes in current retailing compared with the early 1980s are the emphasis upon marketing approaches based on style and differentiation; the careful targeting of markets; and the use of store refurbishment and redesign as a competitive weapon. (Bamfield 1988, p. 28)

Greater efficiency, better shops, a wider range of goods, and higher standards all typify British retailing in the 1990s. During the 1970s sales growth was slow and possibly even negative during 1977–1979, leading to price competition (for example, Tesco's Operation Checkout). During the 1980s, the emphasis on price was replaced by image. Consumer incomes rose leading to demands for distinctiveness, style and higher standards, especially among the upwardly mobile. Dual income households and the decline in the traditional family unit began to be identified as representing key new markets. Bamfield suggests that

> Changes in marketing were accentuated by the need for multiples to differentiate themselves from one another in order to protect their profit margins. (Bamfield 1988, p. 16)

Several distinct factors seem to have affected retail competition: marketing, shop numbers and industry structure.

Marketing

There was a move away from price to upmarket trading with the development of new forms of commercial operation – lifestyle retailers (for example, Habitat, Laura Ashley, Next), niche marketers (or focused retailers such as Tie Rack, Knickerbox, Sock Shop) – often based on new, small businesses. The larger corporations have also restructured their operations by creating separate businesses focused on specific types of customer. Sears for example, operate several distinct types of shoeshop (Saxone, Dolcis, Trueform, Shoe City) catering for the needs of different market segments.

The supermarket chains have also been able to repackage the service they seek to offer by providing a form of scrambled merchandising for the one-stop shopper. Scrambled merchandising simply means that businesses which developed from a traditional product-centred base (bakers, butchers etc) are now offering a wide range of other types of product to allow shoppers to purchase most of what they need under one roof. Today, the large grocers control 70% of the grocery market, 46% of the markets in alcoholic drinks, bakery, fruit and vegetables, and 30% of milk and meat. These are traditional markets for the grocer. However, they also control 38% of the market in motor accessories, 20% of cigarettes, and 8% of hardware, electrical goods and textiles. This trend has led to the refurbishment of stores and the development of new marketing concepts. In the 1990s key marketing strategies are likely to be developing markets for children, the home, leisure and recreation.

Shop numbers

There was a decline in shop numbers for all types of retailer during the 1980s (Table 3.5) but most especially for members of Co-operative Societies (48% down over 1976–1984). This is mainly explained by the concentration of business in larger, more carefully sited superstores. In 1986, 396 superstores accounted for 25% of all grocery sales, and 85% of these were owned by just five companies. From 1972 to 1985 the average size of stores owned and operated by corporate chains increased by more than 300% to 10,000 square feet of sales area. Grocery superstores are considerably larger, with the average sales area of Sainsburys exceeding 18,500 square feet. These large stores need careful siting and many have been developed on the edges of urban areas. A superstore providing 45,000 square feet of sales area costs around £20 million to develop but can boost annual turnover by £65 million. There is thus enormous competition for these special sites as only 850 are thought to exist in the whole country.

	1971	1978	1984
One shop independents	338,210	245,000	201,633
Large independents	83,966	67,886	73,670
Multiples	71,162	66,343	62,037
Cooperatives	16,480	10,370	5,813
Totals	509,818	389,599	343,153

Table 3.5   The decline in shop numbers

(Source: After Bamfield 1980, 1988)

Industry structure

Between 1980–1987, £8.5 billion was spent on takeovers between the major operators. Major amalgamations during the 1980s were Burton-Debenhams, Storehouse (Habitat, Mothercare, British Home Stores), the Dee Corporation (Gateway, Carrefour, Fine Fare, Keymarkets, International Stores), and Argyll (Presto, Lo-Cost, Allied Suppliers, Liptons, Safeway). Bamfield (1988) suggests that a key reason for amalgamations was to provide access to first-class sites which are increasingly limited in number. Moreover:

> Retailers who have got the fundamentals right overcome the shortages of sites, diversify, and apply their methods to new business by takeover, often using a focused approach to operate several different shops in the same locality. (Bamfield 1988, p. 20)

Table 3.6   The Ownership of British Retailing – Retail outlets belonging to selected multiple groups

Retail Group	Retail Type	Outlets
1. Sears	Department Stores	Selfridges,
	Women's fashions	Miss Selfridge, Wallis, Warehouse, Together
	Men's clothing	Fosters, Hornes, Your Price, Bradleys, Dormie, Zy
	Children's clothing	Adams
	Footwear	British Shoe Corporation – including Freeman Hardy Willis, Saxone, Trueform, Curtess, Lilley and Skinner, Shoe City, Cable and Co, Roland Cartier, Manfield, Dolcis
	Camping and leisure	Millet's
	Sports Goods	Olympus
	Jewellers	Garrard, Mappin and Webb, In Time
2. Burton	Department Stores	Debenhams, Harvey Nichols
	Women's fashions	Dorothy Perkins, Principles, Top Shop, Evans
	Men's clothing	Burton, Top Man, Collier, Radius, Principles for Men, Alias.
3. Boots	Chemists, Drugstores	Boots the Chemist, Underwoods
	Opticians	Boots Opticians
	Children's clothes, toys etc	Children's World
	DIY	Payless DIY
	Car Accessories	Halfords
4. W H Smith	Newsagents and Stationers	W H Smith
	Booksellers	Sherratt and Hughes, Waterstone's
	Records	Our Price
	Stationery	Paperchase
	DIY	Do It All
	Travel Agents	W H Smith Travel Agents

5. Storehouse	Home furnishings/ Housewares	Habitat
	Department stores	Bhs
	Women's fashions	Richards
	Mothers' and children's clothing	Mothercare
	Men's clothing	Blazer
6. John Lewis Partnership	Department Stores	John Lewis, Peter Jones, Bainbridge, George Henry Lee, Jessops, Tyrrell and Green
	Grocery supermarkets	Waitrose
7. Kingfisher	Variety stores	Woolworths, Kidstore, Volume 1
	DIY	B and Q
	Electrical goods	Comet, Ultimate, Connect, Laskys
	Drugstores	Superdrug, Share Drug, Tip Top
	Auto Centres	Charlie Brown's
8. Ratners	Jewellery	Ratners, H Samuel, James Walker, Terry's, Ernest Jones, Watches of Switzerland, Time, Stephens, Zales
	Handbags and Luggage	Salisbury's

Amalgamation has allowed many rather conservative companies to trade upmarket and establish a wider, more lucrative business base. Burtons and Woolworth, for example, have succeeded in reversing their former images, associated respectively with off-the-peg men's tailoring and low status variety goods trading. By using a mixture of niche marketing, focused retailing and a concentration on a small number of core merchandise areas, both companies have re-established themselves as major forces in the market. The dynamics of these major operators have changed the industry. This has been especially felt in the grocery industry where:

> a small number of multiples have radically changed food retailing in ways that one thousand multiples would not have been able to do. The competitive strategies of multiples, based on the need to increase market share have produced a new retail environment both for the initiators of change and for those who have been forced to change in order to avoid failure. It has been argued also that the most successful retailers have been those who not only perceive new needs, but also have the management and finance to be able to introduce a package of necessary changes quickly. (Bamfield 1988, p. 28)

The ownership of British retailing

Over time, consumers in Britain have become extremely familiar with the names, shop fronts and logos of the major high street retailers. When shopping in stores such as Boots, Dorothy Perkins, Habitat or Woolworths, most people are well aware that they are patronising a multiple. However, it is unlikely that many will realise that these chain stores are often components of much larger retail and business conglomerates. For example, Boots not only incorporates chemists shops, but also operates a chain of opticians, Children's World, Payless DIY and Halfords car accessories. Similarly, Dorothy Perkins is part of the Burton Group, which also includes Debenhams department stores, Principles for Women, Top Shop, Collier and Radius. Many high street retailers are owned by conglomerates better known for their non-retailing activities. For example, United Biscuits, who are better known as manufacturers, operate the Wimpy, Pizzaland and Perfect Pizza chains. The pattern of ownership of many British stores is thus particularly complex. Some features are summarised in Table 3.6. This gives some indication of the concentration of power which characterises the oligopolistic structure of the British retail market.

Conclusions

British retailing is dominated by large corporations operating from large, efficient stores located appropriately to their markets. The traditional image of the small shopkeeper is no longer an accurate one, as the ravages of increased competition have reduced profit margins and culled many thousands of independents. Today, such retailers are only able to operate successfully if they can offer a service not already provided by the corporations. This might mean opening at peculiar times and staying open long hours. Alternatively, they may be able to provide 'topping up' services for products which are needed daily or only a few times a week. But it is not all bad news; small independents offering specialised services can survive and even thrive as the corporations have not yet covered all market possibilities.

CHAPTER 4

The Geography of Supply and Demand

Introduction

The development of a system of retailing requires that suppliers and their customers come together at some conveniently located point. Such points must be accessible and historically have been located at crossroads, fords, and bridging points – indeed at any 'nodal' point where human traffic converges. In the building of the British townscape the most accessible area has tended to be in the centre at a village green, market or meeting place. As retailing is dependent on attracting and retaining customers, the location of retailing facilities depends heavily on access to such central areas.

The pattern of retailing within a single town cannot be studied in isolation from that town's role in its locality, region or nation. Some towns provide retailing for a purely local market, others serve a regional function and carry facilities which are purchased by people of many towns and villages in the area. Still others offer national functions, carrying retailing facilities which have a national or even international market. It is thus possible to picture the spatial structure of retailing as a series of hierarchies, ranging both between different urban areas and within single urban areas. The concept of a hierarchy is relatively easy to describe and understand and has played a central role in the management and planning of British retailing during the twentieth century. It is, however, insufficiently robust to account for all types of British retailing, especially contemporary trends, and has thus been reconsidered in the light of modern developments.

This chapter looks specifically at how retailing attempts to meet demand by developing points of supply within and between towns and cities in Britain. It focuses on some of the theoretical work produced by economists, planners and geographers on the development of retailing systems, specifically, hierarchies, centres and specialist developments, and examines how these ideas relate to modern urban areas in Britain where heritage, concern for lifestyle and the paradox of increased personal mobility and congestion frame many planning decisions. Before considering these issues however, it is necessary to outline how the geography of retail provision has evolved and adjusted to changing demographic patterns.

Supply, demand and space

Nodality

An essential pre-requisite for exchange and trade is the coming together of suppliers and customers at conveniently-located 'nodal' points such as village greens or crossroads. For many British towns, the ability to grow and develop was conditioned to a great extent by their nodality, which influenced both their accessibility to other areas and their 'spheres of influence' (Pahl *et al.*, 1983). For small settlements, the town centre typically lay at the heart of a local route network and would have been the hub around which activities such as trade and retailing would have revolved. With improvements in accessibility brought about by the building of new roads and technological developments in transport, so larger spheres of influence would have emerged, providing a larger market area to be exploited by the town. This process is summarised in Figure 4.1. Such pressures provide the essential spatial demand for retailing facilities.

The intra-urban retail hierarchy

The expansion of British towns and cities to accommodate growing populations and an increasing variety of activities inevitably led to the spatial separation of urban functions and the segregation of land uses into distinctive areas such as residence, retailing and industry. As towns spread outwards from their original cores, not only did people's homes become separated from their workplaces, but much of the population became more distant from the traditional retail focus in the town centre. As a result, their everyday needs could no longer be met so conveniently from town centre shops but required new, more local provision at convenient points in the suburbs (Wild and Shaw 1979).

Continuing urban growth during the nineteenth century led to the laying down of the basic framework of the intra-urban retail pattern. At the top of the hierarchy, central areas grew in response to rising demand by spreading outwards along routes leading in to the town centre. Similarly, in the suburbs, groups of shops became established at accessible intersections leading to the phenomenon of the 'corner shop' as a provider of basic necessities and focal point of the neighbourhood. Further out, the growth of the town by accretion at the periphery frequently meant that surrounding villages became engulfed by urbanization, with their retail functions

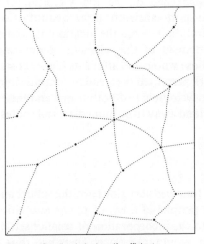

Stage 1. Small, relatively self-sufficient settlements linked by pathways and tracks.

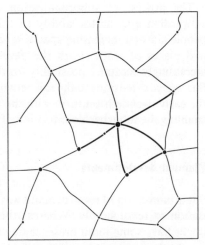

Stage 2. Improvements in transport network enhance accessibility and permit settlement growth.

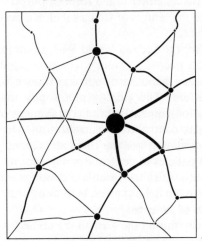

Stage 3. Additional developments to infrastructure (eg. new modes of transport, expansion of route network). Urban hierarchy based on variations in accessibility becoming clearly apparent.

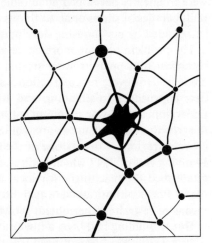

Stage 4. Mature urban hierarchy and sophisticated transport system.

Key • ● – Settlements *(size of dot reflecting relative importance of settlement)*.

.... – transport routes *(thickness of line represents relative importance of routeway)*.

Figure 4.1 Schematic diagrams to show the interrelationship between urban growth and variations in accessibility accompanying transport developments

frequently becoming focal points for further retail development in the larger urban market.

The process of suburbanization quickened during the Victorian and Edwardian eras as the ability to transport efficiently large quantities of people allowed increasing spatial separation between the location of homes and places of work. With the development of the railways, commuting increasingly became a possibility for those who could afford its higher costs. Successive extensions to the rail network permitted the trend to continue into the early twentieth century, with the development of both trams and buses enabling the suburban colonization of land away from immediate rail routes.

Planned developments

Suburbanisation of retail demand was followed very slowly by the suburbanisation of retail supply. Whereas the peripheral areas of towns and cities might have some retail presence due to the incorporation of smaller settlements, there was no guarantee that this would take place. There was thus a need for some form of planned retailing development. Shopping facilities were frequently developed at suitable places either in the form of purpose-built parades of shops or as additions to the centres of villages that had been surrounded by new housing development.

The problem became more acute after the Second World War, as major reconstruction projects were started all over the country to repair bomb damage. However, reconstruction was not haphazard, but was framed by new approaches to planning and welfare. The guiding philosophy that underpinned post-war planning legislation emphasised the containment of the growth of existing urban areas allied to controlled decentralization to less crowded regions. Cornerstone of the legislation was the Town and Country Planning Act of 1947 which instituted policies to control development and established the machinery for local authorities to formulate development plans. Local authorities were also directed to delimit green belts as a further means of restraining peripheral growth of suburbs.

House building had been a low priority during the war. In the immediate aftermath the most urgent need was to make up lost ground and to replace homes that had been destroyed. The state assumed a leading role and between 1945 and 1956 almost 1.5 million local authority houses were built, mostly on vacant suburban land. The New Towns Act 1946 set in train the eventual construction of 32 new towns whose principal aim was to relieve overcrowding in the conurbations of Britain. For each designated town, central government set up a development corporation with extensive powers to acquire land, to lay down infrastructure, to fund house building and to provide a range of amenities. Retail facilities that were built both on estates of local authority housing and in New Towns were located according to the well-established principles of the intra-urban retail hierarchy and reflected the persistence of the concept amongst the planning fraternity.

The state-sponsored shift of population and jobs that took place under the New Towns programme was only part of a much more extensive social and economic restructuring in progress in Britain. From the 1960s onwards, forces working towards the decentralization of population led to dramatic increases in the population of villages, market towns and smaller provincial centres. This turnaround in the emphasis of urban development and employment growth has become known as 'counter-urbanization'. Research into this trend has shown that in broad terms, the smaller the population or employment size of an area, the greater was the rate of population and employment growth during the period (Fothergill and Gudgin 1982).

This drift of population to free-standing towns and quasi-rural areas over the last three decades or so has been prompted to a large extent by forces similar to those which triggered the earlier suburban exodus. Some people moved to live and work in areas of employment growth. The mobility conferred by widespread car ownership and the extension of the motorway network enabled others to reject the negative aspects of city living in favour of life in more placid rural surroundings, whilst continuing to commute to larger centres for work. Although the shift was a country-wide phenomenon it was more noticeable in the South where there was a larger proportion of the population and where there were more small towns that had been all but by-passed by the Industrial Revolution. This left them with ideal characteristics from which to benefit from the social and economic changes that were under way. The combination of images of picturesque townscapes and gentle rurality with other attributes sought by expanding industries and services led to dramatic economic changes in towns along the much publicised M4 corridor as well as many others around the country such as: county towns (Norwich, Chester, Cambridge), inland spas (Harrogate, Bath, Cheltenham), old market towns (Shrewsbury, Cirencester, Banbury) and ancient ecclesiastical centres (York, Exeter, Peterborough and Winchester). Pinch and Williams (1983) suggest that the decentralization process was important both quantitatively and qualitatively in that those moving were frequently professional and managerial workers. They estimate that between 1961 and 1971 the cores of the seven largest urban areas lost 19% of their professional and managerial employees relative to the national average for these groups.

Housing the influx necessitated considerable amounts of suburban house building in the free-standing towns. The shift of population also represented a decentralization of effective demand and undoubtedly had important knock-on effects on the retail systems of the growing towns. Within the new housing estates low order shopping needs were usually catered for by the developers, though sometimes in an inadequate or half-hearted manner. It was mostly in the town centres that the growth in numbers of professional, salaried, white collar residents had most impact. The traditional retail cores of these smaller towns experienced a significant degree of growth and retail revitalization as independents and multiples moved in and established premises from which to serve the expanding market of affluent consumers.

The supply of retail services has, however, been much slower to decentralise, partly because the massive retail investments in the inner areas of cities cannot easily be abandoned and also because local planning authorities, guided by the notion of the intra-urban retail hierarchy, have been unwilling to allow wholesale redevelopment on the edges of towns. Many local authorities rely heavily on the rates they collect from retailing. Dawson (1979) notes that these may be as low as 5% in the case of Stretford, but rise to as high as 18% in Cheltenham and 25% in Chester. Justification for impeding retail decentralisation includes the need to maintain local authority finances, the protection of the green belt, and the need to provide shopping facilities for those who have limited access to transport (frequently the disabled, the elderly and the poor). Wrigley (1988) notes that between 1965 and 1977 major efforts were put into developing city centre retailing and by 1976 Britain lagged behind both Western Europe and North America in developing edge-of-town trading.

The election of Conservative governments throughout the 1980s ostensibly to roll back the boundaries of bureaucracy has allowed retail decentralisation to take place much more quickly. There are several reasons for the change in policy. First, many of the restrictions on development were seen as unnecessary restrictions on trade and therefore removed for ideological reasons. Second, the planners' expectation that edge-of-town developments would have a harmful impact on central shopping has been found to be far too pessimistic. There is some evidence to suggest that the presence of a large peripheral development creates opportunities for smaller operators who can fill some of the gaps not covered by the major firms. Third, the massive decline in British manufacturing performance has meant that any other economic runner has had to be backed. Retailing is now perceived as having a positive contribution to make to urban redevelopment.

Models of demand and supply

It is quite clear from the previous discussion that there are geographies of demand and supply. Attempts to describe these systematically by paying particular attention to space have been important in geography since the 1950s. However, where business and financial accounts of retailing have tended to underplay the role of space, geography has tended to go to the other extreme, simplifying much of the business complexity of retailing systems in an effort to highlight spatial patterns and regularities in urban areas. Theoretical work on delimiting retail market areas using a form of central place theory typifies this process. Brian Berry's classic text, *Geography of Marketing Centers and Retail Distribution*, published in 1967, begins as follows:

> The thesis of this book is that the geography of retail and service business displays regularities over space and through time, that central-place theory constitutes a deductive base from which to understand these regularities, and that the convergence of theoretical postulates and empirical regularities provides substance to marketing geography and to certain aspects of city and regional planning.

The tone of this and subsequent work, especially in the USA, was that the spatial form of retailing was largely determined by the interaction of threshold and range effects associated with particular classes of product. 'High-order' goods (for example, jewellery) attract considerable markets and tend to be sold from a small number of central locations such as city centres. 'Low-order' goods (for example, bread) have smaller ranges and so are found much more widely. This idea is neat and is reasonably sensible, in that it suggests the hierarchical arrangement of shopping facilities based on types of goods being sold which we have already seen has some basis in fact in the spatial history of British retailing.

Central place theory

The purpose of central place theory is to describe the economic forces which lead to an hierarchical supply of shopping facilities in urban areas. The concept of such a hierarchy has been demonstrated frequently in the past and it has been widely accepted by the planning profession as a model of retail organisation. Underlying the theory is the belief that all goods may be ordered qualitatively in terms of their 'threshold' and 'range'. By threshold, geographers usually mean the population needed to make the supply of the good worthwhile. By range, geographers mean the distance consumers are typically expected to be prepared to travel to purchase it (Figure 4.2). By putting the two ideas together, market areas are defined within urban spaces in which 'high-order' goods requiring large thresholds and ranges are only supplied from populous 'central' places while 'low-order' goods (smaller thresholds and ranges) are available more locally (Figure 4.3). The landscapes associated with central place theory are typically described by maps of interlocking and overlapping hexagons, the geometry being the result of the economic processes implied by the model (Figure 4.4 and 4.5). (For further details of this theory, see Christaller 1933, Berry 1967.)

The theory is rather more elegant than practical. Dawson (1979, p. 190) notes:

> Whilst the theory serves to describe and, in part, explain locational patterns developed prior to the 1960s it can no longer be used as a basis either for the

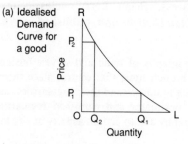

(a) Idealised Demand Curve for a good

Although there are many determinants of demand, *ceteris paribus* ("other things being equal"), demand varies inversely with price – that is, when price goes up from P1 to P2, the quantity demanded goes down from Q1 to Q2.

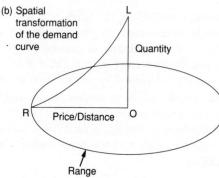

(b) Spatial transformation of the demand curve

The "real" cost of the good is made up of the purchase price *plus* the cost of getting to the shop or central place in order to make the purchase. Thus, quantity of goods purchased or frequency of shopping at a store or central place will decrease as distance from the store or central place increases. By tipping graph (a) over to the left through 90° we can see that demand falls with increasing distance ("real cost") from the store until a point is reached, beyond which the store will not be patronised, i.e. the *range* of the particular good in question. By rotating graph (b) through 360° about OL, a market area will be delimited within which goods from that store will be bought.

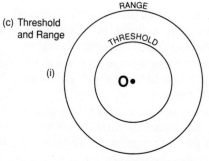

(c) Threshold and Range

(i)

In (c)i, the *threshold* lies within the *range* i.e. there is enough demand to support the business within the maximum distance over which the shop can reasonably expect to sell its goods – therefore, the business can function profitably.

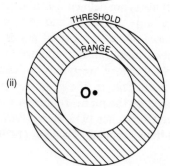

(ii)

In (c)ii, the *threshold* lies outside the *range*. Consumers living within the shaded area would not patronise shop O because of the travel cost, inconvenience or closer proximity to an alternative shop. The business would fail due to insufficient trade.

Figure 4.2 The relationship between threshold and range

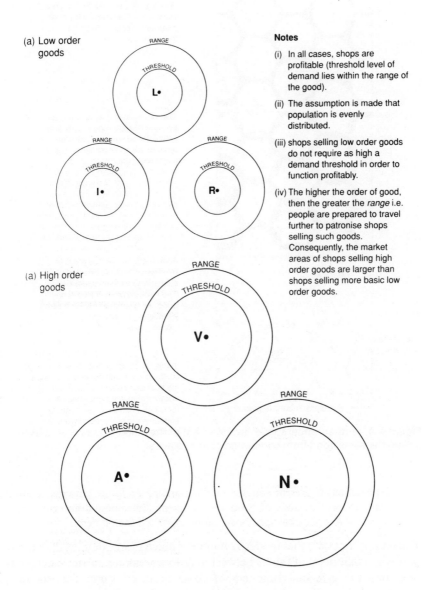

Notes

(i) In all cases, shops are profitable (threshold level of demand lies within the range of the good).

(ii) The assumption is made that population is evenly distributed.

(iii) shops selling low order goods do not require as high a demand threshold in order to function profitably.

(iv) The higher the order of good, then the greater the *range* i.e. people are prepared to travel further to patronise shops selling such goods. Consequently, the market areas of shops selling high order goods are larger than shops selling more basic low order goods.

Figure 4.3 Threshold and range for different orders of good

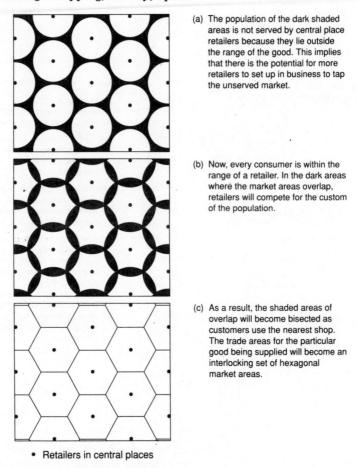

(a) The population of the dark shaded areas is not served by central place retailers because they lie outside the range of the good. This implies that there is the potential for more retailers to set up in business to tap the unserved market.

(b) Now, every consumer is within the range of a retailer. In the dark areas where the market areas overlap, retailers will compete for the custom of the population.

(c) As a result, the shaded areas of overlap will become bisected as customers use the nearest shop. The trade areas for the particular good being supplied will become an interlocking set of hexagonal market areas.

• Retailers in central places

Figure 4.4 A theoretical spatial arrangement of the market areas of retailers selling the same good from competing central places

explanation of present patterns or the planning of future patterns. Central place theory, because of these measurement difficulties, disintegrates and merely states that some places are more important than others.

The reason for this is that modern retailing is much more complex than in the past with traditional divisions between retailers breaking down. Whereas at one time the principal suppliers of basic products were, for example, butchers, bakers, drapers, grocers, all trading from their own identifiable premises, the modern situation is less clear-cut. Many shops now employ scrambled merchandising in which a wide variety of products are sold by a single retailer under one roof. Supermarkets, for example, sell groceries, electrical goods, pharmaceuticals, garden furniture, meat and vegetables,

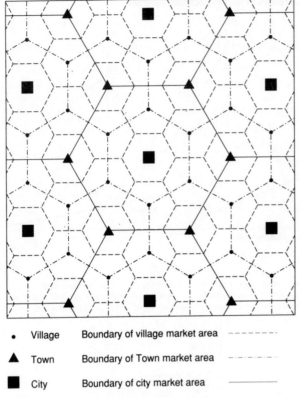

- •   Village   Boundary of village market area   – – – – – –
- ▲   Town   Boundary of Town market area   – ⋅ – ⋅ – ⋅ –
- ■   City   Boundary of city market area   ———————

Notes:

(a) Clearly, different types or orders of good supplied from different levels of central place will have different ranges and thresholds and thus sizes of market areas as in **Figure 4.3**. As a result of the space-packing process shown in **Figure 4.4**, a nested hierarchy of various sizes of market area will be produced as shown above.

(b) This pattern of central places is known as a K=3 hierarchy. The K value is determined by the number of lower order centres served by the next higher level of central place. In the case of the K=3 hierarchy based on the marketing principle, the relationship between centres at progressively less specialized levels in the urban hierarchy follows a geometrical progression (1,3,9,27... etc).

Figure 4.5   The hypothetical arrangement of market areas for three levels of central place according to Christaller's Marketing principle

and provide a level of service which makes measuring thresholds and ranges very difficult. Simple comparisons cannot easily be made between the remaining shops specialising in these products and the multiple chain stores. As Dawson (1979, p. 189) notes:

Central place theory has been derived in a period of specialist retailing with the

(i)   Bid-Rent curves for five different types of land use.

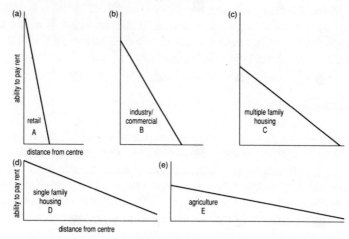

(ii) Here, the bid-rent curves for the five different types of land use have been superimposed. The two-dimensional graph can be rotated through 360° about O to show how a concentric spatial arrangement of land uses might come about.

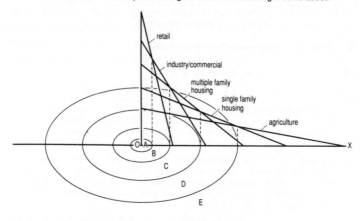

Figure 4.6   Bid-rent curves for five land uses

(Source: After Hamnett, 1977)

few general merchandise stores carrying a deep assortment of a rather limited mix of products. This is no longer the case and to suggest that the provision of a few, rapid-turnover record stands in a supermarket should be treated in the same way as a specialist record shop is to fail to appreciate how retailing really operates.

The attraction of central place theory was that it provided a theoretical model for the hierarchical arrangements in retailing one can see in urban networks and within urban areas. It explains why London contains the major fashion houses and the top stores, and why small places such as Durham do not have department stores. However, apart from describing these patterns it does not really relate them to the behavioural world of real retailing and so cannot be a full explanation.

Bid-rent theory

An alternative spatial model of intra-urban retailing which has been used by geographers is Bid-rent theory. This attempts to explain the spatial patterns of shopping within a town using rent levels as a spatial filter. Figure 4.6 illustrates the basic idea. It suggests that rent levels for retailing property largely depend on centrality and the number of customers they can attract. In general, central areas are more accessible than peripheral areas because all the roads and bus routes concentrate on them. Rent levels in central areas are thus likely to be higher than in peripheral areas and will only be payable by businesses whose mark up on products or level of turnover allows them to pay. Figure 4.7 illustrates a typical arrangement of businesses.

This model is easy to understand but again is too simple. Improvements may be made to incorporate the architecture of real cities rather than the hypothetical city. It is well-known that rent levels are associated with accessibility but that accessibility can vary significantly depending on location even within central areas. Corner sites having two shop fronts are likely to be

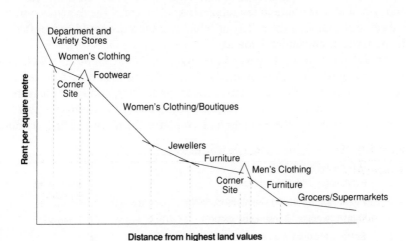

Figure 4.7   A hypothetical rent gradient in one direction across a town centre retail core from the point of highest land values

(Source: After Scott, 1970)

able to advertise their products to a wider audience than shops having only a single front. Rent levels are therefore likely to be higher.

In addition to site, distance from bus stations and bus stops can also affect the potential rent levels for sites. Pedestrian surveys show that the numbers of people passing a shop front can affect the rent levels charged, in that shops in favoured sites should be able to sell to a larger market than those in less-favoured locations. This idea is particularly important in choosing the tenant mix of planned shopping centres.

Shopping models

A third important contribution made by geographers to the study of retailing is in the development of numerical models of retailing. Alan Wilson (1988) describes some of the major contributions in an important review article. He notes that two distinct types of model have been suggested: models which attempt to assess the locational problems of individual shops, and those of shopping centres. These are separate issues operating on different scales and involving different sorts of problems.

The purpose of these models is to add an element of rigour to 'rules of thumb' approaches based on the experience of retailers. By measuring a series of hypothetical relationships between consumers, products and stores, the modeller attempts to provide a simplified description of how the key aspects of retailing operate. Should such a model be discovered, it may be manipulated on computer to simulate a variety of different retailing strategies and contribute to the retailer's knowledge of the dynamism of the market. For example, the effects of relocating the store could be assessed on the patterns of consumer demand.

Three elements lie at the core of the large family of techniques which have been developed: measures of demand at differing distances from a store (centre), measures of the attractiveness of the facility, and some measure of the flow of money or people between them both. Providing numbers to define and calibrate the models and compare them with actual retailing

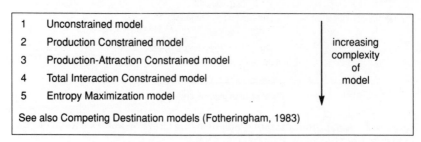

1	Unconstrained model	
2	Production Constrained model	increasing
3	Production-Attraction Constrained model	complexity of
4	Total Interaction Constrained model	model
5	Entropy Maximization model	
See also Competing Destination models (Fotheringham, 1983)		

Table 4.1　The family of Spatial Interaction models (after Senior, 1979)

practices is rather more complicated than it might appear at first sight. However, a variety of models has been developed which vary in their complexity and degree of abstraction (see Table 4.1).

Consumer behaviour studies

During the 1970s and 1980s geographical contributions to retailing, particularly in Britain, became rather less concerned with central place theory as such, and more concerned with the functioning of retailing as a business which operates in space. Work by geographers such as Bowlby, Davies, Dawson, Guy, Kirby, Potter, and more recently, Wrigley, have focused attention on the organisational and commercial structure of the industry and its relationships with other types of land use. While centrality is still regarded as an important element in understanding certain aspects of

Beaujeu-Garnier, J and Delobez, A (1979)	Geography of Marketing, Longman, London.
Berry, BJL (1967)	Geography of Market Centers and Retail Distribution Prentice-Hall, Englewood-Cliffs
Davies, RL (1976)	Marketing Geography, Retail and Planning Associates, Corbridge.
Davies, RL (1984)	Retail and Commercial Planning, Croom Helm, London.
Dawson, JA (1979)	The Marketing Environment, Croom Helm, London
Dawson, JA (ed) (1980)	Retail Geography, Croom Helm, London.
Dawson, JA (1982)	Commercial Distribution in Europe, Croom Helm, London.
Dawson, JA (1983)	Shopping Centre Development, Longman, London.
Guy, CM (1980)	Retail Location and Retail Planning in Britain, Gower, Farnborough.
Nelson, RL (1958)	The Selection of Retail Locations, Dodge, New York.
Potter, RB (1982)	The Urban Retailing System: Location, Cognition and Behaviour. Gower, Aldershot.
Scott, P (1970)	Geography and Retailing, Hutchinson, London.
Wrigley, N (ed) (1988)	Store Choice, Store Location and Market Analysis, Routledge, London.

Table 4.2   Some key texts in retail geography

retailing, its position of primacy has gone. Today, retailing geographers work more readily on the spatial effects of issues such as consumer behaviour, planning legislation, information technology, and national and international distribution systems. Table 4.2 lists some of the key contributions.

One of the thorniest problems facing the modern retailing analyst is accommodating the quality of shopping provision in their models. Early work on consumer behaviour by, among others, Downs (1970) and Golledge (1970), has shown that demand patterns are affected by consumers' perceptions of the quality of products and shops. The main difficulty in quantifying this is accommodating the varied aspects of quality, many of which may be incompatible. Components of quality may depend on the product itself – reliability, price, after-sales service, ease of use; and on the shop selling it – convenience to car parks, cleanliness, efficiency and courtesy of staff. These may be mutually incompatible in that the cheapest prices may only be available in shops with a poor reputation for after-sales service. Some of these issues are considered in greater detail in Bates (1988).

Contemporary trends in retail location

The development of new styles of retailing and marketing has distinctly spatial implications. The principal spatial manifestation of these trends is the restructuring and decentralisation of shopping provision. As recently as the 1950s the town centre or high street was considered to be the unchallenged pinnacle of the intra-urban retail hierarchy. Considering that the suburbanization of population and thus consumer demand has been taking place at a significant rate since the late nineteenth century, it is surprising that suburban consumers still had to look to the town centre as the main place to go shopping until relatively recently. The intra-urban retail hierarchy was viewed by retailers and planners alike as a robust and enduring feature of the British townscape. Consumers too had come to associate certain kinds of retail functions with particular levels of shopping facilities.

However, the increased pace and scale of suburbanization and decentralization processes in conjunction with related socio-economic changes over the last thirty years led to growing pressures for retail investment to follow consumer demand to the outskirts of urban areas. This does not mean that the high street has disappeared, but that its role has changed and is continuing to change. At the same time, peripheral developments are gaining ground and are becoming increasingly visible components of the built environment. General agreement exists about the processes underlying the trend towards the greater decentralization of retailing activities (Davies 1976; Kivell and Shaw 1980).

Population decentralization

The population moving to the suburbs and freestanding towns has generally been made up of young to middle-aged, affluent professionals with their families (Fothergill and Gudgin 1982). The less well off have been required out of circumstances to remain in older, often more run-down housing in less salubrious parts of the inner urban areas of the established towns and cities. They are thus forced to rely on more traditional elements of the intra-urban hierarchy to meet their needs, which in the case of retailing, may place them at a disadvantage.

Increased personal mobility

The importance of transport has already been emphasised as an explanatory variable in determining the location of retailing at accessible places *within* urban areas. Up until the 1960s in Britain, public transport focused on town centres played an important part in reinforcing the intra-urban retail hierarchy. However, over 60% of British families now have access to a car. This has been an important element both in permitting post-war suburban expansion and the shift of population to smaller towns. What is perhaps more significant is that post-war suburbs tended to be ill-served by public transport because, owing to the design and layouts of the estates, bus operators did not find it cost-effective to establish services. So, not only did one have to be a car owner, but suburban residents increasingly came to depend heavily on their cars for all manner of journeys – to work, for entertainment, for holidays and of course, to shop. Furthermore, increased car ownership and use led to increasing congestion in town centres as customers attempted to make use of traditional shopping facilities; this gave rise to demands for more conveniently located shops that were more easily accessible to cars.

Social and demographic factors

A number of changes in many peoples' way of life can be seen to have affected shopping habits. Of particular significance for retailing has been the changing role of women in British society. Female participation in the workforce has shown a marked increase over the last two decades. The reasons for this are complex. Some families require two incomes to service high mortgage repayments and this may necessitate the deferment of child bearing. A person in these circumstances has popularly become known as a DINKY (Double Income No Kids Yet). On the other hand, those with no intention of having children who require both partners to be earning in order to satisfy more materialistic desires are termed DINKI (Double Income No Kids Intended). In addition, there is a growing number of 'women returners' who, having raised children to school age, decide to seek rewarding employment away from the home.

Whatever the motives for being in paid work it is inevitable that there is less time available for routine convenience shopping. Role sharing has increased and it has become far more familiar to see both partners going on shopping trips together. The drudgery of running the home is eased by the availability of labour-saving equipment such as dish washers, microwave ovens and freezers stocked with ready-prepared gourmet meals. The trend is away from daily shopping for food purchases towards weekly one-stop, bulk-buying grocery trips using the car. Consumers are better educated, more sophisticated and discerning in what they demand of the shops they patronize. As well as seeking greater variety, quality and choice they are attracted by the comfort, convenience and novel retail experience offered by new edge-of-town shopping facilities (see Chapter 6).

Implications of changes in the scale of retailing

The ascendancy of the multiple chains and growth of retail conglomerates has already been introduced in Chapter 3. Paralleling this strengthening of corporate power within retailing there has been a tendency for large firms to concentrate their activities into larger stores in order to gain economies of scale in operation. This is especially apparent in the grocery sector which has witnessed the evolution of the supermarket into the superstore. Larger floor areas are needed to accommodate the wider variety of goods that are typical of these scrambled merchandising operations. Wider aisles are necessary to allow the easy movement of larger shopping trolleys and greater customer throughput, which in turn requires the installation of more checkouts in order to prevent irritating bottlenecks building up. Retailers selling goods such as furniture, carpets and electrical appliances are also moving into larger premises where there is greater potential for designing elaborate room setting displays. Land on which to build the kinds of stores that incorporate these features is cheaper and more readily available on the outskirts of the built-up area. Sites on the periphery are also more accessible to potential customers – the affluent, car-borne suburbanites for whom conveniently located car parking adjacent to the store is of prime importance.

Implications of changes in marketing channels

Another aspect of the growth of multiples has been the extension of their control over the marketing channels in which they are active (see Chapter 2).

The considerable negotiating power of large retail organisations has permitted them to by-pass the wholesaler and deal direct with manufacturers. Multiples have established their own centrally located warehouse premises from which to redistribute stock to their various branches. Keeping branches fully serviced depends on the efficient integration of sophisticated stock control and re-ordering systems. Sales data captured from electronic point of sale (EPoS) terminals permit a lower inventory of stock to be carried on site at the branches, providing that just-in-time deliveries from the central warehouse can be efficiently coordinated (Chapter 7). Delivery by large articulated trucks to branches in town centres can be a real problem because of antiquated road networks, access problems at unloading bays at the rear of the stores as well as having to contend with tortuous one-way systems. On the other hand, stores on the edge of town are much more easily reached by bulk deliveries. Road layouts are designed to modern standards and traffic specifications, making branches more accessible to trucks and so allowing quicker unloading and rapid turnaround times.

Summary

Taken together, the points set out above may appear to represent a reasonably convincing and logical justification for accepting the inevitability of a restructuring of the retail pattern to take account of social and economic evolution. Without doubt, many town centres have lost their pre-eminent position as the dominant accessible location within the urban area. Yet although the pressures for decentralization have been increasing since the 1960s the reaction of the key actors involved has been mixed. Even amongst retailers, responses have varied considerably. Many who had major town centre investments in property feared that their businesses would suffer from the new competition. Some adopted an ambivalent attitude whilst others became enthusiastically espoused to the idea of relocating to the outskirts of the town. Concern about the closure of high street shops and the effects this would have on the overall vitality and appearance of town centres together with the erosion of rateable values was expressed by many local authorities. Finally, working within the framework of national legislation, local authority planners have been charged with making decisions on proposals for new peripheral retail developments. Over time, the changing ideology and view of central government regarding retail decentralization has caused local planners, who were initially fairly hostile to decentralization, to ameliorate their attitude quite considerably.

Retailing and land use planning

Although pressures for retail decentralization have been experienced widely throughout western society, there has been considerable variation between nations in the extent to which it has been permitted and controlled. It is probably in the USA where the decentralization of retailing has had the greatest impact. The aspirations of the white population to live in the suburbs have increased, especially since the end of the Second World War with the arrival of large groups of Black and Hispanic immigrants into urban areas. The availability of vast tracts of building land outside cities has meant that these aspirations were relatively easily satisfied. Because the new suburbs were so spacious and extensive, high levels of car ownership and usage became an essential element of suburban living. Additionally, retailers were able to follow their markets fairly easily partly owing to the fact that land could be readily acquired, but also because the liberal federal and state planning controls imposed negligible restrictions on development. As a result, malls and regional shopping centres proliferated in edge and edge-of-town locations. This is in sharp contrast to the situation in Britain where the slower pace of suburbanisation led to the more gradual emergence of the pressures for retail decentralization. Of even greater significance has been the influential part played by the British planning system in shaping the location of retailing.

The tone was set with the passing of the Town and Country Planning Act 1947, which instituted restrictive containment policies and development controls to ensure that there would be no repeat of the rampant ribbon development and urban sprawl that had been allowed to take place in the inter-war period. The commitment of architects and planners to traditional retail patterns was reaffirmed in towns established as a result of the New Towns Act 1946 where the location of shopping provision was based on the concept of the intra-urban retail hierarchy. Much of the planning legislation enacted since 1947 was subsequently incorporated into the Town and Country Planning Act 1971 which reiterated the broad tenets of control and containment.

In the particular context of retailing, Thorpe (1974) has identified four constituent elements of the rationale behind the application of planning controls to retail development. These are:

(1) The retail case: free market forces need to be carefully controlled in order to prevent the construction of an excessive quantity of shops and to achieve an optimum mix of shop types at the various levels of the retail hierarchy.

(2) The urban case: due care needs to be given to planning the distribution of shopping facilities because of the influence they have on complementary land uses as well as on the overall urban morphology. Town centre

vitality is heavily dependent on the complex web of interactions between the diverse central functions.

(3) The social planning case: retail planning is necessary in order to ensure equity in shopping provision such that no socio-economic groups should become disadvantaged.

(4) The environmental case: town planners should attempt to separate retailing from non-conforming or incompatible land uses and minimize the environmental impact of new retail development.

These four fundamental principles have become entrenched in retail planning policy in Britain and have been reinforced by a philosophical consensus amongst the majority of planners regarding how the retail pattern should be organized. Three main objectives stand out. First, there has been an unswerving commitment to the maintenance of the town centre as the prime retail focus. Since the mid 1960s most of the investment in retail facilities has taken place in town centres (Hillier, Parker, May and Rowden, 1989a). Second, the belief in the robust immutability of the intra-urban retail hierarchy has ensured its perpetuation and enhancement. Additions to the hierarchy have taken place where necessary, for example, by the insertion of new retail facilities on structure plans to take account of areas of population growth and residential development. Finally, through the greater part of the period since the Town and Country Planning Act 1971, there has been a presumption against new peripheral retail development that could contribute to urban sprawl and undermine the established retail hierarchy.

No hard-and-fast prescriptive policy on shopping has been laid down by central government. Instead, the Department of the Environment has issued a series of policy notes setting out general guidelines for planners and retail developers (for example, Department of the Environment 1972, 1974; Department of Environment and Welsh Office 1988). Development Control Policy Note 13 was the first real attempt to address the pressures for edge-of-town retail development (Department of Environment 1972). Though this slim document was open to somewhat ambiguous interpretation and the Department was criticized for not giving clear enough guidance, it did establish the requirement for all proposed development of more than 4,645 square metres (50,000 square feet) to be submitted to the Department of the Environment for inspection. Policy notes are periodically revised by government to take account of its changing attitude to particular issues. For example, in 1977 the floorspace area criterion of Policy Note 13 was doubled to 9,290 square metres (100,000 square feet), implying a greater flexibility in the Department of the Environment's approach to edge-of-town retailing (Department of the Environment 1977).

Although government guidelines are of major significance in regulating the pace and direction of retail change, it is probably fair to say that the part played by the Department of the Environment has generally been more reactive than pro-active. This is because planners and central government have been taken unawares by the rapidly changing social trends and market forces that have underpinned the recent dynamism of the retail sector.

The election of Conservative governments in Britain after 1979 and through the 1980s on a platform of free market, non-interventionist policies has led to some liberalization of planning guidelines and a more permissive attitude to edge-of-town developments (Department of the Environment and Welsh Office 1988). Furthermore, the determination of these governments to reduce public sector spending enabled them to reduce the rate of income tax which had the effect of increasing the disposable income of large sections of the population. This in turn led to a consumer boom which indirectly increased the demand for new shopping provision. Also, the Conservatives' staunch belief in increasing individual choice and promoting competition and efficiency led them to favour the idea of there being a greater variety of retail facilities available. Retailers and developers were quick to exploit this opportunity and the tempo of edge-of-town retail development was accelerated. Following an inevitable time lag during the early 1980s whilst land was assembled and construction took place, the rate of growth of floorspace in edge-of-town retail developments of one sort or another increased spectacularly after 1985 (see Figure 4.8).

However, it would be erroneous to think that the protagonists for edge-of-town development have triumphed completely and now have the wholehearted support and backing of local authority planners and central government. The high street versus edge-of-town debate continues, though not with the same fierce intensity or desire to prohibit development as

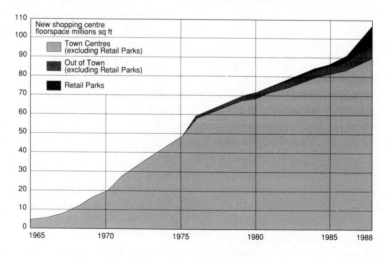

Figure 4.8   Cumulative Retail Floorspace 1965–1988

(Source: Hillier, Parker, May and Rowden)

prevailed in the early 1970s. Over time the pendulum has swung more in favour of peripheral development and the nature of the issues has become modified. The three broad areas of debate as identified by Davies (1976), remain appropriate headings under which to summarize the main points at issue.

Economic considerations

From the late 1960s to the early 1980s the consensus amongst planners was that the granting of permission to peripheral shopping developments would lead to harmful competition with the traditional high street and would destabilize the established intra-urban retail hierarchy. The experience of the decline of central shopping areas in North America was held up as evidence of the deleterious effects that large edge-of-town retail developments could have. Additionally, it was argued that the built environment of town centres was the result of a great deal of public and private investment in fabric and infrastructure over a lengthy period which it was imperative to protect in order to maintain the rateable values. Flowing from this it was felt that changes in the retail composition of the high street such as the loss of a large anchor supermarket would have a harmful effect on other functions and lead to a slump in shopping activity.

Opposing this view, retailers and developers argued that the obsolete buildings and crystallised route networks of town centres were often out of keeping with the requirements of modern retailing. They pointed to the congestion costs and inefficiencies associated with central sites such as traffic circulation, lack of customer car parking and the difficulty of arranging bulk delivery by lorry during the working day. Additionally, expensive land and rates in town centres add to overheads which are passed on to the customers, who could benefit both from cheaper prices as well as easier access at peripherally located shops. Retailers contended that properly planned edge-of-town development could complement existing shops and could be seen as a logical restructuring of the intra-urban retail hierarchy. For example, in areas of brand new suburban development a superstore could be integrated in order to provide for new local demands that had not existed or needed to be catered for before. At the same time, the town centre would benefit from drawing on the enlarged suburban population for its higher order comparison goods shops.

Environmental considerations

Influenced by the containment policies inherent in the Town and Country Planning Act 1947, planners have developed an aversion to proposals that might add to the problem of urban sprawl and harm the semi-rural character of the urban fringe. They have also been concerned that new developments would generate a large volume of additional traffic that would overburden the existing road network, necessitating the loss of even more land for the building of additional roads to channel cars to and from the new shopping developments.

On the other hand, retailers and developers argue that not all land on the edge of town is rural in character by any stretch of the imagination. They have cited cases where derelict land, redundant railway yards and obsolete industrial premises that are ripe for demolition and clearance could be put to more efficient and environmentally attractive uses if recycled for retailing. They also justify the decentralisation of certain types of retailing such as food and bulky items, for example, furniture and Do-it-Yourself (DIY) material from the centres, reasoning that this will liberate valuable space and premises which can then be used for more comparison goods shops, thus enhancing the shopping provision and adding variety to the townscape.

Social considerations

Given that edge-of-town shopping developments are designed principally for the car-borne consumer, concern has been expressed by planners that unbridled decentralization would lead to dual standards of shopping facilities. Affluent, suburban consumers would benefit most from the new retail provision whilst accessibility would be more difficult for poorer, less mobile groups who are more dependent on public transport. The problem of two tiers of retailing would be compounded by the fact that the facilities might, as a result of their more competitive position, lead to the demise of certain stores in the town centre, further reducing choice for the less mobile segments of the population. Furthermore, the generally lower prices in edge-of-town shops would not be so readily available to the less well-off who actually need the benefits of reduced prices even more than the affluent suburbanites.

Retailers contest that, because of the nature and structure of the intra-urban retail hierarchy, there have always been different standards of shopping provision and access inherent in the traditional retail system. Protagonists of edge-of-town retailing argue that it is simply not justifiable to prevent peripheral developments on simplistic grounds of social equality because, by so doing, you will deny all segments of society the opportunity to shop there. A more satisfactory answer would be to plan for an equitable distribution of new facilities such as superstores throughout urban areas, providing that appropriate sites accessible to both private and public transport could be found. In this way all members of the community could benefit from greater choice and lower, more competitive prices.

Conclusion

Times have changed since Davies asserted that 'there is no other country in Western Europe which has sought to contain the process of decentralisation to the same degree as in Britain' (Davies 1976, p. 177). The climate of opinion regarding edge-of-town shopping development has changed and some degree of reconciliation has been achieved between planners, retailers and developers.

Being firmly wedded to the idea of the free-market, successive Conservative governments since 1979 have reduced state intervention in many aspects of social and economic activity, including planning. One aspect of this has been the Department of the Environment's willingness to be more favourably disposed to edge-of-town development. In the face of de-industrialization and the falling contribution of manufacturing to the economy and to employment – down from 8.7 million in 1966 to 5.4 million in 1984 – governments have encouraged any developments that would create wealth and generate jobs. Service sector activities such as retailing, leisure and tourism have come to be seen as having an important part to play in resuscitating the economy. The realization that older development plans had been by-passed by events has led to greater readiness to permit land that was formerly designated for industry to be used instead for retailing. Now, coherently planned and located peripheral developments incorporating retailing, office space and leisure facilities are viewed as potential growth points within restructured local economies.

Planners too have shown themselves willing to develop more flexible responses to pressures for retail decentralization against this backcloth of free-market ideology and reduced state intervention. Edge-of-town developments are no longer seen as ephemeral aberrations, temporarily distorting the intra-urban retail hierarchy, but as permanent and substantial elements within a restructured retail system. The perceived devastating effects of edge-of-town superstores has come to be seen as much less severe than had been predicted. There is also an acceptance of the fact that it makes more sense to locate shops selling bulky goods such as furniture, carpets and DIY materials away from town centres (Gibbs 1981). With the guidance of planners, retail development has been channelled into areas of derelict land. Although retailing was not initially anticipated as a use of land in Enterprise Zones, it is certainly more efficient, visually attractive and preferable to the atmosphere of decay that preceded redevelopment. Examples of large scale retail development on Enterprise Zone land include: Merry Hill (Dudley), Metro Centre (Gateshead), and Meadowhall (Sheffield), whilst retail parks have been developed in Enterprise Zones in the Lower Swansea Valley, Scunthorpe and Corby (see Chapter 5). Additionally, planners have been impressed by a changing commitment and attitude on the part of retailers and developers. In marked contrast to the early uninspiring converted factories and warehouses, developers have progressed to constructing higher quality, more stylish buildings in sensitively landscaped surroundings which harmonize with the rural fringes of urban areas.

The changed attitudes and responses of central government, planners, retailers and developers have culminated in considerable changes occurring in the spatial pattern of retailing in Britain. Many of the old certainties and preconceptions about the intra-urban retail hierarchy have been reassessed and found to be wanting in the light of recent demographic, social and economic changes. The principle of protecting the high street to the exclusion of all else is no longer held to be sacrosanct. Town Centres still have a major part to play in the retail system but their role is changing and will continue to change. Now, there is a greater awareness that the aim should be to create a sensibly balanced mix of shopping facilities, both in and on the edges of towns in order to accommodate the various needs of consumers and the dynamism of retailing.

CHAPTER 5

Shops, Shopping Centres and the Built Environment

Introduction

The pattern of land use in most British towns and cities includes buildings from several different phases of retailing development. Some of these still offer their original function (for example, churches and cathedrals), but most have been renovated or converted to meet changing needs. The realisation that a building's structure and fabric has become obsolete can lead to reduced expenditure on maintenance, progressive deterioration and subsequent dereliction. Eventually, it may be most economical to simply demolish the building and redevelop the intrinsically valuable site. However, prior to the Second World War, changes in most British towns were slight and incremental. Developments were frequently vertical rather than spatial as new construction methods such as steel-framed buildings, and new technical advances such as lifts and escalators made multi-storey retailing practicable.

Since the late 1950s though, a considerable amount of retail development, refurbishment and redevelopment has taken place. Initially, most efforts were focused on town centres as these were widely accepted as the highest level within urban shopping hierarchies (Ministry of Housing and Local Government 1962). More recently however, there has been a major decentralisation in the supply of retailing facilities, leading to radically different forms of development in the suburbs and edges of towns. This chapter describes some of these spatial expressions of retailing in Britain beginning with the town centre and the development of the planned shopping centre. After that, some consideration is given to edge-of-town developments such as the hypermarket, retail warehouse and retail park. Third, the effects of design and corporatism are considered. These have led to a uniformity in shopping styles which many find dull and unattractive. Finally, some reactions to this are considered, in particular, the development of retailing in historic buildings and conservation areas.

91

Shopping centre development

Definition

Although people often use the expression 'shopping centre' to refer to the cluster of shops they visit either in town or in suburban neighbourhoods, the term is used here to mean 'a group of businesses, the majority of which are retailers, located in a unified architectural unit which may be a single structure or related group of buildings' (Dawson, 1979, p. 289). Most centres of this type are planned and have been developed since the Second World War. However, precursors may be found in the shopping arcades that date from the nineteenth century (Mackeith, 1986; Geist 1983). The best known British example is probably Burlington Arcade in London but excellent examples may also be found in Cardiff, Leeds and Birmingham. In Europe, the ornate *galeries* of Paris and Brussels and elaborate *gallerias* of Milan and Naples are similar examples of the trend.

Evolution of the planned shopping centre

The planned shopping centre as defined above only really began to have a profound effect on urban morphology from the late 1950s. At the end of the Second World War many European countries embarked on a period of massive reconstruction, both to rebuild blitzed parts of cities and to catch up on development that had taken a low priority during the war. Housing, industry and infrastructure were tackled as first priorities before attention turned to retail provision. When it came to designing and constructing new retail facilities, architects and planners were influenced to some extent by the experience of the USA where the concept of the planned shopping centre was already well established. Simmons (1964) suggests that Roland Park, built in Baltimore in 1907, was the first of the modern genre of shopping centre. This innovation diffused rapidly in the USA, where the growth of car ownership and suburban expansion also resulted in planned shopping centres being built in edge-of-town locations as early as 1923 when Country Club Plaza opened in the suburbs of Kansas City (Mills 1974).

The evolution and growth of planned shopping centres as elements of the townscape in Britain has been succinctly charted by Schiller (1985). Planned centres first appeared in two different types of setting. One group comprised places such as Bristol, Coventry and Plymouth where severely bomb-damaged city centres and traditional retail cores were demolished and redeveloped. The other set was made up of the first generation New Towns established under the 1946 New Towns Act. In places such as Crawley, Hemel Hempstead and Basildon, planners were able to start with a clean sheet and design shopping centres according to contemporary principles and ideals. The most common form of these centres was the open air pedestrian precinct. When first opened, these spacious pedestrian precincts attracted considerable interest from retailers and were popular with consumers because they were such a novel form of shopping facility. The innovation caught on and during the 1960s precinct schemes of various sizes were incorporated into the intra-urban retail hierarchies of a great many towns and cities.

In this early phase of development the public sector tended to be the prime mover in instigating the construction of shopping precincts. The local authorities of the blitzed cities were keen to rebuild their centres in an imaginative and efficient way, acknowledging that a vibrant retail core is an essential element of urban dynamism. Similarly, the New Town Development Corporations wanted to create shopping facilities in keeping with the ethos of their planned showpieces. Numerous other towns and cities also jumped on the pedestrian precinct bandwagon in the hope of enhancing the attractiveness of their town centres to consumers. An indication of the significance of the pedestrianised shopping centre on retail structure is given by Roberts (1981) who has identified over 1,300 such schemes in Britain.

The opening of the Elephant and Castle Centre in London and the Bull Ring Centre in Birmingham in the mid-1960s marks the beginning of the second phase of shopping centre development in Britain, which Schiller (1985) suggests lasted until about 1972. These centres were landmarks in that they were enclosed and weatherproof, representing the beginning of a shift away from the open-air pedestrian precinct format. Though it was not realised when they were being built, many of the early pedestrian precincts and enclosed centres possessed architectural and stylistic features that were to become outmoded and characteristics that were later perceived as inadequate. Part of this was due to the fact that developers (principally inspired by local authorities) were working to limited budgets in the post-war period of austerity. They were also driven by a desire to fulfil immediate needs as quickly as possible with the inevitable result that many of the built forms now seem unimaginatively conceived with scant attention having been paid to fine detail.

The 'modernist' style of these early developments was characterized by rectangular, geometrical shapes and clearly defined lines. Use of simple mathematical proportions conveyed an impression of order and rigour, producing a boxy appearance to building elevations. Expressed in terms of precinct and shopping centre architecture, this gave rise to a uniformity of proportions in the ground plan and layout, whilst the regularity of dimensions could also be seen in design details such as standardized, modular shop frontages. Extensive use was made of concrete because of its cheapness and ready availability. Pre-cast sections of curtain walling were convenient and permitted rapid construction of buildings. However, concrete does not mellow with age but quickly acquires a stained, grubby appearance, especially when subjected to atmospheric pollution.

The 'golden age' of shopping centre development

According to Schiller (1985), the period 1972–1980 was the 'golden age' of shopping centre development in Britain. Whereas previously local authorities had paid relatively little attention to the design details of centres, by this time they were more astute and better experienced in managing the development process. In particular, they began to take a more pro-active role by determining the location and form of the shopping centre in relation to existing retail provision. Development took the form of a competition, with developers being invited to submit proposals for the designated site, which was frequently an infill development attached to the existing core. Criteria for judging competing proposals included the merit of the architectural design of the shopping centre as well as its projected financial return to the local authority. To see the project through to completion, a triangular partnership was typically formed between the local authority as owner and landlord of the site, the successful property development company, and its financial backer who was usually a pension fund or similar institutional investor. As the completion of building approached, shopping centre managers would be appointed to work with letting agents in order to achieve a balanced and appropriate mix of retail tenants.

Several trends in the evolution of shopping centres distinguish this phase

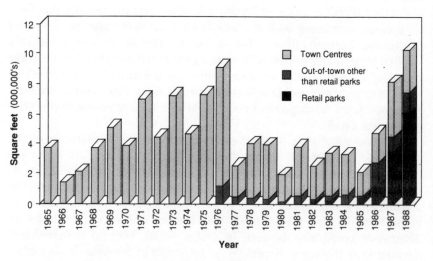

Figure 5.1   Total floorspace opened in retail schemes

(Source: Hillier, Parker, May & Rowden)

of their development. As the name 'golden age' suggests, these were the peak years in terms of the numbers and size of town centre shopping schemes built (Figure 5.1). Some of the largest and best known examples of British shopping centres were opened during this period, including Eldon Square in Newcastle-upon-Tyne, The Arndale Centre in Manchester and the Victoria Centre in Nottingham. Throughout this period, there was a steady increase in the number of fully enclosed shopping centres, with the trend being particularly pronounced amongst the larger schemes (Hillier, Parker, May and Rowden 1987). Many of these incorporated features such as air conditioning and a controlled microclimate to ensure year-round comfort for shoppers. At the same time, there was also a marked improvement in their appearance and quality. Design styles were based on 'post-modern' architecture, and the monolithic brutalism of the early concrete blockhouse-style buildings was progressively replaced by higher quality, more varied building materials with greater attention being paid to detail and finish.

Schiller (1985) suggests that 80% of British towns with a population of 75,000 or more have experienced shopping centre development with their central areas. In spite of a drop in the number of completions since 1976 (the peak year), there is evidence to suggest some recovery in investment in town centre development since 1986, fuelled largely by government financial and fiscal policies (Hillier, Parker, May and Rowden 1989a).

Tenant mix

The purpose of a shopping centre is to create a convivial atmosphere for shopping. It is therefore important that the centre is managed to create the best image possible, with the result that customers are encouraged to return time after time. The attractiveness of a centre depends on the types of shops found there (the 'tenant mix') as well as on the design and appearance of the buildings. Usually, centre managers will attempt to locate one or two key tenants at strategic points so that they maximise the pedestrian flows between them. Such anchor tenants are usually multiple retailers such as Marks and Spencer, Debenhams, BHS and Sainsbury. The remainder of the tenants depends on the size and shape of the centre.

In general, a centre will try to offer a range of chain stores together with some local independents such as speciality shops or retailers selling craft goods or products associated with the town or region. Their purpose is not only to meet the shopping expectations that are cultivated by national advertising, but also to be sufficiently different from other centres in the region so that they can create their own distinctive identity.

Development consortia go to considerable lengths to include features that will help to differentiate their particular centre from others. Architectural features such as glass barrel-vaulted roofs to let in natural daylight have become popular as have atria and wall climber lifts. Standards of fixtures, fittings and decorative finish are constantly improving and materials such as marble are increasingly being used for wall cladding and flooring. Water features and lavish planting schemes add to the overall ambience and aura of elegance. Novelty focal points such as the Wishing Fish clock in the Regent Arcade in Cheltenham have been shown to be attractive elements that are worthwhile incorporating because of their potential for stimulating shopper interest and pedestrian traffic.

Centre revitalisation

There is no doubt that the shopping centre of the 1990s is a very different place from the pedestrian precincts of the 1950s. An important consequence of the contrast between the stylish modern shopping centres and the drab monotony of many of the early examples is the realisation that periodic refurbishment is vital if shopping centres are to maintain their attractiveness to an increasingly sophisticated shopper. From studies of shopping centres in the USA, Lord (1985) notes that centres may become structurally or functionally obsolete quite quickly and be out of tune with prevailing retail trends. In extreme cases this may result in important anchor tenants deciding to move out. Also, should the demographic structure of the shopping centre's trade area change markedly then there may be serious implications for certain of the tenants who find themselves either having to reassess their offering or question the viability of staying in business.

   Lord has identified a number of shopping centre revitalisation strategies that have been attempted in order to address these problems. These include:

(1) Enclosing a centre that was formerly open to the weather.
(2) Reducing the floor area of individual retail units that occupy the shopping centre in order to increase their number and in doing so broaden the variety of tenants.
(3) Restructuring the tenant mix in order to restore the centre's competitive position.
(4) Improving the energy efficiency of the centre.
(5) Expansion of the centre at the same time as refurbishing the old fabric.
(6) Redesigning the internal layout and external vehicular facilities of the shopping centre, and
(7) Developing an innovative marketing strategy to update the centre's image.

A recent survey of British shopping centres has shown that many of those built as recently as the 1970s are already undergoing extensive refurbishment programmes involving the sort of techniques listed above (Hillier, Parker, May and Rowden 1986). Since the late 1950s the planned shopping centre in its various guises has become a common feature of British townscapes. In spite of the increasing trend towards retail decentralization, local authorities have maintained a steady determination to enhance the viability of traditional town centre retailing with the result that 'most of the shopping centre floor space completed since 1965 is still in town centre schemes' (Hillier, Parker, May and Rowden 1989, p. 2). In the face of increasing competition from edge-of-town facilities, developers must be responsive to the changing needs of retailers and shoppers. Successful shopping centres are consumer led and success

> depends on thinking from the start in terms of creating a balanced living concept of a place where customers find it natural to shop – not just once, but time and time again because basic retailing principles have been recognised and applied from the very outset. (Stewart McColl quoted in *The Times*)

Edge-of-town retail developments

The decentralisation in demand for retailing services has already been noted in Chapter 4. However, though this began in the Victorian and Edwardian eras, the decentralisation in the supply of retailing has been much more recent. Most of the outward movement has occurred since the Second World War, with an acceleration in the numbers and types of suburban developments occurring since the mid 1970s (see Figure 5.1). A particular economic impetus to relocate premises or develop entirely new types of retailing on the edges of towns came with the abolition of Resale Price Maintenance in 1964, which heralded a new era of price competition. Retail firms could now buy in bulk from suppliers at favourable rates and then sell the product on to consumers at discount prices. Supermarkets incorporating self-service methods to keep overheads down spread rapidly in this newly competitive environment.

In town centres and suburban residential areas the new supermarkets were frequently former grocery stores whose internal layout had been redesigned to permit the introduction of self-service selling techniques. Though self-service can be significantly cheaper than personal counter service, space limitations on the high street seriously restricted what could be achieved. Many entrepreneurs therefore sought larger, more spacious premises away from the high street where they could store, display and sell the produce they bought in bulk from manufacturers. Their solution was to model a form of retailing on the wholesale cash-and-carry warehouses that had grown in number since the end of the Second World War. This cash-and-carry system had been set up by wholesalers to cater for small, independent grocers who drove to the off-centre warehouse to select stock for their shops which they paid for at a checkout before carrying it away in their own vehicles. With minimal modification, the cash-and-carry concept became fused with self-service supermarket techniques, evolving into the discount food store.

Phase 1: The 1960s discounters

The rise of the discount store represents the embryonic phase of retail decentralization in Britain. Asda and Kwik Save are two classic examples of retail organizations that started selling groceries in this particular way. Kwik Save was established at Prestatyn, North Wales in the early 1960s. In the beginning, to speed the expansion of the chain of stores and to keep development and construction costs to a minimum, existing buildings were used wherever possible. Various types of building were acquired. As long as they had large floor areas and could be quickly adapted they were suitable candidates for conversion into discount stores. Old cinemas, car showrooms, garages and auction salerooms, usually in off-centre rather than edge-of-town locations, were recycled into Kwik Save premises. Standards of decoration and shop fittings were kept to an absolute minimum to help keep prices down. Kwik Save prospered and set Albert Gubay, its founder, on the road to joining the ranks of Britain's two hundred wealthiest people (Beresford *et al.*, 1990).

Grocery retailers were the first to make this move into discounting but, before long, astute retailers of durable goods such as carpets and furniture picked up the innovation and tailored it to their particular merchandise and methods of selling. Examples include the discount warehouses associated with Allied Carpets and MFI. These were more likely to be found occupying converted factories and industrial warehouses which were located towards the edges of towns. Their earliest discount warehouses were often tucked away on industrial estates, mixed in with manufacturing land uses. As a result, and often to the consternation of planners and conservationists, they needed garish signs and large hoardings to advertise their presence. The sheds were soulless but the prices were attractive and the young, aggressive firms grew rapidly.

Phase 2: The entry of the multiples

The second phase of decentralisation is characterized by several distinct types of development each of which is associated with multiple retailing: superstores, hypermarkets and retail warehouses. The attitude of planners and central government has been particularly important in assisting or hindering these developments. There is thus a varied spatial pattern of these facilities around the country.

Much of the impetus for the entry of the multiple stores came from the decision of the Leeds-based grocery discounter, Asda, to trade up-market and embark on an extensive expansion programme of brand new store development. The major grocery multiples had seen the success of the early discount stores but had not taken the threat very seriously. However, Asda's decision meant that the large grocers could no longer stand by and risk seeing their hard-won market shares eroded. From about the late 1960s firms such as Sainsbury, Tesco, Fine Fare and the co-operative societies began to seek edge-of-town sites. Not only did these well-established companies have money to invest in retail facilities but they were not prepared to risk their reputations by occupying obsolete, down-at-heel buildings. As a result, the multiples began to search systematically for suitable sites for brand-new, purpose-built stores away from their traditional town centre arena of operation.

Though the climate for retail decentralisation at the time was largely hostile, in practice, local authority planners adopted one of three approaches to proposed developments: outright prohibition, restriction of new development to designated locations, and the assessment of each application on its merits (Burt *et al* 1983). Planners in different regions of the country also varied in their opposition to new peripheral developments with those in the South being generally more hostile and inflexible (Bamfield 1980). The arrival of the major grocery multiples on the scene also made for some moderation in planners' viewpoints. Whether they were more disposed to look favourably on proposals submitted by multiples because they were less suspicious of established retailers than they had been of the earlier discounters, or if it was more due to the discreet flexing of corporate muscle, is debatable.

The entry of the multiples into the decentralisation process led to the development of the 'superstore'. Essentially, superstores are much enlarged supermarkets. Definitions vary but the term has generally come to mean a freestanding store of between 2,325 square metres (25,000 square feet) and 4,650 square metres (50,000 square feet) gross floorspace, selling a wide range of food and general household requirements with extensive adjacent car parking. Permission was also sought for stores of greater than 4,650 square metres gross floorspace. Though smaller than their counterparts in Europe, these British 'hypermarkets' were often significantly larger than superstores and so aroused commensurately greater opposition from planners. This was partially due to their size and likely impact on the built environment and also because of the nature of the goods they were expected to sell. Hypermarkets were designed to be large enough to accommodate not only a wide range of groceries and household requirements but also an extensive range of higher-order durables such as 'white goods', televisions, audio equipment, bicycles, toys and clothes.

Because of its size and product range, planners tended to view the hypermarket with hostility. By 1983 there were only 39 hypermarkets in Britain, whereas 240 superstores had been opened (Unit for Retail Planning Information 1984). The controversy surrounding hypermarket development at this time is reflected in the number of public enquiries into applications for edge-of-town development and in academic interest in this particular retail innovation (see for example: Bristol City Planning Department 1972, Lee *et al.*, 1973, Thorpe and Kivell 1971).

A third feature of this phase of decentralization was the evolution of the retail warehouse. In similar ways to those in which the grocery discount store evolved into the superstore, so, during the 1970s the basic discount warehouse concept became transformed into the retail warehouse. The refinement in store format was evident in a number of ways. Instead of merely converting redundant factories and warehouses into serviceable retail space, the emphasis gradually shifted towards the construction of buildings specifically designed for retailing. Although one cannot get away from the fact that the new retail warehouses were essentially very large open-plan sheds, they were not as crude or cavernous as the early discount warehouses. Greater attention was paid to architectural details such as cladding materials, exterior decoration and interior design. This upgrading of quality had the added advantage of helping to calm the fears of planners who came to accept that retail warehouses selling bulky goods such as furniture and carpets to the 'hatchback and roof-rack' trade had a part to play in the intra-urban retail hierarchy. They could see the logic of locating stores that needed extensive space for storage, display and customer car parking on more accessible, cheaper sites away from town centres (Gibbs 1981). Firms such as Comet (electrical appliances), MFI (self-assembly furniture), ELS and Queensway (furniture), and Allied Carpets grew rapidly and soon developed national networks of retail warehouses in order to make the most of the profitable growth opportunities.

However, the most dramatic expansion was experienced by relative newcomers to the retail scene – the 'Do-it-Yourself' (DIY) retail warehouses, for example, B & Q and Dodge City – which were established in 1969 and 1973 respectively. Both were subsequently acquired by the Woolworth company, which in turn became part of the Kingfisher group (Jones 1983). A combination of circumstances favoured the exceptional growth of the DIY sector. Rising affluence since the 1950s and increased disposable income led to a large proportion of the population having spare money for discretionary expenditure on items such as home improvements. Coupled with this, shorter working weeks and longer paid holidays meant increased leisure time that could be spent on pursuits such as gardening, woodworking, painting and decorating. An ever-increasing range of power tools and gadgets removed the need for certain of the craft skills formerly required to tackle major projects around the home. Technological developments such as quick drying, non-drip paints and ready-pasted wallpaper enabled the keen amateur to match professional standards of decorative finish. Furthermore, because more people were now employed in sedentary, non-manual employment (see Chapter 1), large numbers turned to home improvement activities as a therapeutic and physically demanding outlet. Against this backcloth, the DIY sector flourished and other firms such as Texas and W. H.

Smith Do-it-All moved in to exploit this growth area.

The final characteristic of this second phase of development was the gradual readjustment that took place in the location of edge-of-town retailing. With the entry of the multiples and the growing number of purpose-built superstores and retail warehouses, there tended to be a shift away from obscure locations in the middle of industrial estates to more accessible and visible sites alongside arterial and ring roads. As more enlightened planners came to accept the new forms of retail outlet as valid components of a restructured intra-urban retail hierarchy, it became increasingly common to find a few retail warehouses clustered together along main roads on the outskirts of towns.

Phase 3: Acceleration and agglomeration in the 1980s

The most recent phase of retail decentralization began in the early 1980s and is still in progress. Trends established during preceding phases have generally continued but with a tendency towards an increased intensity, pace and scale of development. As has been shown earlier, the more permissive approach towards edge-of-town developments that stemmed from the election of Conservative governments committed to free-market ideology has played an important part. Developers responded enthusiastically to this changed attitude and energetically sought out suitable sites in peripheral locations, whilst an increasing range of retailers began to consider the potential of decentralization. The increasing availability of retail floorspace on the edge of town led to a considerable broadening in the variety of retail firms leasing premises or investing in the new developments.

The new arrivals fell roughly into four groups. First, there were a number of new chains of specialist retailers such as Textile World, Shoe City, World of Leather and Lounge House. Second, new stores such as Sainsbury's Homebase (DIY, home improvement and garden centres) and Boots' Children's World exemplified established firms' attempts to diversify their activities away from their original core businesses and into fast growing markets. Third, and probably most significant was the increasing edge-of-town presence of retailers that had traditionally been associated with the high street, for example, Habitat, Halfords, Argos, Currys and Olympus. Without doubt though, it was the radical decision in 1984 of Marks and Spencer, considered by many to be the flagship of the high street, to establish a number of edge-of-town stores that indicated the extent to which retailing patterns were changing. The fourth group of edge-of-town stores was distinctive in that they were branches of foreign controlled retailing companies. Examples include Toys R Us based in the USA and Ikea (home furnishings) which has its headquarters in Sweden.

The DIY retail warehouse sector has continued to experience strong growth during the current phase of decentralisation. Here too, government policy has played an influential part. Conservative governments since 1979 have been committed to meeting the aspirations of the population for private home ownership (Department of the Environment 1988a). The pursuit of financial policies aimed at controlling interest rates led to a substantial increase in mortgage lending for home buying. Furthermore, the ideologically-motivated sale of local authority houses to tenants further increased the numbers of private homeowners. Together, these processes benefited the DIY sector by boosting demand from new homeowners who were naturally keen to protect and enhance their investment in bricks and mortar. Retailers responded by building newer, larger stores stocking a wider variety of merchandise.

Retail parks

Towards the end of the second phase of retail decentralisation the beginning of a shift away from the freestanding superstore or retail warehouse had become discernible. In some towns, guided by imaginative planning policies, small groups of retail warehouses were established either in a cluster or strip form adjoining main peripheral roads. From these origins, further development and refinement took place resulting in the emergence of the retail park.

Property consultants Hillier, Parker, May and Rowden have prepared a useful working definition of retail parks. They suggest that in order for an edge-of-town development to qualify as a retail park it:

> Should have at least 50,000 square feet (4,645 square metres) gross lettable area, and be built and let as a retail entity. It should be sited outside the town centre and contain at least three retail warehouses, defined as single storey retail units of at least 10,000 square feet (929 square metres). It should also include some purpose built pedestrian area or joint car parking facilities. (Hillier, Parker, May and Rowden 1990, p. 11)

Apart from retail warehouse tenants, retail parks may also include a grocery superstore, for example, Sainsburys in the Arnison retail park on the outskirts of Durham.

The first retail park proper was opened in Aylesbury as recently as 1982 (Hillier, Parker, May and Rowden 1989b). Between 1982 and the end of 1985 the number grew fairly slowly owing to the time taken for the effects of the liberalization of the planning process to work their way through the development pipeline. However, since 1986 there has been a surge in retail park development (see Figure 5.2). By the end of 1989, 174 retail parks had opened in Britain, representing over 20 million square feet (1,858,000 square metres) of retail space. An indication of the growing significance and

a) Retail Park Openings

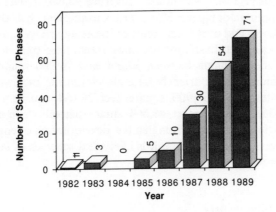

b) Retail Park Floorspace

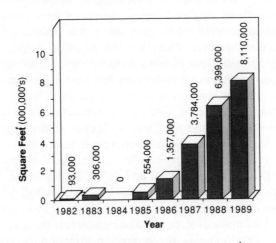

Figure 5.2 Retail Park Development 1982–1989

(Source: Hillier, Parker, May & Rowden)

pervasiveness of the retail park as an element in the retail system is revealed by the fact that in 1989 alone, 71 retail parks were opened, together representing over 57% of all shopping centre floorspace completed during that year. No slackening in the trend is anticipated and another 80 retail parks were forecast to open in 1990 (Hillier, Parker, May and Rowden 1990). Inevitably, larger towns are generally favoured by retailers seeking to expand their edge-of-town operations, but, as suitable sites become more difficult to find, retail park development is likely to filter down the settlement hierarchy.

According to the Hillier Parker definition, a retail park may be occupied by as few as three retail warehouses covering 50,000 square feet (4,645 square metres) gross floorspace. However, an example such as this would be placed at the lower end of the size range as the average development in 1989 was 114,225 square feet. In spite of this, most recent retail park developments have been smaller, ranging between 50,000 and 74,000 square feet. The average thus hides some extremely large developments such as the 'Retail World' at Gateshead (367,000 square feet/34,094 square metres) and Rotherham (436,000 square feet/40,504 square metres) which are amongst the largest developed to date. Though a few developments of equivalent size are in the process of construction, it is likely that schemes as large as these will remain the exception.

Regional shopping centres

Although the majority of edge-of-town retail developments lie somewhere along a size continuum ranging from the individual freestanding superstore through to the large retail park, there are a few examples that are in a different league altogether. These are the so-called Regional Shopping Centres, varying in size from 70,604 square metres (760,000 square feet) up to 167,200 square metres (1.8 million square feet). The first of these was Brent Cross, opened at Hendon in North London in 1976. Although having extensive car parking facilities, Brent Cross resembles the blockhouse style of enclosed shopping centre that was in favour at the time. It is more reminiscent of the North American shopping mall than the two recently built edge-of-town regional shopping centres, Gateshead's Metro Centre and Merry Hill at Dudley, where layout and design owes more to post-modern influences. This trend is even more noticeable at Meadowhall on the outskirts of Sheffield which opened in the autumn of 1990. In fact, not only in the largest regional shopping centres, but also right across the spectrum of edge-of-town retail development, much greater attention is being paid to standards of architecture, design and layout.

The contrast between recently constructed retail facilities and much of the earlier unprepossessing development on the edge-of-town can be seen in a number of ways. The increasing use of materials such as brick rather than sheet cladding, slates or pantiles for roofing and the incorporation of features such as gabled roofs, spires and clock towers gives buildings a more attractive, substantial appearance. The functional austerity of some of the early retail warehouses and discount stores has given way to brighter, warmer, more convivial environments in which to go shopping. In regional shopping centres considerable expenditure is made on all aspects of internal decoration and finish in an effort to create an air of opulence and comfort. Attention to detail also extends to the area outside the premises. Instead of the bare expanses of car parking that were to be found adjoining the early developments it is now far more common to see car parking spaces interspersed with areas of hard and soft landscaping including cast iron bollards and lamp standards, flagstones, cobbles, brick paving, trees and shrubs.

Apart from being carefully designed to be attractive to potential customers, regional shopping centres also need to be readily accessible to a large market. As befits their position at the top of the edge-of-town retail continuum, regional shopping centres have all been strategically located on major routeways so that they can draw from the largest possible catchment. Brent Cross benefits from proximity to both the North Circular Road and the southern end of the M1, Metro Centre is linked to Newcastle-upon-Tyne and to the A1(M) by new dual carriageway roads and Merry Hill has excellent access to the Midlands motorway network via the M6. Located right alongside the M1, Meadowhall has a brand new direct link to the motorway whilst, in the south of England, the Lakeside Centre is being constructed close to the M25 at Thurrock.

Being the largest of the edge-of-town developments, it is not surprising that the regional shopping centres should contain the greatest variety of shops. Not only do the tenants consist of multiples that have come to be firmly associated with an edge-of-town location, for example, B & Q, Comet, MFI and Sainsburys, but also a wide selection of the major high street names such as Marks and Spencer, House of Fraser, Debenhams, BHS, C&A, Habitat and Next. Regional shopping centres occupied by such retailers undoubtedly draw some trade from existing town centres within their catchments. However, the potential for developing additional regional centres of the scale of those either built or nearing completion would seem to be limited (Figure 5.3). The chief constraint is the dearth of suitably large areas of land with good regional access.

Without doubt, it was the availability of extensive sites in Enterprise Zones together with generous rates reductions that played a crucial role in the development of Metro Centre, Merry Hill and Meadowhall. The completion of the M25 London orbital motorway stimulated a spate of proposals for large regional shopping centres at motorway intersections in this prosperous area. To date, only the Lakeside Centre at Thurrock has received the support of planners and the Department of the Environment. In spite of going to appeal, schemes proposed for Bricket Wood near St. Albans, Hewitts Farm near Orpington and at Wraysbury near Staines have failed to get planning permission, principally on the grounds that these developments would have been in the Green Belt. Clearly, even though the Conservative government is committed to free-market policies, there is a point at which intervention is felt to be necessary and desirable.

Similarly, the Secretary of State for the Environment refused permission for regional shopping centres at Leicester (Centre 21), Southampton

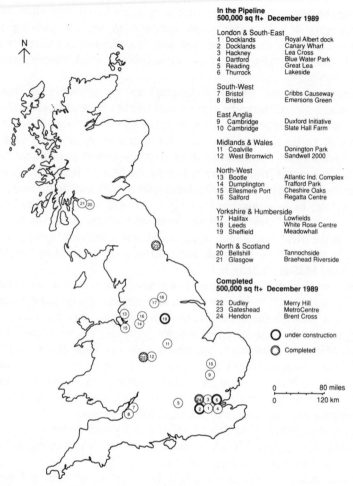

In the Pipeline
500,000 sq ft+ December 1989

London & South-East
1 Docklands   Royal Albert dock
2 Docklands   Canary Wharf
3 Hackney   Lea Cross
4 Dartford   Blue Water Park
5 Reading   Great Lea
6 Thurrock   Lakeside

South-West
7 Bristol   Cribbs Causeway
8 Bristol   Emersons Green

East Anglia
9 Cambridge   Duxford Initiative
10 Cambridge   Slate Hall Farm

Midlands & Wales
11 Coalville   Donington Park
12 West Bromwich   Sandwell 2000

North-West
13 Bootle   Atlantic Ind. Complex
14 Dumplington   Trafford Park
15 Ellesmere Port   Cheshire Oaks
16 Salford   Regatta Centre

Yorkshire & Humberside
17 Halifax   Lowfields
18 Leeds   White Rose Centre
19 Sheffield   Meadowhall

North & Scotland
20 Bellshill   Tannochside
21 Glasgow   Braehead Riverside

Completed
500,000 sq ft+ December 1989

22 Dudley   Merry Hill
23 Gateshead   MetroCentre
24 Hendon   Brent Cross

◯ under construction

◉ Completed

0   80 miles
0   120 km

Figure 5.3   Out-of-Town Regional Shopping Centres

(Source: Hillier, Parker, May & Rowden)

(Adanac Park) and Bristol (Cribbs Causeway) because of the threat they posed to the vitality and viability of the respective city centre shopping facilities. However, this apparent change in viewpoint does not signify a U-turn in Government policy regarding edge-of-town development. It is merely that the very *scale* of the large regional shopping centres requires there to be a carefully detailed assessment made of likely positive and negative effects. In the case of the regional shopping centres that have been built in Enterprise Zones (that is, Metro Centre, Merry Hill and Meadowhall), approval hinged on the view that the benefits of employment growth and economic regeneration outweighed any harm that might be done to nearby town centres.

Hybrid developments

Schiller (1988) suggests that a more likely threat to the town centre could be posed by what he terms 'hybrid centres'. Schiller envisages these on the edge of towns of 100,000 people or more, containing branches of firms such as Marks and Spencer, Tesco, Toys R Us, Habitat, Allied Carpets, MFI, Comet, together with a multi-screen cinema, fast-food restaurants and a bank. Being smaller in scale than regional shopping centres, but still containing a balanced mix of retailers, hybrid centres in Schiller's view, have the potential to become quite numerous. In terms of the edge-of-town retail continuum outlined above, a hybrid centre would lie somewhere between a large retail park and a regional shopping centre. They could present a formidable threat to the established high streets of medium-sized, free-standing towns, especially those where retailers did not consider the market to be sufficiently large to justify maintaining branches both in and on the edge of town. Whether such hybrid centres are developed in significant numbers remains to be seen. Much will depend on the attitude taken by local planners and the Department of the Environment.

It is not inconceivable, however, that larger retail parks may grow by a process of accretion with the construction of successive phases of retail development, thus acquiring the characteristics of Schiller's hybrid centres. A pointer to such a scenario is provided by the example of Cribbs Causeway on the outskirts of Bristol where a retail agglomeration has developed in stages since the late 1970s. Commencing with the construction of a Carrefour hypermarket (which is now trading under the Asda banner following takeover from Gateway in 1989) the cluster has gradually expanded with the addition of a variety of retail warehouses including B & Q, Toys R Us, World of Leather and Argos. As was noted above, plans for a full-blown regional shopping centre (in addition to this existing retail provision) have been recently turned down by the Secretary of State although an appeal is currently pending. Whatever the eventual outcome, it is plain to see that Cribbs Causeway is even now in fact almost a hybrid centre, requiring only limited additional development to fully qualify for this status. In Leicester, where the Department of the Environment refused permission for the large Centre 21 regional shopping scheme, there is even clearer evidence for advancing the view that the hybrid centre is gaining ground. A smaller edge-of-town retail complex named Fosse Park was given the go-ahead and amongst the major retailers who have taken premises are Toys R Us, Habitat, W. H. Smith, Do-it-All, but, most significantly of all, Marks and Spencer, whose presence has set the seal on the development, guaranteeing that it will have a considerable impact.

Incorporation of leisure facilities such as bowling alleys, multi-screen cinemas, ice rinks and restaurants has already started to occur, not only in regional shopping centres, but also in retail parks, for example Craig Park

(Edinburgh) and St. Andrews Quay (Hull). Yet another indication suggesting that an accretionary trend towards hybrid centres is underway is revealed by a recent survey which indicates that retail parks are gradually evolving with a steady influx of retailers who have not previously considered location on the edge of town (Hillier, Parker, May and Rowden 1990).

The signs are thus becoming apparent that the emergence of the hybrid centre could well constitute a major element in the next phase of retail decentralization. Although talk of retail saturation might be premature, the massive growth of edge-of-town development cannot realistically go on *ad infinitum*. The supply of land formerly designated for industry as well as accessible derelict land is not inexhaustible and, assuming a maintained commitment to the Green Belt, prospects for green field developments look slim. However, a contradictory and extremely controversial view is that because surpluses of temperate foodstuffs are now routinely produced as a result of Britain's increased agricultural efficiency, much more rural land can be devoted for retail and housing development. Similarly, it may seem logical to assume that the relatively stable total national population can only support a finite number of retail facilities. This is an overly simple view, however, because factors such as changing regional demographic structure, social trends, tastes and demands have important implications for the provision of retailing. Undoubtedly, astute retailers will adapt to meet changing market conditions and will target the resulting growth opportunities. Thus, there will inevitably be changes in the make-up of edge-of-town shopping provision, just as the retail composition of town centres has evolved over time.

Some of the existing occupants of retail parks and regional shopping centres may fall by the wayside as trading conditions change. An increase in merger and acquisition activity is probable as aggressive companies endeavour either to expand their market share by taking over faltering companies, or to acquire the valuable sites of underperforming competitors. Alternatively, the growth in number of new, dynamic retail firms will broaden and revitalise the edge-of-town offering. Existing firms with a successful retail format can be expected to want to move to larger and/or more modern stores in more prominent positions on retail parks, leaving their original premises vacant and available for a new tenant.

Although superstores and retail warehouses are relative newcomers to the retail scene, some of those built as recently as the early 1980s already seem outdated and in need of refurbishment if they are to compare favourably with recently built additions to edge-of-town developments. Companies such as Asda, Great Mills and W. H. Smith Do-it-All have recently embarked on extensive upgrading projects. Finally, even if it is accepted that the numbers of distinct schemes cannot increase indefinitely, this does not rule out all forms of peripheral growth. A more probable eventuality is the expansion of existing retail parks due to the addition of new phases of development.

Providing that suitable adjacent space is available, planners would be far more likely to permit an extension to an existing retail park rather than to countenance the construction of a new and entirely separate scheme. But if this supposition is borne out by events, then the emergence of fully-fledged hybrid centres becomes even more certain.

Multiples and the built environment

The decline of the independent retailer and the rise of the multiple chain has been dealt with earlier (see Chapters 2 and 3). The market share of multiples has grown consistently and has been accentuated further by the formation of powerful retail conglomerates such as Storehouse, the Kingfisher Group, the Burton Group and Sears Holdings. In the highly segmented, competitive market place, multiples want to be easily recognized by customers and so make strenuous efforts to establish a distinctive identity. The development of a powerful corporate image permeates all aspects of their retail presentation. Outside the premises this includes elements such as the colour and design of the fascia and shopfront, whilst the corporate theme is continued inside the shops, extending from decoration and layout, to own-brand labelling, employees' uniforms and carrier bags. For example, long established companies such as Boots and Marks and Spencer have developed a strong identity over time, making their branches instantly recognisable from familiar features such as logos and signs. As an inevitable consequence of their market dominance, not only have multiples attained a ubiquitous presence, but also, because they all engage in strategies to make themselves readily identifiable, the retail environment has become boringly similar throughout Britain.

Since the 1970s the creation of distinctive corporate identities has depended increasingly on the application of skilful design principles (Gardner and Sheppard 1989). To differentiate themselves from the opposition, multiples have engaged the services of specialist design consultancies whose brief has been to produce an exciting, seductive shopping environment and individual personality for their shops. Though merchandise obviously remains important, the aim is to produce the right atmosphere and give the chain a strong visual identity and appeal. In their pursuit of a distinctive image, retailers are very conscious of the radical changes that have taken place in the structure of the retail market since the 1950s. Changing from a fairly homogeneous, mass consumption market to one that is fragmenting according to changing tastes, attitudes, aspirations and lifestyles, it reflects a very much more multi-faceted society. Consumers are better educated, more sophisticated and more demanding with the result that quality, style, ambience, service and reputation have become more important variables in the retail mix.

Recognising this changing situation, retailers no longer attempt to service the whole market. Instead, multiples narrow their offering and trade with the needs and expectations of a particular market segment such as teenagers, working women, the 'thirtysomethings' or male executives very firmly in mind. In turn, the designers have to pay particular attention to the characteristics of the intended target market in their efforts to devise inviting retail environments that will tempt the customers back to the store time and again. Careful consideration is given to every imaginable aspect of the retail operation that can in some way influence the consumers' perception of the chain. This starts outside with the facade and continues inside with decoration, displays and fittings, the use of colour and graphics, right down to lighting and background music. Multiples see it as essential to keep track of the shifts occurring in the retail market and to adjust not only their merchandise, but also their image, to take account of discernible trends. From time to time, total refurbishment will be necessary to update the retail formula. In extreme cases it may even be beneficial to relaunch the entire chain if a major departure from the former operation in terms of merchandise and image is planned. Probably the best example of such a process was the conversion of the entire Hepworths chain of mens' outfitters into Next stores under the inspired guidance of George Davies.

The visible consequence of all the effort being expended on retail design and image creation is that all round the country, bright new shops are emerging from cocoons of scaffolding and hoardings, their old frontages gone forever and their interiors revamped in the pursuit of distinctiveness. Although it might seem entirely logical for a company to try to gain an edge on competitors by investing in a facelift programme for the chain, the irony is that only a short term advantage at best can be obtained. As soon as a chain is seen to be revamping its image, so competitors will feel it necessary to jump on the refurbishment bandwagon in order to protect their market share. For example, the outstanding success of Next triggered an imitative response from the Burton Group who launched Principles, whilst even Marks and Spencer was forced to rethink its marketing strategy for fashion wear. Inevitably, the whole process turns into a zero-sum game in which innovative retailers and designers can only gain a temporary lead before the rest catch up with them.

A retailing system dominated by multiple firms thus has an unfortunate tendency to produce a chain of clone-like offspring. The result is that high streets are becoming almost indistinguishable from one another. Even in enclosed shopping centres where careful management assures the assembly of a balanced tenant mix, the same shop names feature prominently. On the edge of town, the same process is occurring with retail parks becoming composed of a predictable set of tenants whose premises are only too familiar in appearance.

Retail gentrification

Although the characteristics of corporatism and standardization predominate in the retail system, there are examples of retail environments which have a greater degree of individuality. In recent years local authorities and property developers have come to appreciate the fact that certain historic buildings and areas of architectural merit lend themselves to transformation into retail facilities of great character. As has been the case with many retail innovations, the earliest examples of this trend were seen in the United States. Probably the first of these was the conversion of the buildings of an old chocolate factory in to the Ghirardelli Square shopping centre in San Francisco, which opened in 1964. Here, the shells of the original buildings were retained whilst the space inside was divided up into numerous small retail premises. The area between the buildings was carefully landscaped to provide a pleasant environment for pedestrians. Other similar developments dating from this period are The Cannery, also in San Francisco, and Trolley Square in Salt Lake City. On the East Coast the Faneuil Hall-Quincy Market scheme was developed purposefully as part of a conservation project aimed at the restoration and rehabilitation of the historic urban fabric of central Boston. The Quincy Market building opened in 1976, providing accommodation for a wide variety of food retailers. It was followed two years later by the North and South Markets that were tenanted by small specialist craft and gift shops (Mackeith 1985). The recent, imaginative conversion of Union Station in Washington DC provides another excellent example of how historic buildings can be recycled for retail uses.

In Britain, the best known example of this form of retail gentrification, where the architectural quality and style of the redeveloped and refurbished building becomes the key element in the creation of a new shopping environment, is Covent Garden in Central London. Faneuil Hall and Covent Garden have similar origins in that formerly they were both centrally-located urban wholesale produce markets. Increasing traffic congestion, access difficulties and lack of space for expansion to accommodate the growing volume of trade led to the relocation of their traditional functions to other areas within the cities, leaving the original buildings redundant. At Covent Garden, over three hundred years of wholesale fruit, flower and vegetable trading ended in 1974 when the Market Authority sold the site to the Greater London Council (GLC) for £6 million. Numerous suggestions were put forward for the future use of the market buildings. After much debate the brief set out in the Covent Garden Local Plan proposed that the buildings should be converted into small shops, galleries and workshops. The first floor was to be occupied by office studios whilst the halls were envisaged as providing space for pavement cafes on similar lines to those found in the arcade-style *galeries* of Brussels and *gallerias* of Milan (Wacher and Flint 1980).

The project was organised and co-ordinated for the GLC's Covent Garden Committee by the GLC Covent Garden Team, a multi-disciplinary group of architects, planners and surveyors. Painstaking attention to detail and quality went into the implementation of the re-development and restoration projects (Thorne 1980). As the GLC was sole owner, the Covent Garden Team was in the fortunate position of being able to ensure that its clear philosophy concerning the retail structure and mix of the completed project would be fulfilled. It was decided that the scheme should be an integrated unit and that its retail composition should be sufficiently distinctive to attract trade from the London area as well as from tourists. It was felt to be pointless having shops that could be found in a typical high street and so most multiples were actively discouraged from acquiring premises (Wacher and Flint 1980). From one thousand applications for premises, specialist retailers were carefully selected on the grounds of their compatibility and potential for contributing to a balanced, integrated whole. The intention that Covent Garden was to be an area of leisurely shopping was reflected in the allocation of six units within the scheme for restaurants, wine bars and the like. The majority of the redeveloped Covent Garden opened for business in 1980. A year later it was established that the annual retail turnover was something in excess of £10 million with an additional £2–4 million from catering (Flint 1981). Since then Covent Garden has gone from strength to strength and now figures prominently as a retail destination in London.

Apart from Covent Garden Market, retail gentrification has occurred in many other smaller schemes in Britain. A number of types can be identified and, broadly speaking, these include:

(1) Impressive historic buildings such as Briggait, Glasgow (former fish market); Piece Hall, Halifax (former cloth trading hall); Crown Passage, Worcester (former corn exchange and coaching inn); St. Peter's Market, Chichester (former church).

(2) Refurbished Victorian and Edwardian Arcades such as the Great Western Arcade, Birmingham; St. Michael's Arcade, Chester; Barton Arcade, Manchester; Westminster Arcade, Harrogate; Royal Arcade, Norwich; Makinson Arcade, Wigan.

(3) Dockland and waterfront redevelopments such as Tobacco Dock and St. Katherine's Dock, London; Albert Dock, Liverpool; Swansea Maritime Quarter; The Watershed, Bristol.

(4) Architecturally distinctive districts, streets or quarters in towns and cities such as The Rows, Chester; Clifton, Bristol; The Lanes, Brighton; Stonegate, York; Montpellier, Cheltenham; The Pantiles, Tunbridge Wells; Burgate and Buttermarket, Canterbury, and several parts of central Bath.

Although every project is unique, a number of similarities can be teased out. Obviously, all retail gentrification schemes are based on the rehabilitation of an architecturally significant but redundant or neglected element of the urban landscape. They tend to be located off-centre in most towns, sometimes being found at quite a distance from the traditional core. Therefore, they must have a significant measure of aesthetic appeal and retail distinctiveness so that they can attract sufficient customers to confirm their viability. Their traders are most likely to be speciality retailers, with the range of products on offer typically including; crafts, books, pictures and prints, fashion clothing, shows, flowers and plants, health foods, jewellery, objets d'art, speciality foods and so on. Another common feature is the presence of a variety of restaurants, coffee shops and wine bars. Shop units are usually smaller than many multiples require and so there is generally a good representation of independent retailers.

Retail gentrification schemes included in types (1) to (3) above are usually carried out as complete entities by property development companies who oversee the project from start to finish. In managed schemes such as these, developers are able to work in close collaboration with the letting agents responsible for finding tenants. They can afford to pick and choose from amongst prospective retailers in their efforts to assemble an attractive mix of speciality shopping. Unlike the other forms of shopping centre mentioned earlier another policy usually pursued in managed retail gentrification schemes is the decision not to include large multiples acting as anchor tenants. Arguably, the essence of speciality retailing in gentrified schemes is the very diversity of shop types trading in a relatively well-defined area. It is the clustered nature of compatible and complementary tenants that gives such developments their viability, graphically illustrating Nelson's (1958) 'principle of cumulative attraction', which has at its heart the application of the concept of external economies of scale to retail clusters.

On the other hand, in the case of the distinctive streets or districts (retail gentrification type 4), achieving a suitable tenant mix is rather more difficult simply because there is no overall control or management. Although speciality retailers are attracted to premises in these architecturally desirable parts of towns, the eventual composition of the retail agglomeration cannot be predetermined or planned. Instead they grow organically in an *ad hoc* fashion. Unlike managed schemes where the creation of a carefully balanced tenant mix minimizes the likelihood of direct competition between shops selling similar goods, the retailers who operate in historic streets or districts are far more exposed to the rigours of free market forces. Furthermore, it is these unmanaged areas of gentrified retailing that are most vulnerable to change and therefore erosion of their individual character. If, for example, they gain a reputation as profitable retailing locations, then multiples with their higher rent paying abilities may well move in and come to dominate the scene.

By virtue of their specialist nature gentrified facilities do not exist to provide for day-to-day shopping needs but to offer a leisurely and recreational shopping experience in a pleasant environment. Consequently they flourish in areas that are popular with tourists and also in places that are accessible to affluent customers who have sufficient leisure time and disposable income to spend on seeking out unusual or luxury goods.

Several factors help to explain the increasing numbers of gentrified retail schemes around Britain. With their high proportion of distinctive independent shops they represent a reaction to the predictable and standardized look of the typical high street. For many consumers, the customized and individual goods on offer are a refreshing change from the mass-produced goods sold by multiples. Finally, they have benefited from an increased awareness of urban conservation issues. In recent years, developers and retailers have turned this interest in the architectural heritage to their advantage, unashamedly capitalizing on the nostalgia for more human scale, richly textured streetscapes.

Conclusion

The structure of the retail system at any time mirrors the complex inter-relationships between economic, social, technological and political factors. Since the 1960s, such has been the pace and scale of changes in the web of linkages binding retailers and consumers together that the period has been dubbed the 'retail revolution' (Dawson 1988, Harris and O'Brien 1988). Changes in the size, structure and organization of retail firms have led them to acquire new sets of locational priorities, whilst increasing numbers of mobile, affluent customers have become more demanding and adventurous in their shopping behaviour. Together, these have led to changes in the spatial patterns and built environments of retailing, resulting in considerable visible impacts on townscapes.

Contemporary retail patterns are more elaborate than those implied by the concept of the retail hierarchy. With its long history of evolution, the traditional intra-urban retail hierarchy inevitably remains very much in evidence although its role is changing. Processes associated with the retail revolution have caused readjustments to occur within the intra-urban retail hierarchy such as the development of enclosed shopping centres aimed at maintaining the vitality and attractiveness of town centres. In addition, new layers of investment have produced innovative shopping facilities such as superstores, retail parks and regional shopping centres in peripheral locations which hitherto would not have been considered appropriate for retail development.

Both in and on the edge of town the successful retailers will be those who respond most positively to the changing patterns of shopping behaviour. Retailers need to plan for the future in imaginative ways that will allow them to maximise their potential for incorporating the most appropriate permutations of the 'Three Cs' – comfort, convenience and conviviality – into their offerings. However, retailers cannot do this single handedly. Attracting customers into a shop is only one stage in a broader process. First, consumers need to be attracted to particular towns and then to parts of urban areas such as the town centre or a peripheral retail park. Consequently, attention needs to be paid to the appearance of the *overall* townscape because of its importance in contributing to consumers' perception of towns and thus to the viability of retailing in them.

Local authorities, often in collaboration with retailers' associations, promote their towns in a variety of ways, for example: by embarking on major projects such as International Garden Festivals (for example, Glasgow, Liverpool, Stoke-on-Trent and Gateshead), by entering competitions such as 'Britain in Bloom' in order to mobilise local community efforts to enhance the towns' appearance and through imaginative campaigns designed to raise general consciousness and increase local civic pride (for example, 'Glasgow's miles better', 'I love New York'). Commendable as these pump-priming activities are, their effects may only be ephemeral. In the long run the prosperity of towns and cities principally hinges on factors such as the condition of their infrastructure and quality of their environment. Here, useful lessons can be learned from managed areas of gentrified retailing, where careful planning leads to the creation of an attractive built environment for shopping.

In spite of the effects of decentralization processes, town centres continue to be of major importance, playing host to a considerable range of social and economic functions. Undoubtedly, they can still have an important part to play in the retail pattern. Smith (1972) has identified four sets of potential consumers that centrally located retailers can target: metropolitan area shoppers, downtown employees, city-centre residents and visitors to the central area including tourists and businessmen. However, if retailers are to be able to capitalise on these markets, then much depends on the initiatives and actions of local and central government.

Carrying out schemes to improve consumers' perceptions of the comfort, convenience and conviviality of town centres such as traffic management, pedestrianisation, landscaping and environmental rehabilitation depends not only on the motivation of the local authority, but ultimately on the national political will. This is because the financial resources for local programmes to revitalise town centres are allocated from the uniform business rate and community charge, the levels of which are closely monitored by central government. In determining the shape of the retail environment in the years to come, government will need to pay close attention to the dynamics of retailing in order to ensure that changing consumer demands are satisfied effectively, and to reconcile the sometimes conflicting views of retailers, planners and conservationists.

CHAPTER 6

The Modern Consumer

Introduction

The motivation for retailing as an economic activity is meeting the needs, wants and desires of consumers. Consumers may take many forms: individuals, families, households, companies, banks, government, hospitals and so on. In general, the principal consumers of the services provided by retailing are individuals and households, though intra-industry trading does take place between different parts of marketing channels. This chapter will therefore focus on the relationships between household consumers and the retailing system.

Though households are the primary customer of British retailing they are not an homogeneous group. Consumers come in many forms reflecting the differences in disposable income, age, health, sex, mobility and opportunity around the country. Their propensities to consume are therefore dependent upon many factors external to retailing itself, for example, their family structure. Women shopping with children are likely to behave differently from women shopping without children, or men shopping with children. Increasingly, retailers have begun to realise that non-monetary factors are involved in a consumer's choice of where to shop. Comfort, convenience and conviviality are also important. Comfort may be provided by suitable lighting and decoration, convenience by creches and accessible car parks, and conviviality by the friendliness and helpfulness of the staff and the appearance of surroundings. The traditional economic model of free markets has very little to offer in understanding why consumers shop in the ways they do. The purpose of this chapter is thus to consider who are the British consumers and what factors seem to be important to them.

The rule of the market

The most well-known conception of consumer behaviour comes from the theories of micro-economics (see Lipsey 1975 or Samuelson and Nordhaus 1989, for further details). In traditional economic theory, a consumer is a rational human being who attempts to meet his or her needs by buying goods and services which help to maximise his or her satisfaction. These goods and services are not always available in the form or quantity wanted: they are said to be 'scarce'. To obtain them, the consumer must make use of a market. This may be a physical entity such as an open space or a series of buildings, or an economic mechanism (whose characteristics are largely invisible to the consumer) which exists to get goods and services into the shops.

Economics textbooks generally recognise the following four types of market: perfect competition, imperfect competition, oligopoly, and monopoly. These are distinguished by the behaviour of the supplier. In perfect competition, both consumer and retailer are linked together by a self-adjusting price mechanism. If consumers increase their demand for products, prices will rise initially until checked by a compensating increase in supply. Conversely, if retailers increase their supplies, prices must fall if sufficient demand is to be generated to clear the market. This is the economic ideal. Reality is rather different.

In monopoly situations, the retailer is sufficiently powerful to overrule the regulation of the self-adjusting mechanism and can set the price in the market merely by withholding supply. As the retailer controls the supply, the product is removed from the market to create an artificial scarcity, leaving consumers with the choice of either not consuming or paying the going rate. Monopoly trading is widely seen as anti-competitive and is regulated around the world by a variety of national bodies and laws. Unfortunately, as many of the companies achieving near monopoly situations are transnational in character, they still retain some ability to hold whole domestic markets to ransom.

Lying between the two extremes are imperfect competition and oligopoly. The former corresponds to a situation where the market operates under inadequate or imperfect information about what is available where and at what price. The self-regulating price mechanism may thus be corrupted by local circumstances. One of the most significant of these circumstances is where suppliers band together to operate as a quasi-monopoly though none of them actually can perform that function in their own right. Such oligopolistic practices are distinctly possible in a market such as exists in British retailing today, where a small number of very large multiple chains dominate trading.

However, it would be wrong to believe that the role assigned to the consumer in these economic models actually relates to reality. These models are idealist, they have been created by a process of deduction and simplification to suggest what might happen were the world to operate in this way. As a means of understanding consumer motivations they are distinctly lacking. However, as political concepts they are particularly significant. The debate over 'free markets' is extremely strident with strongly-held views on all sides. Two examples illustrate the core of the debate. For former Conservative, Enoch Powell:

> The free enterprise economy is the true counterpart of democracy: it is the only system which gives everyone a say. Everyone who goes into a shop and chooses one article rather than another is casting a vote in the economic ballot box: with thousands or millions of others that choice is signalled to production and investment and helps to mould the world just a tiny fraction nearer to people's desires. (Powell, quoted in Donaldson 1973, p. 152)

Conversely, socialist Tony Benn suggests:

> Today, capitalist monopolies in Britain and throughout the world have long since 'repealed the laws of supply and demand' and have become centres of political power concerned principally with safeguarding the financial investors who have lost the benefits of shareholder democracy and the great self-perpetuating hierarchy of managers who run them. (Benn 1980, p. 42)

Shopping as a psychological process

Habit and motivation

The description of a consumer as a purely rational animal is too simplistic, however elegantly portrayed in the economics literatures (Engel *et al.*, 1978). As long ago as 1952, psychologists such as Herbert Simon were suggesting that maximising behaviour was not appropriate as a model of psychological health. Instead, most consumers (as well as businesses and governments for that matter) accept an element of sub-optimality in return for a less arduous task. 'Satisficing' rather than optimising is the key. From the perspective of retailing this may mean buying something which is not quite what was wanted, or using the nearest shop even though it is relatively expensive.

Katona (1953) suggests that a better approach to understanding consumer behaviour is to consider habit formation, motivation and group belonging. He argues that consumer choices are rarely made in the context of full knowledge of what is available in the marketplace and that past experience frequently influences what will happen. Habit-formation rather than problem-solving is the key psychological process being based on the frequent repetition of the same sort of buying task. However, the development of new shopping opportunities, for example, the opening of a new shopping centre, can require some rethinking of old habits. New opportunities create problems which can be solved by consumers making one or two visits. If they present a considerable easing of effort, then the prior habitual practices may change to accommodate the new context. New opportunities may create new shopping aspirations and these, especially if reinforced by group pressure, may lead to new forms of habitual behaviour.

Shopping itself has become a much more diverse activity. In the past, shopping was often categorised according to the types of good being sought on a shopping trip, for example, for convenience goods, shopping goods or speciality goods. This distinction was presented in Chapter 2. In the light of modern developments this classification seems simple and ignores the fact that shopping performs social as well as economic functions – a point that is amply demonstrated by a visit to a street market, corner shop or wine bar. Today, 'shopping has become a positive activity linked very skilfully to lifestyle, self-image and leisure' (Harris and O'Brien 1988, p. 36). In addition to essential chore shopping for food, Dawson (1988) identifies four other types of shopping in which consumers may be involved at different times, namely; purposive shopping, time-pressured shopping, fun shopping and experimental shopping; whilst Sargent (1988), emphasising the leisure dimension proposes; gift shopping, leisure shopping, holiday shopping, speciality shopping and festival shopping.

This observation that shopping activity is fragmenting is also significant because each sort of shopping has become associated with particular types of location and built environment. Examples might include:

(1) Chore shopping: major food/grocery purchasing at supermarkets or superstores.
(2) Top-up shopping: buying small quantities of urgently-needed items, for example, bread, milk from corner shops and neighbourhood convenience stores.
(3) Research shopping: for hi-fi, video equipment and cameras – comparisons made between specialists who are often found in clusters for example, Tottenham Court Road, London.
(4) Leisure or recreational shopping: browsing for special gifts in a pleasant environment or town.
(5) Destination shopping: where a visit may be a day out for all the family – for example, coach trips organised from Edinburgh to Gateshead's Metro Centre incorporating shopping, ten pin bowling and a cinema visit.
(6) Hobby shopping: for example, for DIY material at retail warehouses; for gardening requisites at garden centres; for jogging or aerobics equipment at town centre sports goods specialists.
(7) Lifestyle/statement shopping: for example, shopping at designer boutiques or shops such as Habitat, Laura Ashley and The Body Shop.

It is important to emphasise that these types need not be mutually exclusive. For example, a visit to Hay-on-Wye, which is renowned for its second-hand bookshops, could well embody elements of research, recreational and hobby shopping. Similarly a recreational style shopping trip to Covent Garden may result in the purchase of expensive gifts or merely a simple staple such as a wholemeal loaf made by an independent craftsman baker (although the purchase of a wholemeal loaf in Covent Garden has different connotations from, say, buying a loaf in a supermarket).

Shopper types

Dawson (1983) suggests ten different reasons underlying shopping behaviour. These may be classified loosely into personal motives and social motives. The personal motives include: obtaining personal knowledge about what is new in the shops; raising morale; making a change in a routine; role playing; having a walk, and basic stimulation. Shopping thus offers information and a break from the other routine areas of personal life. The social motivations are: shopping to meet friends or make new acquaintances; social contact with peer groups; the pursuit of social status, and participation in a social event. These reflect the need to meet others and participate more widely than in the context of the household.

From these it is possible to suggest that there are a variety of types of shopper whose behaviour reflects different combinations of these personal and social attributes. The following are some examples: the economic shopper, personalising shopper, ethical shopper and apathetic shopper (Stone 1954). Alternatively, Johnston (1974) suggests pragmatic shoppers, satisfied shoppers, shopping trippers and bargain hunters. Kotler (1965) focusing on economic/behavioural motivations suggests Marshallian shoppers, Freudian shoppers, Pavlovian shoppers, Hobbesian shoppers, and Veblenian shoppers. Haley (1968) suggests yet another classification based on the perceived benefits of shopping to consumers: the status seeker, the swinger, the conservative, the rational consumer, the inner-directed

The Status Seeker	...a group which is very much concerned with the prestige of the brands purchased.
The Swinger	...a group which tries to be modern and up to date in all of its activities. Brand choices reflect this orientation.
The Conservative	...a group which prefers to stick to large successful companies and popular brands.
The Rational Man	...a group which looks for benefits such as economy, value, durability, etc.
The Inner-Directed Man	...a group which is especially concerned with self-concept. Members consider themselves to have a sense of humour, to be independent and/or honest.
The Hedonist	...a group which is concerned primarily with sensory benefits.

Table 6.1 A classification of consumers according to Haley's (1968) Benefit Segmentation Hypothesis

consumer, and the hedonist. Some of the supposed characteristics associated with these distinct types of shopper are outlined in Table 6.1.

Shopping addiction

For many, shopping can become an addiction. Research suggests that women tend to suffer addictive shopping rather more than men and that it may be due to a lack of self-esteem. There are no simple reasons for this. Some may do it out of anger or spite to get back at a partner by hurting them in their wallets. For others, shopping may become some form of emotional support, offering them an escape into a world of fantasy which seems more attractive than their reality. Wilkie (1986) notes that this is a form of 'hedonistic consumption' which is principally concerned with 'the rich and detailed fantasies that are inspired by products'. Conversely, many elderly people seem to become addicts because shopping provides them with a way of meeting people and maintaining reality. Shopping therefore offers a mechanism, however superficial, to overcome temporarily the loneliness of old-age.

However, Cozens (1990) argues that these reasons are relatively minor compared with the systematic attempt by retailers to win consumers for their products. She notes that:

> perhaps the main reason for compulsive shopping lies in the pressure put on us by advertising and the media. Young and old, rich and poor, we are told constantly that there is something better for us – even that there is a better us – available at a price. (Cozens 1990, p. 100)

and that it is:

> often hard to withstand the images which constantly bombard us, insisting that the door to happiness is easily opened, that a new shape, colour or style will provide the magic key to a better you and that loans will oil the lock. The bottom line is that we are all susceptible to the modern philosophy that maintains: I shop therefore I am. (Cozens 1990, p. 102)

Retailers focus specifically on creating positive images for their products which attempt to associate them with successful people, youth, happiness, health and wealth. In effect, Cozens is arguing that the retailer's task is to turn the possibility of a demand into a necessity. The fact that these products are available in shops means that they should be bought. This is a moral imperative; greed is being marketed as an acceptable motive, the 'naughty-but-nice syndrome'.

Consumer spatial behaviour

Different types of retailing develop because consumers behave in many different ways. Some shop regularly, buying small amounts of goods such as milk, bread and papers which they get from a variety of stores. Others shop much less often (possibly once or twice a month) and may utilise only one shop or shopping centre. The variability in behaviour which is likely to be encountered by retailers and planners has meant that considerable efforts have been expended trying to describe and model consumer spatial behaviour. The 'shopping trip' has been particularly important as it is the mechanism which brings shoppers and retailers together, and which involves overcoming the 'tyranny of distance'. Implicit in the study of trip-making behaviour is the study of its length, destination, mode of transport and frequency. These factors, if analysed systematically, can provide retailers with an understanding of how shoppers actually behave when faced with a variety of competing shops, centres and products.

Predicting shopping trips

The problem of predicting the nature of shopping trips has taxed planners and retailers rather more than most. As we saw in Chapter 4, some of the spatial procedures developed by economists, planners and geographers have made use of simplistic assumptions about the threshold and range of products and the stability of relationships within central place systems. These may be criticised technically (Openshaw 1975, Lierop and Nijkamp 1980) and theoretically (Dawson 1979) for their failures to represent the subtleties of spatial shopping behaviour. Both spatial interaction approaches and central place theory only provide aggregate descriptions of retailing and even these are of limited use in describing segmented markets. Indeed, Guy and Wrigley (1981, p. 5) note:

> the factors which appear to influence shopping behaviour are so many and varied that any attempt to devise a model of behaviour reliable for individuals and for single trips would seem doomed to failure.

They suggest that a better approach is to focus on methods which are designed to predict trip frequencies over a time period (that is, how often particular types of consumer shop at particular types of facility).

Frequency prediction

Guy and Wrigley (1981) suggest four possible approaches which might offer solutions to the trip-prediction problem. These are: effort minimising models, revealed preference models, discrete choice models, and stochastic shop-choice models. These differ in the ways they seek to represent the trip-making process but are all heavily dependent on the availability of medium to large data collections in which trip-making behaviour is disaggregated by product type and shopper type. Information on the transport network and location of consumers is also required. Such data sets are collected by commercial agencies for their own needs. An attempt to produce an equivalent for academic use was made in the Cardiff Consumer Survey conducted over six months during 1982 (for details, see Guy *et al.*, 1983 and Wrigley *et al.*, 1985).

Effort minimisation modelling involves deducing a pattern of shopping trips over time using information on three distinct types of variable: the frequency with which shoppers purchase particular products, the availability of these at accessible locations, and the distances of these locations from the shopper's home. The underlying model has been set out in Bacon (1971) and shown to be equivalent to a linear programming problem in which total distance travelled to meet the household budget is minimised (Evans 1972). An extensive account of this modelling approach is outlined in Bacon (1984).

The revealed preference approach is based on the assumption that the observed pattern of shopping trips made by a spatially dispersed sample of consumers reveals underlying preferences for particular types of activity. These preferences could allow for shopping 'rules' in which consistent trade-offs in behaviour were permitted. The model was first applied in geography by Rushton (1969) and tested empirically in a study in Watford by Pankhurst and Roe (1978). The particular theoretical difficulty with this form of modelling is that observed patterns of behaviour may have little or nothing to do with underlying rules of shopping activity. Such models eliminate the context of shopping which may vary drastically within so-called homogeneous shopper categories. The trade-offs implied by these models may be nothing more than an averaging of diverse and widely deviating shopping behaviours.

These comments apply equally well to discrete choice models, one form of which derives directly from revealed preference modelling (McFadden 1968). The methodological development proposed by these procedures is the ability to model behavioural activities which are categorical and indivisible in form rather than continuous (for a discussion of these issues, see Hensher and Johnson 1980 and Wrigley 1985). During the 1960s and 1970s it became possible to link models based on random utility concepts of behaviour (Luce 1959, Lancaster 1971, Rosen 1974) with numerically tractible statistical models such as logit and probit regression. It was thus assumed to be possible to model observed behaviour statistically and interpret model results systematically in terms of consumers' preferences for alternative products or services. Evidence from the experiences of traffic and transport engineers who use these types of models as key analytical tools is that certain types of behaviour may be sufficiently consistent to be modelled successfully. A retailing example of the methodology is provided in Fotheringham (1988) who uses logit models in store market-share analyses (examining why and how consumers select particular stores).

The fourth type of model suggested by Guy and Wrigley is stochastic choice models such as the negative binomial distribution model. These have been developed by market analysts principally for the analysis of brand choice (Ehrenberg 1968, 1972). The object of such models is to develop empirical norms in retailing behaviour which can be used to predict how consumers of given types are likely to behave in the future. Perhaps surprisingly, it can be shown that in spite of the much-vaunted variability in retailing, consumers do indeed appear to organise shopping trips or exhibit particular types of behaviour such as repetitive buying in ways which are sufficiently stable in time. Models based on this class of procedures have been developed to study the problems of store choice rather than brand choice (Wrigley 1980, Kau Ah Keng and Ehrenberg 1984, Uncles and Ehrenberg 1988).

Store choice

The models outlined above all attempt to predict aggregate frequencies in product purchasing over time periods of varying length. The locations of the stores being patronised are usually excluded from such models, being assumed as given. However, Fotheringham (1988) notes that this assumption need not be made as extensions to the basic models can allow for contemporaneous analyses of store and product choice. This development brings the modelling environment rather closer to reality.

The work of Wrigley and Dunn (1984a–c, 1985) is particularly significant in this respect in that it provides a major test of the combined effects of spatial choice and product choice in grocery retailing. Their work uses the data collected in the Cardiff Consumer Survey mentioned above and allows modellers the opportunity to focus on individual stores rather than groups of stores, store types or shopping centres. The technicalities of their work are too detailed to present here. However, their results are relatively easy to interpret. For example, by using the negative binomial distribution model on shopping behaviour at a single store they were able to show how it had failed to convert a sample of Cardiff householders into regular customers. In particular, the model suggested that advertising had indeed attracted customers to visit the store but only for a single, exploratory visit. Furthermore, they also found that in analysing the performance of stores located in different parts of an urban area, great attention has to be given to defining the catchment area properly. Without a clear perception of the market area for a store of a given size, retailers run the risk of losing considerable quantities of money through ineffective advertising and poor market research.

Complicating factors

Though the models outlined above are useful in producing empirical norms which are sufficiently tractible to allow retailers to investigate the effects of consumer behaviour, they are not particularly suitable for analysing its causes. The literature on causes of consumer behaviour is enormous and clearly identifies factors such as income, aspirations and lifestyle. Income is the lubricant of any capitalist system and very little can be done in the formal economy (see Chapter 1) without it. Aspirations and lifestyle help to fashion particular types of retailing where particular types of products become associated with styles or assume symbol status.

Guy (1984) suggests that time, shopper age and attitudes towards shopping are major factors in determining how consumers organise their retailing behaviour. In the Cardiff study young people typically found shopping a chore and consequently tended to shop as infrequently as possible using relatively few shops. Older shoppers on the other hand tended to view shopping as something to be enjoyed (possibly for its social benefits). They tended to shop more frequently and use a wider variety of stores. Shoppers living on the outskirts of the city also seemed to find shopping relatively unpleasant in spite of having higher levels of income and car ownership. Guy suggests that these factors are difficult to interpret satisfactorily because of other spatially dispersed factors such as the range and variety of stores available. Of course, the restriction to grocery shopping in the Cardiff survey is also likely to affect the results.

He was also able to identify five distinct types of shopping trip in the Cardiff data: home-based trips; trips made during the journey to or from work; work-based trips; 'other' and 'unclear'. The latter pair refers to trips in which some other origin-destination pair was involved ('other') or the origin, destination or both could not be inferred from the survey returns ('unclear'). Taking all trips into consideration, he was able to show that the panel of Cardiff shoppers made 5.2 food and grocery trips on average per week. This figure compares with the 4 trips per week found in a 1969 study in Watford (Daws and McCulloch 1974), and 4.34 trips in a 1976 study in North London (Bruce and Mann 1977) and the 4.5 trips in a 1969 study in Coventry (Davies 1973). Guy suggests these differences may be due to differences in survey methodology. However, a particularly interesting finding from Cardiff was that car ownership, number of children and certain personal characteristics had no statistical significance at the 0.05 level upon trip frequency. The differences in trip-making between large and small households was significant (4.68 trips per week for a single person household compared with 5.56 for a six-person household), as was location and ownership of a freezer. The influence of location was particular important for consumers without access to private transport. Indeed, Guy (1984, p. 52) notes 'much of the variability in store use appears to reflect accessibility to types of store rather than other factors'.

Access to credit

Credit cards and plastic money

One of the mechanisms oiling consumer behaviour is access to personal credit. The idea behind the use of credit is that payment for goods and services can be deferred for a period of time allowing consumers the luxury of consuming products they could not otherwise afford. This is such a potent notion in a materialist society that the current Conservative government claims it is the principal reason why they cannot control the rate of inflation.

In the 1960s credit arrangements were largely restricted to department store accounts and hire purchase agreements, usually with electrical goods suppliers. These limited the customer to a particular store or to the purchase of a specific product. Though these arrangements still exist, their inherent limitations led to the development of more flexible systems based on the use of credit cards and charge cards administered by banks, building societies, American Express and Diners Club. Credit cards have been particularly important for the ordinary shopper in that they were available on application without the payment of an annual fee and provided holders with extended interest-free credit. Barclays Bank led the way by issuing Barclaycard. This offered existing customers the chance to purchase goods and services at registered suppliers up to the value of an agreed personal credit limit.

With a credit card, holders are expected to repay the bank each month a sum which can range from the whole amount to a minimum payment determined as a percentage of the debt. Interest is charged on the outstanding amount, providing the bank with additional income. In effect, Barclaycard and the equivalent systems, Access and Mastercard, offer holders systems of free extended credit should the outstanding debt be paid off in full each month. The flexibility provided by these cards considerably increased the attractiveness of credit in the domestic market during the 1970s, leading to the banks creating international credit organisations such as Visa to extend their use abroad. Barclaycard as a member of international Visa can now be used at more than 6 million places worldwide and has helped reduce one important headache for the foreign traveller. The Visa system is thought to be more acceptable to the general public than Access, but more than 23% of all card holders now have two or more cards anyway (*The*

Times, January 31st, 1989). Between 1984 and 1988 the number of Visa cards issued in Britain grew from 7.2 million to 9 million but their share of the credit card market fell from 30% to 21% in the face of increasing competition (*The Guardian*, 24th February, 1990, p. 14).

While the use of extended credit is a valuable asset for the consumer, it is only of interest to the banks if significant numbers of customers fail to repay within a month. Income generation requires some defaulting which, though allowed, attracts relatively high levels of interest. With the market for credit booming in the late 1980s and the major credit companies offering very similar deals, it is no surprise to see emerging a new range of credit cards, offering modified facilities from the originals, as well as new types of card. One significant modification has been the introduction of annual fees, initially associated with newer credit cards such as the Save and Prosper Visa card, but now fairly standard across the range. The original Access and Barclaycards are now only available for an annual fee of around £8 to £10, but attempt to offset this by providing lower annual rates of interest than previously as well as some new facilities. Barclaycard, for example, now provide insurance for 100 days against the loss, damage and theft of goods bought using the card. Emergency cash, card replacement, medical and legal help abroad are also available, as is the chance to obtain a Barclays Mastercard at no further expense. All of this may seem attractive to the user but the Consumers' Association suggest that 'Barclaycard's "New Deal for the Nineties" is a raw deal for many of their customers' (*Which? Magazine* June 1990 p. 303).

Table 6.2 lists some examples of 'plastic money' available in 1990. It is not possible to compare these cards exclusively using just one measure such as the annual percentage rate (APR) of interest because their conditions of use differ. The Barclays Assent card for example is a budget card rather than a credit card. Similarly, some APRs are calculated by excluding the interest-free period so are more expensive than they may look. The 'New Deal' from Barclaycard involves a change in the way interest is calculated. Whereas previously interest was charged from the statement date, it will now begin from the date the purchase appears on the bill. The effect of this is that products will be being charged over different time periods with the possibility that rather more is paid in interest than the customer may expect.

The importance of 'plastic money' to the consumer has also been recognised by retailers. Department store chains have traditionally offered account cards which allow favoured customers the chance to defer payment for a period of time. By offering convenience in payment, the companies hoped to encourage a degree of consumer loyalty and an increase in sales, partly due to the status that a prized account card seems to attract. During the 1980s most of the major multiple retailers began to offer similar financial arrangements based on the use of budget, credit and charge cards. By the late 1980s more than 2 million people had acquired a Marks and Spencer Charge

Card	Annual Percentage Rate (APR)(%)
Access Cards	
Bank of Ireland	29
Clydesdale Bank	29.8
Lloyds Bank	29.8
Midland Bank	29.8
NatWest Bank	29.8
Northern Bank	26.8
Royal Bank of Scotland	29.8
VISA Cards	
Allied Irish Bank	23.1
Bank of Scotland	29.8
Barclaycard	29.8
Chase Manhattan Bank	24.6
Cooperative Bank	29.8
Girobank	28.3
Halifax Building Society	27.5
National and Provincial Building Society	22.8
NatWest Bank	29.8
Royal Bank of Scotland	29.8
Save and Prosper	22.7
Town and Country Building Society	19.5
TSB Trustcard	29.8
Yorkshire Bank	29.1

Table 6.2   Credit Cards and the cost of borrowing (at January 1990)

Card. Once again, it is difficult to assess the deals being offered simply on the basis of APR. However, as Table 6.3 shows, in-house cards tend to be more expensive than their bank counterparts.

Charity cards

A major innovation in the late 1980s has been the introduction of charity credit cards which are designed both to increase the acceptability of credit as a means of payment and increase revenue to chosen charities. Table 6.4 lists some of the types of cards which were introduced in 1989. The idea behind these cards is that customers will be more likely to use credit arrangements if they know that a percentage of the money made using them will be donated to their favourite charities. To operate the system, a charity makes its mailing

Retailer/Card	Annual Percentage Rate of Interest (APR)	
	Monthly/Minimum payment by Direct Debit	Monthly payment by other means
Marks and Spencer Budget card	29.8	29.8
Marks and Spencer Chargecard	29.8	34.4
Burton Group Option Account card	34.4	36.8
House of Fraser Frasercard	–	34.4
Rumbelows Chargecard	34.9	–
Storehouse – Storecard	29.8	34.4
Next Budget Account	36.0	39.9
Littlewoods Personal Account	30.5	36.5
Sears Card	29.8	34.4

Table 6.3   Cost of some retailers' in-house credit cards (July 1990)

list available to a bank or building society who use it to approach named subscribers directly. A typical arrangement is that the charity receives a donation for each credit card taken up and thereafter a small percentage of the gross takings made using it. According to *The Times* (January 24th, 1989), the arrangement made in 1988 between the National Society for the Prevention of Cruelty to Children (NSPCC) and the Bank of Scotland ensures that they receive £5 directly when one of their subscribers joins and a further 25p from every £100 of sales made using its special charity Visa card. This can be a potentially lucrative source of funds for the charities with annual receipts running to hundreds of thousands of pounds.

Debit cards

At the same time as banks and retailers have been offering alternative forms of credit card, an entirely new form of plastic money has been developed: the debit card. This makes use of improvements in telecommunications which allow retailers to be connected directly to their customers' bank or building society current accounts. Instead of writing a cheque, paying cash or using a credit card, the customer can use a debit card to authorise a cash transfer from his/her account directly to that of the retailer. The whole transaction involves linking the shop till to the retailer's computer and from there to bank or building society computers. In spite of the apparent complexity, it is now a very simple and straightforward operation.

The advantage of using a debit card such as Switch (offered by Nat West, the Midland, the Royal Bank of Scotland and the Bank of Scotland) or Barclay's Connect is that it may lead to a significant reduction in cheque and

Bank/Building Society	Charities
Bank of Scotland Visa	NSPCC
Coop Visa	RSPB, Help the Aged
Girobank Visa	OXFAM
Leeds Permanent Building Society	British Heart Foundation, Imperial Cancer Research Fund, MENCAP.
Midland Bank Care Card	Age Concern, British Diabetic Association, British Red Cross, Cancer Research Campaign, Multiple Sclerosis Society, NSPCC, Royal National Institute for the Blind, Royal National Institute for the Deaf, Save the Children Fund, Spastics Society, St. John Ambulance, Terence Higgins Trust.
NatWest Visa	World Wide Fund for Nature
Royal Bank of Scotland Visa	Royal National Lifeboat Institute, Woodland Trust, Canine Defence League.

Table 6.4   Examples of Charity Credit Cards

credit card fraud as the transaction is only authorised if the customer has sufficient funds to cover the bill. From the point of view of the customer, debit cards allow the flexibility of paying by cheque (principally free credit for three working days) without their inflexibility (fixed cheque guarantee limits which are smaller than the monthly shopping bill). They are also becoming more widely accepted at superstores, petrol stations and department stores.

Promotions

The need to remain competitive in the credit market has forced many of the companies to develop special promotions which encourage card holders to use their cards in preference to other forms of money. The charge cards – American Express and Diners Club – have traditionally provided their holders with various 'perks' as well as status, but most other companies have now begun to enhance their cards too. The Visa system now offers home shopping, a travel and insurance service, and perks in the form of Profile Points and Air Miles.

The Barclays Profiles promotion entered its third issue in March 1990 offering a profile point for every £1 spent using Barclaycard. These points can be converted to gifts or Air Miles tokens allowing reductions in the costs of air travel. Typical gifts include merchandise, short air trips and, as a star prize, a hot-air balloon trip with England cricketer Phil Edmonds. *The*

Guardian (24 February 1990) points out that this particular prize costs the cardholder £12,500 to amass the required number of points. The cheapest gift requires points totalling £1750.

Customer-friendly shopping

Modern marketing is aimed at selling large quantities of produce to clearly defined market segments. These may be defined by the capacity to purchase particular types of product marketed to emphasise status or prestige. One aspect which is seen as increasingly important is the quality of shopping environments. Bidder (1989) reports the results of an *ad hoc* survey of supermarkets by mothers with children. She notes that:

> it seems mothers are put through considerable strain while shopping at supermarkets: Not enough help at checkouts, dangerous products within reach of little fingers, sweets provoking battles and not enough loos were the major complaints. (Bidder 1989, p. 185)

This survey was reported in *Good Housekeeping* and makes no attempt to be scientific. Its purpose was to assess how effectively a group of supermarkets are responding to the needs of family shoppers who frequently have to cope with several children on shopping trips. The surveyors were shoppers with children, the group who are most likely to know about these things. Interestingly, Bidder notes that in six regions where the survey was to take place, finding volunteers to take part was not easy: 'a total of six mothers turned us down because they couldn't face their local store with both children in tow' (p. 178). Newer, larger stores fared rather better than smaller ones, but these too have their own particular problems: poor car-parking, inadequate separation of roads from footpaths in car-parks, insufficient help with packing goods and helping customers to cars, revolving doors, unprofessional staff.

Supermarket chains are beginning to realise the importance of comfort, convenience and conviviality, and the need to emphasise the services they provide to promote and maintain a strong market image. Good service increasingly means personal service and help – help with packing and getting the products to the car, crêche facilities and play areas for children, wider aisles and checkouts to remove the claustrophobic atmosphere of many stores, better positioning of dangerous items to stop children tampering with them, the provision of toilets and changing facilities for babies which are accessible to both parents. The survey suggests that for all their market research the big multiples are still some way from providing this level of service.

Conclusions

The aim of this chapter was to examine some of the factors which affect modern patterns of demand for the products and services of retailing. It is clear that there is not a modern consumer as such, rather there are many types of modern consumer with specific characteristics which distinguish them to the marketing managers. Retailing is increasingly becoming focused towards providing goods and services for such groups rather than tackling the more amorphous needs of a mass market. The implication of this is that products which were previously perceived as utilitarian are now invested with image quality, and are differentiated to provide a range of images. What was once a single product now becomes a series of products, each competing with each other to offer increased choice and satisfaction. While this is the key feature of the 1990s consumer it should not be thought that marketing managers can continue to segment markets indefinitely. Market segments which are thought to be of limited commercial value are unlikely to be targetted seriously unless those in them pool their resources and consume collectively against recalcitrant retailers. Mothers with children are likely to be in this group.

CHAPTER 7

Information and Retailing

Introduction

More than ever before, success in retailing depends on access to up-to-date information. This includes information on who buys what, where and how often, how consumers organise their shopping behaviour, what motivates them to purchase one type of product rather than another, and how they pay for shopping. Answers to these questions help retailers to assess the demand for their services and allow them to plan for the future. However, they also need to know about the availability of land around the country which could be used for shopping development, how that land relates to existing and planned transport facilities, how the site relates to the distribution of the population who might become customers, and what types of competition are already present or may be anticipated in the future. Answers to these questions help retailers to assess the supply of retailing services.

The future of retailing in Britain will depend on how effectively retailers can turn geographically-based economic, social and psychological information into profitable products. An adequate supply of information may give a retailer the edge over competitors who are less well organised, thus helping to maintain or even increase market share. Furthermore, by paying particular attention to general behavioural information, much of which is not directly concerned with shopping behaviour, retailers may be able to anticipate potential patterns of future demand for their services, possibly even changing the nature of their services by skilful marketing.

The aims of this chapter are therefore to review some of the types of information which seem to be particularly important to retailers and to indicate how changes in shopping and computer technology may lead to new ways of selling. It also considers some of the techniques used by retail planners to make sense of this information, especially those developed from a geographical and planning perspective.

The need for information

All types of retailer make use of information on their customers, who they are, where they live and what they buy. However, the effort they put into collecting and 'analysing' such data varies considerably. The most useful way to collect information, and to determine what is and is not relevant to the needs of the business, is for retailers to get to know their customers as individuals.

For small, single-outlet businesses such as the traditional 'corner shop', the main source of information on customers comes from the daily round of selling. Such businesses usually operate by providing a service not currently available from the larger firms (perhaps a local delivery service for small purchases or late opening times), or by appealing to consumers who cannot or will not travel to use supermarkets and shopping centres. Traditionally, these businesses have tried to operate by creating cosy and convivial atmospheres for shopping. Customers would be served rather than processed, with the owner often being the principal shop assistant. The advantages of such a system are that commercial decisions for the business are made by people who know their customer-base (and may actually know many of their customers personally) and who can know their tastes with sufficient accuracy to stay profitable.

The situation for larger companies is likely to be very different. Simply because of their size and complexity, they need to develop specialised 'professional' functions within the firm to run it efficiently. The key decision-makers on the Board, and the senior store managers who define business strategy, may rarely, if ever, be involved in face-to-face selling on the shop floor. Their function is the development of a business strategy for the company and not serving customers. Consequently, they may have little or no recent personal knowledge of the problems associated with selling, indeed, many of them may have no training in the business at all, having joined the company for their marketing, personnel or financial skills. Similarly, those who have the daily experience of dealing with customers may have limited responsibility for commercial decisions and none at all for strategic planning. Though they can pass their knowledge up the hierarchy, there is no certainty that the quality will be good by the time it arrives at the top. To compensate for this, such businesses have tended to develop some form of statistical 'information supplement' to help their planning. This usually consists of aggregate data on customer-types rather than individuals but is better than no information at all.

A useful insight into the types of information required by large companies is provided by Penny and Broom (1988) based on their experiences in the retail food business. They describe some of the workings of Tesco's Research Unit, a specialist body of analysts employed by that company to assess likely locations for future store development. They argue that Tesco needs this sort of unit to continue to expand. Growth in the market for food items is possible by introducing new products and selling them from stores that are fully equipped to handle them. Many of these require new sites well-away from the traditional clutter of the high street. This has meant that Tesco and their competitors are involved in a major search for sites on which to develop superstores, but these are both limited in number and potentially very expensive to acquire. Land prices have been particularly high, with figures of between £2 million and £3 million an acre being commanded in South Oxford and Watford. Clearly, with prices as high as these, the investment needed to develop these new stores is very large. Even companies the size of Tesco cannot easily afford the costs of getting the site hopelessly wrong.

Tesco require the Unit to provide three functions: to direct the search for new sites for building superstores; to screen the probable sites from the possibles; and to provide sales forecasts for the probables which can contribute to a profit and loss analysis. These forecasts must be accurate to within 10% of actual performance because profit margins are so fine. These functions are met by the creation of a locational modelling system which requires information on the following topics to produce forecasts: consumer demand, household expenditure on product types, delineation of catchment area boundaries, purchasing power of catchment population, competitive activity (including its quality), and transport media. The information fed into the computerised system comes from a variety of government statistical collections, in-house surveys, competition shopping, and surveys of competitors, as well as customer and store performance data held by Tesco. Information on transport is provided by linking the data sets with a digitised road network for the country, and information on new sites for development comes from contacts established with local authorities, staff fieldwork, the property development industry and the media. To run the Unit effectively requires a staff of between 20 and 30 professionals, many of whom are graduates in geography and planning.

The effectiveness of this system is seen in the speed and accuracy with which it can provide information for senior management in terms which they most easily recognise. For example, questions such as 'Which of Tesco's stores with over 20,000 square feet of sales area are within ten minutes driving time of an Asda?' are easily and immediately answered. More complex questions obviously take longer, but the production of sales forecasts for potential development sites may have to be done in days. Added to the annual development budget of £150 million, such short time horizons impose particular organisational and technical difficulties. However, management questions are not technical or philosophical; they are simply demands for factual information which can help develop strategy. The answer has to be provided in the same terms as the question was asked if management is to spend time assessing it.

This suggests that large companies not only need specialist information but also a 'communication culture' within the organisation which can allow such specialists to meet their tasks and communicate findings efficiently. Penny and Broom note that the impetus for developing the Unit within Tesco came alongside other strategic concerns within the company. It was not simply a case of Tesco deciding it needed a unit; strategic administrative changes were taking place which transformed the organisation of the whole enterprise and made it possible to advance the concept of a unit. They note:

> The culture of retail decision-making is especially receptive to answers and advice; however it does not appreciate esoteric analytical problems which invariably surface in any detailed research and modelling problem. (Penny and Broom 1988, p. 109)

Analysts are thus obliged to turn essentially esoteric techniques originally developed in the abstract into business tools and ensure that in communicating their results, the language of business is used.

The cost of obtaining this type of information can be considerable involving, among others, the employment of specialist staff, computers, and adequate computer memory to store large quantities of data. The latter is often overlooked by analysts who see hardware costs falling but fail to look sufficiently closely at storage (see Blakemore *et al.*, 1985 for further details). These costs may be prohibitive for small companies, and seem excessive to large companies which do not have the 'communication culture' displayed by Tesco.

Sources of information

There are three major sources of information providing contemporary data for retailers. First, there is official socio-economic and demographic information which is collected and published by central and local government. Typical sources are the Census of Population, Census of Employment, Census of Distribution, Family Expenditure Survey and General Household Survey. Trends in employment and society can also be picked up from publications such as *Social Trends* and *Employment Gazette*. Collectively, these sources can provide useful background information on the socio-economic structure of the population. This information may also be available for small geographical areas such as census enumeration districts and wards allowing retailers the possibility of area profiling (see later section). Second, there is the information on retailing provided by commercial agencies and academic consultancies such as Hillier, Parker, May and Rowden, Nielsens, URPI, CACI, Pinpoint Market Analysis, Goad, Dun and Bradstreet and the Oxford Institute of Retail Management. These provide a variety of types of information on the state of retailing markets which can be of particular use in identifying trends in retailing.

Companies such as CACI and Pinpoint in particular have developed computer-based information systems which can be of significant help in researching retail markets.

However, the third and generally most useful of the sources are the 'in-house' information systems based on customer surveys, credit application forms, and the analysis of till transactions. These tell the company what they are selling (product and volume), when and to whom. By putting these sources together, a company can produce its own tailor-made socio-economic and demographic profile of its customer base and use this to examine market segments which are being targetted well or badly. Because this information is available in the form most suited to the commercial needs of the company it is likely to be of greater use than the government sources. However, these may be used in conjunction with 'in-house' surveys to provide information on areas not currently covered by the company and for which no 'in-house' data are available. This may be crucial information in assessing expansion or relocation plans.

Sources of data based on the trading experiences of specific companies are closely-guarded secrets. The following notes therefore briefly describe some of the features of the main official data sources.

Population items	
1	Name
2	Sex
3	Date of Birth
4	Marital status (single, married, remarried, divorced, widowed)
5*	Relationship in household (husband/wife/son/daughter, other: specify)
6	Whereabouts on Census night
7	Usual address (including postcode)
8	Usual address: 1 year ago (including postcode)
9	Country of birth (present name of country)
10	Whether working, retired, housewife, etc., last week (full-time, part-time)
11*	Name and business of employer
12*	Occupation (includes description of work)
13	Employment status (apprentice, supervisory role, self-employed)
14*	Address of place of work (including postcode)
15*	Daily journey to work (train, tube, bus, van, foot, etc.)
16*	Degrees, professional and vocational qualifications
Housing items	
H1	Number of rooms
H2	Tenure (freehold, leasehold, renting, other)
H3	Amenities (fixed bath or shower connected, WC)
H4	Shared household
H5	Cars and vans (number)

*Questions marked with an asterisk were included on all forms, but only a 10 per cent sample of the replies was processed.

Table 7.1 The 21 questions in the 1981 Census

(Source: Thatcher 1984, p. 9)

Census of Population

A Census of Population is conducted in Britain every ten years to document the demographic structure of the population. Its principal purposes are to provide government with information which will help to assess the future demand for public services such as schools and hospitals, and to allow economic planners to assess trends in labour supply. The first such Census was conducted in 1801, and there has been a continuous sequence since then except for 1941. Mid-term 'sample' censuses were held in 1956 and 1966 but were abandoned on the grounds of cost in 1976 and 1986. The 1991 Census is expected to maintain the format used successfully with the 1981 Census (HMSO 1988). This obtained information on 21 topics from some 18 million households in Britain (Thatcher 1984). These are listed in Table 7.1.

Census of Employment

A census is conducted in Britain every three years by the Department of Employment. The last published data refer to 1987. The purpose of this Census is to provide an industrial analysis of the British economy which can be used to assess employment trends and changes. The raw data collected from business firms by sample census or enumeration, depending on the size of the firm, are classified according to the Standard Industrial Classification (1980). This describes industrial employment according to a variety of classification schemes, ranging from industrial divisions (11 in number) to industrial activities (several hundred in number), allowing a detailed breakdown of industrial employment by chosen classification.

The data from both the 1981 Census of Population and the 1984 and 1987 Censuses of Employment are stored in computer-readable form in the National Online Manpower Information System (NOMIS) – a large geographically-based information system run by the Training Agency in Durham University. The advantage of this fully on-line system is that detailed locational breakdowns for demographic and employment data are available. The ability to investigate how socio-economic classifications change spatially as well as temporally is vital labour market information and can help retailers identify the hot-spots and the areas of stagnation for their products. For details of NOMIS, see Townsend *et al.*, (1986) or O'Brien *et al.*, (1988).

Family Expenditure Survey

The Family Expenditure Survey is a unique source of household data on expenditure, income and other aspects of household finance. It is based on a representative sample of about 12,000 households in the country and has been running continuously since 1957. Data are available at regional level and above.

Information in the Survey is organised by 14 commodity/service groups defined to be consistent with the classes used in the calculation of the retail prices index. Occupational data are also available based on the 1980 standard industrial classification. Initially, the survey was used to collect information with which to weight the components of the retail prices index (*Employment Gazette* 1989). However its contemporary function is rather broader and has included credit card expenditure by acquisition from 1988. While it is able to provide analyses of the earnings of broad groups of individuals, its sample size is too small for studying the distribution of earnings in the country. This can be obtained using the Department of Employment's *New Earnings Survey*.

General Household Survey

The General Household Survey is a continuous survey of the non-institutional population and has been running since 1971. Data are collected by interview from roughly 20,000 people (10,000 households) aged 11 + . The purpose of the survey is to monitor changes which occur over time in variables most related to social policy. Since its inception, data have been collected on fertility, housing, employment, education and health. Recent additions to the list include share ownership, attendance at arts performances, museums and historic buildings, dental health and the take up of occupational pension schemes. An interesting finding from the 1988 Survey, published in 1990, shows that the percentage of people reporting a long-standing illness has increased from 21% in 1972 to 33% today. Not all of this is attributable to age, indicating that some of the traditional assumptions about the mobility of the population may be changing. This could have important implications for so-called 'disadvantaged' shoppers (Guy 1984).

Profiling

Demographic profiles

The ability of retailing to meet customer needs hinges on its being able to perceive and anticipate them. The last section introduced the concept of a socio-economic 'profile' as being one important way in which a company can get to know its customer base. Essentially, profiling involves subdividing the population into non-overlapping and mutually-exclusive subgroups which

Category	Social Status	Typical occupation of head of household
A	Upper middle class	Higher managerial, administrative or professional
B	Middle class	Intermediate managerial, administrative or professional
C1	Lower middle class	Supervisory, clerical, junior managerial, junior administrative or professional
C2	Skilled working class	Skilled manual workers eg. have completed apprenticeships or equivalent training
D	Working class	Semi-skilled and unskilled manual workers
E	Subsistence level	State pensioners, widows, casual workers and lowest grade earners

Table 7.2 An example of class segmentation

(Source: Based on JICNARS National Readership Survey, January to December 1987)

are thought to share some distinctive characteristics. Ideally, these should be characteristics which relate closely with patterns of shopping behaviour or consumption. If this can be achieved, a company can attempt to exploit the vast quantities of government data in order to find out where its chosen customers live. Profiling therefore has a clear spatial component.

There are a number of alternative ways of attempting to subdivide the population into economically distinct classes. One approach which has been particularly important is to use class segmentation or demographic segmentation. This involves classifying households according to the occupation of the household head and typically results in a sequence of the type displayed in Table 7.2. The basis of the classification is an hierarchical arrangement of work skills. Those at the top work in prestigious, well-paid occupations. Those at the bottom either do not work and so rely on benefit, or are only tangentially related to the economic system. They thus do not have prestigious jobs or high incomes.

The principal problem with this scheme is that it is out of step with the character of the modern economy. Devised originally to describe class relationships in 19th century capitalism it fails to account satisfactorily for the development of new types of working or new types of living arrangement which effectively eliminate the association between status and income. Higher-level managers in one type of company may actually earn less than junior management in other companies. Class status has little direct relevance to spending potential.

Stages in Life Cycle	Typical Purchases
Young singles	Fashionable clothing, records, cassettes, mountain bikes.
Young marrieds (no children)	Durables and housewares to equip the home eg. carpets, furniture, white goods, hi-fi, video cassette recorder, pictures and prints etc.
Married with young children	Baby requirements eg. clothing, toys, games, furniture, holidays.
Married with older children/adolescents	Leisure and recreation eg. sports goods, home computers, video camcorder, bicycles, holidays, clothing, larger cars.
Married with children of student age	Home redecoration, holidays, replacement of durables, subsidising education.
Older married, children left home ("empty nest")	Holidays, home redecoration, gardening and other leisure pursuits.
Solitary survivor	Holidays, visiting family and relatives, house move to smaller home and fitting it out.

Table 7.3   Family Life Cycle stages and consumption patterns

An alternative to this classification is one which emphasises the consumption patterns of families. A life cycle classification based on the consumption patterns of families might look something like Table 7.3. In this approach, each class is defined in terms of family stages with young singles at one end and solitary survivors at the other. Each stage is associated with a whole range of familial responsibilities which can dominate its spending behaviour. For example, expenditure on children's clothing and toys is highest in families which have young children. Expenditure on long-haul holidays is highest among those who are least tied to family or work commitments.

Compared with the class-based profiles this is an improvement as it reflects the changing nature of family consumption as the numbers, ages and sexes of members change. However, its principal problem is that the classes used are tied too closely with a traditional model of the family-formation process which is no longer appropriate to Britain or other western countries. British people are still forming families and having children, but they are also getting divorced more readily than in the past or failing to establish formal marriage arrangements in the first place. Increasing numbers of people are choosing to live single lives, are pursuing careers rather than families or are deferring child-bearing until they are older. The consequences of this for spending patterns is that the associations between age, sex, occupation and spending behaviour may be very different depending on the motivations of the individuals concerned. Two thirty-year old females with the same educational background, living in the same area may behave very differently.

A traditional family may have several types of spending activity associated with its different members. Thus to produce meaningful information on the association between life cycle and spending requires far more data than can be obtained simply by demographic profiling.

Psychographic profiles

Demographic profiling is insufficient to help retailers understand the motivations of their customers because it fails to pick up causal associations between the spending behaviour of individuals who may be pursuing different life cycles rather than a common one. A better system would permit some form of motivational or psychological profiling, in which the population could be disaggregated according to their spending preferences. An approach which attempts to provide this is termed psychographic or benefit profiling (Haley 1968).

The idea of psychographic profiling is not new. There have been many attempts in the past to differentiate individuals on the basis of personality types which reflect specific types of motivation. Bayton (1958) suggests three major types of motivation need: affectional needs; ego-bolstering needs; and ego-defensive needs. Affectional needs are associated with the need to form warm, harmonious relationships with others. Ego-bolstering needs are needs associated with promoting the personality, to achieve, to gain prestige and recognition. Ego-defensive needs are those associated with preserving one's dignity or minimising anxiety. By focusing its marketing to the two ego categories, retailing can enhance any product it wishes to sell by emphasising how purchasing (or the failure to) can enhance the consumer. As we saw in Chapter 2, goods are not merely functional, they can be status-enhancing as well. The sorts of classifications produced by psychographic segmentation can be humorous (for example: yuppies, Sloane Rangers, nouveau Richards – see Cooper 1979 for details).

Geodemographic profiling

The ability to differentiate the population into subsets which are causally related to spending behaviour is of little use to retailers if they cannot locate them within cities. Aspatial classifications essentially assume that everybody is located in the same place, or conversely, that there is mixing so that each area receives its fair share of the separate types. Experience shows this is not to be the case. Some means of turning the demographic and motivational information on individuals into geodemographic and geopsychographic information on individuals living in given places is thus desirable.

It is possible to link many different types of data together geographically using postcodes or some similar spatial referencing system. Every address in the country can be identified by its 'unit postcode'. This is the most disaggregate part of a spatial referencing system devised by the Post Office to allow the automation of the postal system, and has been described in the Chorley Committee Report (DOE 1987) as the best candidate for a 'basic spatial unit' (see Chapter 8). When a letter arrives at a sorting office, staff retype the postcode as a series of machine-readable dots onto its front cover. The machinery 'reads' this and sorts and transfers the letter automatically to the relevant postman's round. The system is essential if the postal system is to cope with the rapidly expanding volume of mail.

Each unit postcode can be aggregated to higher geographical areas such as postcode sectors, districts and areas (Table 7.4). Some of these geographical areas correspond to areas used by the government for collecting demographic and economic data. It is thus possible to link the areal (spatially-aggregate) information from these sources with the relatively disaggregate information listed by postcode collected by company 'in-house' surveys. The advantage of this for a company is that individual consumer information collected by their credit application forms can be placed in its socio-economic context. Moreover, the buying behaviour of the individual identified by the company may be related to information on where he/she lives. As townscapes are not random features but are the product of economic and social filtering, this matching may help to identify market areas or consumer types with much greater precision.

A considerable amount of work has gone into developing computer retrieval systems which can provide this type of market analysis at reasonable cost. The earliest systems were largely spatial databases which recovered listings and maps of geographical zones displaying some chosen attribute. Two commercial systems offering this type of service have been widely used – the ACORN and PiN systems – based on data from the 1981 Population Census. The former uses ward data and categorises the country into 11 groups and 38 neighbourhoods, the latter uses enumeration district data (much finer spatially than wards) and identifies 12, 25 or 60 PiN types. Examples of ACORN groups include 'modern family housing, higher incomes' which accounts for 17% of the GB population, 'council estates

Spatial Zone	No. of such zones in the U.K.	Example.
Unit Postcode	1.3 million	NE1 7RU
Postcode Sectors	8,900	NE1 7
Postcode Districts	2,700	NE1
Postcode Areas	120	NE

Table 7.4   Spatial Aggregation of unit postcodes

category 1' which accounts for 13% and 'affluent suburban housing' which accounts for 16%. The groups categorised among the 60 PiN types include 'working people with families' (10% of population), 'suburban middle-aged owner-occupiers with elderly' (9%), and 'affluent households' (7%). By mapping at various spatial scales, retailers can begin to see how the spending power of their key customers is distributed spatially. A 'poor-man's' ACORN system known as SUPERPROFILES (Charlton *et al.*, 1985) has also been developed for academic use. This too is based on the 1981 Population Census enumeration district data.

However, there are a number of significant problems with these systems which arise from the attempt to link Census data with postcode geography. In particular, the two geographies are based on different spatial zones and are not always compatible, with postcode boundaries often cutting across enumeration district boundaries. This may lead to areas being described incorrectly. While some attempt has been made to improve the Central Postcode Directory – the database created by OPCS to link postcodes to enumeration districts – and alternatives have been created (for example, the Pinpoint Address Code devised by Pinpoint Market Analysis), the fundamental problem remains. Incompatible zoning systems based on different geographies will always run the risk of producing erroneous classifications. The only thing one can do is attempt to minimise the level of spatial error.

Geographical information systems

The retrieval of spatial information is one thing, using it to predict or forecast is quite another. Most recent technical work in geodemographics has focused on developing 'geographical information systems' which marry the functions of spatial data bases such as those listed above with analytical functions allowing mathematical and statistical modelling. Typically, such systems are built to turn raw data into marketing information by allowing analyses at a variety of spatial scales including that of the individual household, linking this to information on the infrastructure and topography (for example, the layout of car-parks and the road network), and incorporating information on travel times and costs by a variety of different transport modes. Such systems aim to model some of the dynamism of the space-time economy using the sorts of techniques outlined in Chapter 4 and in the section below on analysing retailing information.

The great advantage of these information systems should they be used creatively is that location is given the priority it deserves in socio-economic analysis. Two types of location can be studied. First, there is the absolute location of each piece of data, for example, each car-parking space for the disabled, measured with respect to some benchmark such as the National

Grid. Second, and more important, there is the relative location of each piece of data with respect to other pieces of data. A simple example of this might be the relationship between bus stops and the nearest housing. Lavery (1989) has shown that the working assumption used by planners and transport consultants that no bus stop is more than 800 metres away from housing is incorrect. His studies in Belfast show that many areas of housing in the north of the city are more than 1200 metres away from their nearest bus stop. This makes it difficult for many people to use public transport for shopping because the walk to and from the bus stop limits how much they can carry.

The great advantage of organising geodemographic information in a locationally-integrated computer system is that it has the potential to answer many questions on marketing and spatial behaviour. For example, by linking together information on the built environment and population structure with information on the road network and journey times, retail planners can assess the potential market sizes at varying distances and travel times from specific shopping sites. The Geopin system developed by Pinpoint Market Analysis allows the analysis of branch location and market potential, impact analysis of new stores, sales territory planning, routing and journey planning for a salesforce, direct marketing and distribution planning. By linking together data on residential neighbourhoods with financial data, they claim to have improved the response rate in direct marketing surveys from 0.75% to a high point of 9.4% for specific customer types. This dramatic improvement may be extreme but illustrates what can be achieved by target marketing to specific consumers living in specific areas. The cost of improved marketing was a twelve-fold reduction in unit cost compared with untargetted marketing.

Shopping technology

The attraction of the profiling procedures outlined above is that they provide background data on trends in the social and economic structure of the economy which can help retailers plan for their future. This can be expensive and outside the reach of smaller operators. Moreover, as none of the government data sets were created solely to assist retailers, they are obliged to make the best possible use of whatever information they can collect for themselves. In recent years, changes in the technology of retailing have provided the larger operators with a ready source of up-to-date information on purchasing activity which they can attach to their existing research methods of 'in-house' surveys and competition shopping (purchasing products in competitors' stores to see what is available and at what price). This section describes some of these techniques.

Automation

Wrigley (1988) suggested that automation was one of six technological improvements which led to the major changes in retailing during the 1980s. By removing bottlenecks in the distribution channels, retailers have been able to supply products to consumers when required. The delays and shortages which typified earlier periods have largely been removed. Automation essentially involves applying computer systems to marketing channels. By setting out the nature of marketing channels for scrambled merchandisers, retailers have been able to identify the critical paths for their businesses. Moreover, they have been able to identify the points where these paths are likely to change due to changing market conditions. It is the ability to respond quickly to these changes by reshaping channels or some aspects of them which allows major retailers to remain competitive. Automation has been applied to warehousing, delivery systems and stock-taking. However, it is at the point-of-sale that most of the key developments are taking place.

Automation has become necessary to support modern focused retailing. As companies have amalgamated and developed diversified retailing through different shops in their businesses, much greater control has been needed over stock management, pricing and ordering. Multiple retailers such as Sears and Next, both of whom operate focused retailing from different types of shop thus need to know what is required in which of their stores, when. Without rapid feedback from the stores themselves it would be very difficult to operate the business in its current form.

Computers provide an obvious way of controlling large and diverse data sets, especially as user-friendly software designed around the use of databases and expert systems has become more readily available. The principal advantage of computer networking is that items purchased in stores can be registered immediately and if necessary reordered. Table 7.5 lists some of the computer developments currently applicable to retailing. A summary of the key applications of computer technology to retailing is given in Distributive Trades EDC (1982), Guy (1988) and Lewis (1989). These focus on four distinct topics: EPoS, EFTPoS, private viewdata systems, and remote shopping.

Regardless of what type of service is being provided, all retailers record their business transactions through some sort of till. In the past these were essentially adding machines which were capable of recording sales totals by department or product types. However, the application of microelectronics has transformed tills from adding machines into computer terminals, enhancing their abilities to record and transmit information. The simplest and to date, most acceptable, development is the EPoS – electronic point of sale terminal. Bamfield (1988) suggests that the number of EPoS terminals in use in British retailing is likely to rise from 58,000 in 1986 to nearly 300,000 in 1991 as retailers come to realise their potential benefits. Most important of

---

1. Electronic Point of Sale Terminals (EPoS)

- product information contained in the bar code label is read by either a flat-bed or hand-held laser scanner and fed into the EPoS terminal which is linked to the company computer.

- Increasing use is being made of Graphical User Interfaces (GUIs). These incorporate a mouse and icon-style screen display. This enables the sales assistant to move rapidly between tasks such as; checking stock availability, recording sales, receiving payment and entering delivery details.

2. Electronic Funds Transfer at Point of Sale (EFTPoS)

- The computer technology is similar to that used in EPoS except that the point of sale terminal is linked not only to the retailer's central computer but also to the computers of clearing banks participating in the scheme. This permits cashless transactions to be made.

3. Teleshopping

- is a branch of the new suite of services called Telematics. These make use of developments in computer and telecommunications technology.

  a) Teletext based (Non-interactive) eg Oracle Teletext.

  b) Videotex or Computer text-based (Interactive) eg. Prestel Teleshopping, Gateshead SIS.

  c) Cable Television Networks eg Kays Homeshopping.

  d) Satellite Television eg. The Lifestyle Channel.

4. Geographical Information Systems

- the management and analysis of locationally-based data.

Figure 7.5   Some computer developments applicable to retailing

these is that sales rung through the till can be classified by product type and then transmitted immediately to the company computer which reorders the product if necessary. Economies of stock control and financial management can flow from this sort of information, offering an improved response time to meet short-term changes in consumer demand. Benetton use a sophisticated version of this type of system which involves downloading sales data every night to their headquarters in Italy. Moreover, this centralised system allows them to tailor their products and colour ranges to precisely what is being demanded in their shops around Europe.

EFTPoS systems – electronic funds transfer point of sale systems – are a natural development of the stock control system. These are tills which are linked both to the company stock control computer and to the computers of the major high street banks and building societies (Cane 1983). The idea is that goods may be purchased using a debit card (see Chapter 6) such as Switch or Barclays Connect Card which is passed through a scanner on the till. The details of the bill are then sent to the cardholder's bank which checks to see if there is sufficient money to cover the transaction and debits the customer within three days if there is. In effect, Switch and EFTPoS offers cash-less shopping without the complexities of using a cheque.

Guy (1988) notes that whereas retailers quickly adapted to EPoS there was much less general acceptance of EFTPoS as this is a facility designed by banks to minimise cheque and credit card fraud. In 1985, Marti and Zeilinger suggested that it might be some time before EFTPoS was accepted. They noted that

> It seems likely that automation with point-of-sale systems will proceed cautiously, yet fairly quickly; but adoption of a full electronic funds transfer system is a much more uncertain matter. Relatively few retailers know much about it, and even fewer are eager to adopt it. (Marti and Zeilinger 1985, pp. 357–358)

However, since 1985 the knowledge base has increased considerably with EFTPoS now being available in supermarkets, petrol stations and other retail outlets all around the country. The new Sainsburys at the Arnison Centre in Durham uses EFTPoS as a marketing strategy as none of its competitors in the city currently offer this facility. Recent figures published in the Retail Pocketbook (1989) show that some 972 stores in Britain now offer scanning facilities. Currently some 17% of total turnover is passed through a check-out using some form of scanning device. This compares with the 55% of turnover scanned in the USA, 35% in New Zealand and 28% in France.

Smart cards

One of the most interesting developments in retailing technology which is still at something of an experimental stage is the development of 'smart' cards (Weinstein 1984). As we saw above, many retailers have invested in tills which are automatically linked to the company computer. As products are checked through these tills, the computer is able to update stock holdings and re-order products as necessary. However, they cannot currently link this purchasing data with geodemographic or psychographic information on the purchaser. Purchasing profiles cross-referenced by individual customer would be an invaluable addition to the retailer's knowledge base as the full details of what was purchased, when and by whom could be stored together.

The way to provide such a link is to encourage customers to use some form of 'smart' card containing their personal details. Each time the card is used, details of what was purchased could be added to the card, providing a comprehensive list of purchasing and personal information: in effect, a full panel survey for the individual.

Push button shopping

The two other aspects of automated selling mentioned by Guy (1988) are public and private viewdata systems (Prestel, Videotex), and remote shopping. Both offer the possibilities of shopping from home using computers or adapted television sets. Instead of visiting a shop, customers can simply call up computer pages of information showing goods, quantities and prices. These can be ordered using a computer keypad and the goods paid for either by account or by credit cards. The goods are then delivered either by the firm concerned or by the normal postal service. Telephone shopping linked to commercial television offers a somewhat more sociable version of the same basic idea, and has become big business in the USA (Strauss 1983) but has yet to develop in Britain. Teleshopping services active or proposed in February 1989 include Oracle Teletext (originators include Interflora, Littlewoods and Kays), Prestel (British Telecom, Littlewoods, Kays), Comp-U-Card (AA members shopping service), Gateshead SIS (Tesco and Gateshead Social Services), and Teleshop (WH Smith Television). These have a market reach of between a few thousand (Gateshead) and 4.5 million households (Oracle).

Experiments with remote shopping for the disabled and the elderly have been tried (see for example the Gateshead system mentioned above, developed by Tesco in conjunction with the local authority in Gateshead and described in Davies 1985). Both groups are classed as 'disadvantaged customers', partly because they have difficulties getting to stores or around them should they get there, and partly because they have relatively little disposable cash. The purpose of remote shopping for these groups is to make life easier for them (social function) and create a caring image for the company which can be turned into a commercial image. To date these experiments remain relatively small-scale operations though the lessons learnt have been valuable. In the future rather more creative thinking will be needed as the cohort of disadvantaged elderly is expected to reach 14 million by 2025. Many of these will be relatively rich, having benefited from home ownership and personal pension plans. They will however still suffer from the full range of disabling conditions which correlate with old age. A model based exclusively on social retailing is likely to be seen by them as both preposterous and insulting.

Analysing retailing information

The previous sections have discussed the typical sources and types of information collected by retailers. Some forms of analysis have also been discussed (for example, geodemographics). However, the retailing industry also makes use of several mathematical and statistical procedures to help turn the raw data collected from these sources into useful business information. From the point of view of the geographer (particularly the economic or quantitative geographer) the most interesting procedures are those which help to identify market areas for stores of given sizes and locations. A series of procedures has been developed to help here which range from simple threshold models based on notions of spatial interaction to sophisticated Poisson regression, discrete choice and stochastic process models which attempt to capture aspects of individual consumer behaviour over both time and space (some information on these procedures was presented in Chapter 6).

The earliest of these market share models were based on analogies with Newtonian mechanics in which flows within a network are determined by forces of attraction and impedence. The geographical analogies of these gravity models were simple spatial interaction models in which trip-making behaviour was determined by the attractiveness of stores or centres and the impedences were measures of distance or cost. Flows from particular origins (usually zones within a city) to destinations (again zones or perhaps points representing shops or centres) were determined by the relative attractiveness of each competing destination and the cost of moving to it. While the idea is simple and straightforward, calibrating the models in ways which allowed them to reproduce trip behaviour in realistic ways has proven to be particularly complicated.

As we saw in Chapter 6, recent developments in modelling have been aimed at predicting the frequencies of certain types of behaviour over particular periods of time or areas. The two principal models from the set outlined in Chapter 6 are stochastic process models such as the negative binomial distribution (NBD) model and the family of discrete choice models based on logit and probit regression. Both sets of models supplement the essentially geometric information which lies at the heart of spatial interaction models with data gathered from shoppers themselves. These include information on their shopping behaviour, home location, frequency of shopping, types of products purchased and so on. Both types of model allow standard marketing analyses developed for the study of products to be transferred to space enabling retailers to determine how stores of a particular type located in given environments are likely to perform given information on their likely clientele. Such market share procedures bring together the product information with spatial information in ways which was not possible before the 1980s.

However, though these are major advances in the analytical armoury of locational analysts, they still cannot handle all the subtleties of modern retailing. Key analytical issues for the 1990s are how to incorporate the measurement of retailing quality and attractiveness into such models (Clarke 1984, Wilson 1983). The quality of a shop depends not just on what it sells but on how it looks and how the staff react to customers. Dale (1989) notes that before restructuring by the Paternoster group in 1982, staff at Woolworth's were so disaffected that they appeared to be frightened off by customers. This led many customers to view the company as being of relatively low quality. The position of the shop in its surrounding environment is also important. As we saw in Chapter 5, the atmosphere associated with a high street or a shopping centre can be affected dramatically by poor environmental control. A good store in a poor environment is likely to fare reasonably badly.

However, this is not a clear-cut argument. Most consumers do not have a single measure of quality which always predominates. The attractiveness of a shop or a centre can depend on who is going shopping, when and by what mode of transport. Factors which might make a centre unattractive to family shopping might disappear if only one person is making the trip. Attempts to incorporate quality therefore must recognise the trade-offs which occur between different attributes of quality. As Bates (1988) notes, a retailer may be unable to offer all the desired facilities at their highest level but can only offer some.

Conclusions

Information relevant to retailers may be obtained from a variety of statutory sources, from geographical and psychological information systems, and from the shopping technology present in their stores. Existing computerised facilities for auditing and stock control can be extended to collect and process information on customers, especially if they make use of some form of plastic money. New developments in shopping technology, such as EFTPoS systems and 'smart' cards offer even greater potential for the future. However, retailers still need to be convinced that such high technology is really in their best interests.

Companies which have acquired access to such information on their customers are potentially in a stronger competitive position than companies which rely for strategic planning solely on the gut reactions and personal experiences of senior managers. While such reactions are important and should not be excluded from forward planning, they do not necessarily provide the strongest platform for the development of strategy. Including data on current consumer attitudes and purchasing behaviour in decision-making processes may help to illuminate personal experiences and allow a company to plan from a more objective base. Locating that data in their geographical context provides even greater information as it allows the influences of spatial structure on behaviour to be accommodated in strategic planning.

CHAPTER 8

Green Retailing

Introduction

Sometime during the 1980s the general public became aware that the planet is under threat from some major environmental trends which may be the direct result of western-style standards of living. A key discovery was provided by atmospheric research which identified a 'hole' in the protective ozone layer over Antarctica and the possibility of a second over the Arctic. This finding was widely publicised in the popular scientific literature throughout the western world, but caused an even greater stir when reported on television and the media because of its possible implications for skin cancer. The news was even carried on children's television, providing information to a market segment which frequently has a powerful influence over adult purchasing decisions.

This was not the only piece of 'bad news'. Research on atmospheric pollution by scientists and pressure groups such as Ark, suggested that the emission of 'greenhouse gases' (most notably carbon dioxide) from industrial processes, car exhausts and intensive pastoral agriculture may lead to global warming. This suggested that global climate will be affected with some areas becoming very much warmer and others very much colder. At worst, global warming may lead to the melting of the polar ice-caps which, in turn, may reshape the world map as London and most of the world's capitals would be flooded, becoming 21st century equivalents of Atlantis.

What has all this to do with retailing? The answer is that all these environmental trends may be the result of capitalist industrial processes which have been created to produce goods for economic markets. These processes have been immensely productive and have helped shape the modern western economies as we know them today. However, the laws of economics have rarely paid sufficient attention to their environmental effects (Mishan 1990). Two distinct problems have grown out of this negligence. First, capitalists have placed virtually all their attention on production and almost none on waste disposal with the result that the planet's natural ability to disperse pollutants on land, sea or air is seriously threatened (see Carson 1951 and 1988 for the 'classic' accounts of this issue). Second, the desire on the part of international business to maintain and expand markets has led to an appalling mis-management of land and water resources in many parts of the world. Infertility of land and economic dependence on a grand scale has often quickly followed as a consequence of this. The adverse publicity given these issues has forced many people to appraise their lifestyles and, out of this, has come the concept of 'green retailing' – daily shopping decisions to save the planet.

This chapter considers the implications of a green consumer movement for British retailing. Green consumption associated with specific lifestyles is growing in commercial importance though it is still a relatively small part of the total market for retail products and services. In spite of this, the retailing industry has been forced to take green issues seriously and has produced a range of responses in accommodation. Before introducing these, we consider the development of the green consumer movement.

The green consumer movement

Man–environment relationships

The ability of humankind to adapt to the varied natural environments offered by this planet has been one reason for its success as a species. However, with the twin advances of science and technology (principally in the last two or three centuries), the harmonious relationships which many humans have established and maintained with their environments have been destroyed. Lands which were once able to sustain people are now barren as the direct result of attempts to create a cash economy by importing unsuitable crops or animals. While yields (a western term) are often spectacular in the short-run, after a few years the land turns into an unproductive desert and is incapable of even sustaining what existed before. The destruction of Amazonia to produce hamburgers for the US–European fast-food market caricatures the process particularly well. The cost to the planet is not just loss of land fertility but the loss of those whose lifestyles and culture have been developed in sympathy with nature (for example, aboriginal culture). For them, 'progress' means the loss of their civilisation and world-view, a life of destitution in the towns, or the degradation of being 'saved' by missionaries.

This scenario is familiar to many who live in the Third World, but has been marginalised in the perceptions of most who live in western economies. For these, technology, science and free market economies have ensured the supply of a varied and diverse range of goods and services. A cheap and adequate supply of food and clothing has kept most people happy and content with the system providing it – capitalism. However, there have always been 'cranks' who have spoken out against capitalism, some for its inherent tendency to alienate people, others for their beliefs in alternative political and economic systems, and still others because they see capitalism as exploitative of nature and ultimately doomed to failure. During the 1960s many of these diverse topics became focused issues.

The 1960s

The 1960s was a decade of intellectual turmoil especially among the young. In most western economies there was a significant expansion in the provision of higher education, providing undreamt of opportunities for children from poorer families. The debates occurring on campuses around the world were increasingly political, concerned with issues such as workers' rights, civil rights, and apartheid. Faith in economic success was questioned. Rachel Carson's books *The Sea Around Us* and *The Silent Spring*, questioned the whole basis of international industry by drawing attention to the effects of toxic waste and the use of insecticides. In 1965 Ralph Nader, the guru of the US Consumer Movement, published *Unsafe at any Speed*, calling into question the position of the automobile in American society. Johnson (1983, p. 661) suggests that 'these books were necessary correctives to the harmful side-effects of rapid growth' but that they introduced an era

> in which the protection of the environment and the consumer became a quasi-religious crusade, fought with increasingly fanatical zeal. It had a peculiar appeal to the hundreds of thousands of graduates now pouring off the campuses . . . keen to find ways to express the radicalism they absorbed there. (Johnson 1983, p. 660)

Before the decade was out, most western countries had begun to introduce legislation to curtail the excesses of business and manufacturing practices. The annual cost of this legislation to American business has been estimated at upwards of $100 billion (Wiedenbaum 1980).

Carson and Nader were not the only authors whose work has helped to focus public opinion on capitalist processes. A wide range of authors in a variety of disciplines have produced work on aspects of development and society which quickly became classics. Among these are the philosopher Ivan Illich, economist Fritz Schumacher, and anthropologist Barbara Ward. Some of their 'defining texts' are outlined in Table 8.1. Great media attention was also given to the work of the 'Club of Rome' whose *Limits to Growth* (published in 1972) suggested the possibility of environmental disaster sometime after the turn of the century. While technical arguments about the calibration of their computer models has largely removed the cloud of doom from this work, its spirit still remains fresh in the minds of those who see the world being steered towards destruction by myopic businessmen. Though

1. Ehrlich, P (1968)	The Population Bomb. Ballantine, New York
2. Hodson, H.V. (1972)	The Diseconomics of Growth Earth Island, London
3. Illich, I (1973)	Tools for Conviviality Harper and Row, New York
4. Marcuse, H (1964)	One Dimensional Man Routledge and Kegan Paul, London
5. McLuhan, M (1964)	Understanding Media Routledge and Kegan Paul, London
6. Mishan, E.J. (1969)	The Costs of Economic Growth Pelican, Harmondsworth
7. Packard, V (1960)	The Hidden Persuaders Penguin, Harmondsworth
8. Pirsig, R.M. (1974)	Zen and the Art of Motorcycle Maintenance The Bodley Head, London
9. Schumacher, E.F. (1973)	Small is Beautiful Blond and Briggs, London
10. Toffler, A (1971)	Future Shock Pan, London
11. Ward, B and Dubos, R (1972)	Only One Earth Penguin, Harmondsworth

Table 8.1   A selection of influential radical texts

the motivation for establishing the Greenham Common Peace camp has now disappeared (in the sense that the nuclear weapons have been removed to the USA), the underlying issue remains. Today, the 'greens' provide a focus for a wide variety of people dissatisfied with the modern world.

Shopping to save the planet

Porritt and Winner (1988, p. 9) suggest the following reasons for people turning green in the 1990s:

> The most commonplace is simply to improve the quality of life: to be healthier, to save a lovely old building or to protect the countryside. The most radical seeks nothing less than a non-violent revolution to overthrow our whole polluting, plundering and materialistic industrial society and, in its place, to create a new economic and social order which will allow human beings to live in harmony with the planet.

Greens are a broad church. Some green issues are general, some are specific;

all imply that modern society is not delivering the goods required. This is the key perception because it suggests a form of protest which can be commercially very powerful.

The emphasis on radicalism and revolution which characterised the 1960s has largely been replaced by a powerful weapon with which to challenge established commercial interests: personal consumption. By guiding their daily shopping patterns towards products and companies who show an active interest in saving the earth, the greens have been able to hurt business in its pocket. Elkington and Hailes (1988) in the Foreword to their *Green Consumer Guide* note:

> A new generation of consumer has grown up at a time of increasing concern about the damage we are doing to our local environment and to the planet. The idea that we can use our everyday consumer decisions to influence the world we live in is not new – but the power of the Green Consumer to push industry in more environmentally acceptable directions is. (Elkington and Hailes 1988, p. vi)

This message is extremely simple: everyday consumption decisions about what to buy as food and clothing can be made so as to protect the environment rather than harm it.

Moreover, these decisions can be made for virtually every type of consumption, whether it be about gardening, going on holiday or buying a new washing machine. If these decisions are made by significant numbers of consumers, and appear to be long-term purchasing preferences, a type of niche marketing will have been created. If the level of demand is sufficient, this may become a mass-market. In either case, a significant group of consumers will have made it clear that existing products do not meet their requirements. Table 8.2 lists some of the areas of environmental concern discussed in *The Green Consumer Guide*.

The modern 'greens'

There are a number of shades of green in the modern consumer movement. Porritt and Winner (1988) suggest the following types using three of the psychographic classes outlined earlier: sustenance driven; outer directeds, and inner directeds. The following notes briefly describe these alternatives.

Sustenance driven greens

These are the consumers who aim to get by but cannot really contemplate paying a premium for green retailing. At the moment the products being sold as 'green' (organic vegetables, wines, beers, washing powders) all attract a

Table 8.2   Some key areas of environmental concern associated with western consumption patterns

1. FOOD AND WATER			Concerns
Water	General Use	(a)	Land needed for collection and storage.
		(b)	Distribution costs.
		(c)	Disposal problems eg. treatment capacity of sewage works exceeded – leading to river and sea pollution.
	Domestic	(a)	Excessive use in the home – washing machines, dishwashers etc.
		(b)	Chemicals used in W.C.s
		(c)	Detergents, bleaches etc. used in washing machines.
		(d)	Excessive use in the garden.
	Agriculture	(a)	Increasing demand for irrigation water.
		(b)	Pollution of water courses by slurry, manure and silage effluent.
		(c)	Agrochemicals in ground water.
	Industry	(a)	Use of rivers and sea for effluent disposal resulting in pollution.
		(b)	Increasing demand.
Food		(a)	Residues of chemical fertilizers and fungicides used in commercial fruit and vegetable production.
		(b)	Residues of growth promoting hormones and antibiotics in commercially produced meat.
		(c)	Long term effects of chemicals/treatments used in the storage and processing of foodstuffs.
		(d)	Effect of monoculture and genetic engineering on species reduction.
		(e)	Demand for peat by commercial growers threatening Britain's wetlands.
		(f)	Factory farming methods and animal welfare.
		(g)	Waste produced from the packaging of foodstuffs.
2. CLOTHING			
Natural		(a)	Cotton requires high inputs of fertilizers and pesticides.
		(b)	Problems associated with cash-crop monoculture – eg. uses land that could be used for subsistence agriculture – Third World dependence increases.

		Concerns
Synthetics	(a)	Nylon, polyester, rayon etc. depend upon petroleum as a chemical feedstock – ie. non-renewable resources.
	(b)	Disposal – not biodegradable and if burnt, release toxic fumes into atmosphere.

3. SHELTER

(a) Building industry and DIY use of tropical hardwoods without forest management and reforestation occurring.

(b) Long term effects of toxic chemicals used in preservative treatment of softwood.

(c) Hazardous materials used in construction eg. asbestos, lead.

(d) Chemicals used in paint, CFCs used in aerosols.

(e) Waste of non-renewable energy resources as a result of poor energy efficiency of homes.

4. TRANSPORT

(a) Use of the private car for commuting – congestion, noise, air pollution.

(b) Amount of land required for roads, car parks etc.

(c) Atmospheric and environmental impact of exhaust emissions – especially lead, carbon monoxide, nitrogen oxides, hydrocarbons and particulates.

(d) Inefficient use of non-renewable fossil fuel.

(e) Pollution problems connected with the extraction, transport and refining of oil and oil products.

(f) Built in obsolescence of many cars – wrecked cars in scrap yards are an environmental eyesore.

5. LEISURE

(a) Many aspects of leisure and recreation associated with use of the car (see above).

(b) Batteries for portable stereos etc. contain hazardous elements such as cadmium and mercury – problems of safe disposal.

(c) Gardening – excessive use of hazardous chemicals, peat etc.

(d) DIY – hazardous chemicals used in paints, glues, sprays, wood preservatives etc. Left overs often disposed of thoughtlessly – possible environmental impacts.

premium price. They are thus beyond the reach of many who would otherwise wish to purchase them and register their environmental concerns with producers.

The outer directed greens

Porritt and Winner suggest that the typical outer directed spends much of his/her time seeking social success and financial status. Green expenditure by this group is typically to make a statement about the individual rather than the state of the planet. An article in *The Times* (July 17th 1989) describes a typical outer directed response to green issues. It notes the establishment of a mail order trading company, The Whole Thing, which is concerned to sell to environmentally-friendly yuppies. Examples of products in their catalogue are the waterproof, solar powered Walkman (£199) and vegetable-dyed quilts (£85). Such products do not remove the materialism which so many greens find offensive.

Consumption patterns by the outer directed may well be rooted in the belief that if they live longer and healthier, they will be able to consume more. The materialist trappings associated with this group may include any or all of the following: second houses in the country, Aga/woodburning stoves, Barbour jackets, green wellies, clay pigeon shooting, lead-free Range Rovers, mahogany conservatories and stripped pine furniture. None of these are in themselves green products but collectively provide a veneer of rustic romanticism which can frequently suffice.

The inner directed greens

For Porritt and Winner the inner directed may have the brightest green potential. They are in many ways the driving force behind the green consumer revolution but are otherwise a mixed bunch of malcontents. They suggest a variety of subcategories for this group: the experimentalists, the social resisters and the self-explorers. Experimentalists are generally in favour of the use of technology but see that it might be refocused more effectively on green issues. Many, for example, are interested in solar power and energy efficiency, that is, delivering the types of lifestyle they currently enjoy more economically. Social resisters are in many ways the 'deep greens', being interested in a range of political initiatives. They are described as being rather narrow in view, intolerant and moralistic. Self-explorers, on the other hand, share many of the concerns of the social resisters but are more catholic.

Retailing responses and initiatives

Retailing might have happily ignored all of these developments were it not for the fact that environmental issues are now high on the political agenda in most western countries. In Europe, but most especially Germany, 'green' movements have become vocal and politically attractive to the general voter. The widening appeal of the 'greens' stems from a general dissatisfaction with the character of modern western economies, their materialism and waste, the alienation of the populace, and, perhaps crucially, the distaste for the arms race. A combination of factors as diverse as nuclear weapons, nuclear power, polluted drinking water, crumbling sewers, and irradiated food has led many people to question traditional assumptions about how needs should be satisfied. The size of this dissatisfaction in Britain may be measured to some extent in the 16% of the popular vote polled by the British Green Party in the recent elections to the European parliament. The success of the greens in these elections has forced the established parties to turn green too. Whether envious of the lost votes, or out of enlightened self interest, both the Conservative and Labour parties have begun to emphasise their green policies, suggesting wherever necessary their pedigrees in the party manifestos. Faced with these responses by politicians and legislators, it is not surprising to learn that the retailing industry has also been turning green, partly in response to the changing climate and partly because it sees in the greens a niche market worth exploiting.

Green initiatives

It is useful to distinguish between the responses of established commercial retailing and the initiatives which have come from dissatisfied consumers and small retailers. During the 1960s dissatisfaction with the meat-eating democracy led to the growth of vegetarian restaurants frequently run by young people. Their customers tended to be people of similar persuasion and the whole enterprise was considered odd. Indeed, the name chosen for the famous Crank's restaurant in London illustrated the mood of the moment. Over time, there has been a diffusion of the concept across the country, first to large cities with a student population and thereafter more generally. The peculiarity of vegetarianism has also diminished as more and more people have become concerned about the safety of factory farming and intensive agriculture with its reliance on the chemical industry.

Three areas of concern stand out. First, the concern over agricultural practices such as the use of chemicals, pesticides and fungicides has led many to question the quality of the products arriving on supermarket shelves. Chemical residues have been found on many crops, nitrates have polluted drinking water, growth promoting hormones and steroids have caused concern, and most topically of all at the moment, is the concern over the effects of BSE ('mad cow' disease) and the possibilities that it may be transmitted to humans. The scientific literature is cautious, as it typically is, not just because the research is scanty, but because insufficient time has elapsed since the beginnings of the Industrial Revolution to assess how far low chemical contamination has affected human genes.

A second area in which greens have taken the initiative is in the pursuit of animal rights. For many people animals and humans have equal rights and therefore the former should not be used to test products for the latter. Organisations such as Anti-Vivisectionists, Campaign against the Fur Trade, League against Cruel Sports and so on have sought via a variety of means to persuade people that animals should not be used to test the safety of cosmetic or pharmaceutical products. There is a popular groundswell of opinion in favour of some of these arguments which led in part to the development of The Body Shop, a company whose products are specifically not tested on animals.

A third area of green concern is the workings of the food industry and what many see as its rather comfortable relationship with the National Farmers Union (an employers' organisation) and the Ministry of Agriculture. There is a cost to be paid in having full supermarket shelves stocked with products whose character and taste can be assured. The cost is the processing of the product. Canning, freeze-drying and concentrates offer three ways of ensuring the product reaches the shops in the state it left the factory. However, it is what happened to it in the factory which concerns many greens. Processing often involves removing natural aspects of the raw material and replacing them with preservatives, colourings and other additives to enhance the product. It is argued that without these the product might not be saleable as processing removes much of the natural colour and flavour. For many the convenience which is offered by processing is only available at the expense of adulterating the product.

Conventional retailers

Enthusiasm among retailers for green consumption has been varied. Some responses have been organised to protect whole areas of trade, while others have been attempts to encourage a powerful environmental image for company products and to increase market share. In other words, some retailers are using the opportunity provided by the emergence of the greens to segment the existing market in new ways with the lure of increased profits to those who can curry the best image. An example of the former approach is the creation of a *Good Wood Guide* by the National Federation of Retail Furnishers and Friends of the Earth, which awards an annual seal of approval to retailers who trade in sustainable timber products (that is, timber produced in a well-managed, environmentally-sensitive way). An example of the latter is that of the supermarket chain, Safeway, which topped the *Green Consumer Guide* list as the greenest supermarket chain in 1988. By the time the *Green Consumer's Supermarket Guide* was published (Elkington and Hailes 1989), Tesco had joined Safeway at the top.

The supermarket is in many ways the battleground of green consumption. Food shopping is a major component of shopping behaviour, requiring considerable effort and expense. It also takes place frequently. Shopping for food is thus likely to be the main arena in which green consumers and retailers meet. Brown (1990) notes that most of the major operators now have a senior manager or director responsible for green issues. Their initiatives appear to fall in three main areas: the promotion of environmentally-benign products, often as own labels; the recycling of glass and plastic; and the refurbishing of stores to remove, for example, greenhouse gases in refrigeration plants.

Green retailers

The Body Shop, mentioned above, is perhaps the best example of a retailing organisation which has been based on green principles. It began in 1976 from a single shop in Brighton and has grown into an international business with outlets in over 30 countries many of which trade as franchises. In 1985, its founder, Anita Roddick, was awarded the Businesswoman of the Year Award, and in 1987 the company became the Business of the Year. The sparkling success of The Body Shop is a timely example of what can happen when an idea is pitched into its perfect market niche.

The spirit of green consumerism dominates the company. Products are produced from natural materials and ingredients (cocoa butter, jojoba); they are not tested on animals (see above), and are offered for sale in minimal packaging. Advertising is not used and the products for sale are described in information leaflets, clearly to contribute to public education. Because of its success, there have been imitators such as the Nectar chain. Even Boots has introduced a natural range of cosmetic products into its stores.

Green producers

The concerns expressed above have not been ignored by commercial foods producers. Some have attempted to focus specifically on convenience products which limit the amount of processing to 'essentials'. Jordans of Biggleswade for example have developed a useful business out of the cereals market. These are dominated by convenience foods producers such as Kelloggs and Nabisco and are not immediately associated with green products. Jordans have attempted to fill what they see as a gap in the market by producing wholefood cereals and snacks. The experience to be gathered from this is that pressure for new products can lead to green developments further back in the food chain.

Green consumption and capitalism

The responses and initiatives outlined above have gone some way towards creating a form of green consumption and retailing. Conventional retailers whose businesses are based on traditional capitalist practices have taken some elements of green consumption on board, partly to maintain market share and create an environmentally-friendly image. For many consumers green consumption is predominantly an image that acts as a foil for their personality. For others it is based on a broader concept of the relationship between mankind and the planet. For these there will always be a problem because there are inherent contradictions between the aims of green consumption in its darkest form and capitalism.

The dark green has two major difficulties. First, everything that is made requires some form of processing. Thus, there cannot ever be a wholly environment-friendly product. Resources are invariably used in extracting, manufacturing or distributing products, even green ones. However, it is clear that there are forms of extraction, manufacture and distribution which are more environment-friendly than others. The issue is finding the point of compromise in which the damage done to the planet is outweighed by the benefits of production and consumption.

Second, the notion of a no-growth economy held by many dark greens contradicts the purpose of capitalism which is the creation of needs which are satisfied by an increasingly global production process. Capitalism requires the creation of new wants and needs, and the replacing of products which have passed through the growth and take-off stages of the product life-cycle. These products cannot be allowed to lapse, they have to be developed in a new guise. Manufacturers need consumers to want to buy them in order to keep themselves in business and perpetuate the company. Retailers also need consumers to want to buy these goods so that they too may stay in business. Dark green consumption challenges the belief in consumption for its own sake; capitalism requires it.

This conflict of interest between business and the dark greens is unlikely to be resolved in favour of the latter. Retailers will not feel the need to dismantle everything to satisfy a group which is probably relatively small in number. However, the idea that capitalist retailing can fully embrace green consumption is also questionable. How green are many of the green products currently on sale?

An interesting example is bottled mineral water which has become particularly important commercially because of its strong, healthy image, and because of increasing concern about the quality of tap water. In 1989 there were about 500 million litres of mineral water sold in Britain compared with 10 million litres in 1979. This rapid increase in consumption corresponds to a rapid increase in production. Bottled water is an industry and has industrial needs. Take Perrier for example. This major producer uses non-returnable glass bottles, requires thousands of tons of glass, plastic and cardboard to package the product, has a huge advertising budget to sell the product, and makes a major demand on natural resources to produce the bottles (fossil fuels) and transport them from France. The cost of the product has been estimated to be 600 times that of an equivalent amount of tap water.

Aqua Libra goes rather further. This is a product marketed as green for a largely materialistic market. The mixture of springwater and fruit juices costs over £2 a litre and has been designed specifically for the health-conscious, lifestyles market. The company is owned by British conglomerate Grand Metropolitan but is registered in Switzerland (mountains, pure snow, fresh air) so gaining health appeal. The British launch was a very low-key affair, suggesting to many consumers that this continental product had been available for years (*The Independent* on Sunday 28th Jan 1990).

Conclusions

Retailing in the early 1990s has become concerned about environmental issues affecting the viability of the planet. Topics such as the warming of the atmosphere, environmental pollution, acid rain, food irradiation and safety, the melting of the ice-caps and water quality have all become major political issues. Traditional politicians, bred solely on a diet of unemployment, trade deficits and inflation, now recognise the importance of the green vote and are determined to win it for themselves with a range of policies which constrain what can and cannot be done industrially. This trend has important implications for retailing, as the industry is, in a real sense, the mediator between the voters and environmental degradation.

Many retailers have chosen to go green before they are forced to by legislation. In the past many consumers have been unprepared to use their purchasing behaviour to make political statements (for example, about South Africa, Chile, Afghanistan) but this seems to be on the wane. The public are increasingly concerned to know how products are made, where and by whom. They particularly want to know whether their buying a product will make it more or less likely that their grandchildren will have a future. When the issue is expressed in this way, British retailing has little choice but to respond.

CHAPTER 9

Conclusions

Introduction

Our aim in this text has been to examine some of the processes (social, economic, environmental and historical) which underlie the contemporary retailing system in Britain. As we have seen, retailing is a varied industry ranging from international conglomerates to single person operations. Some retailers specialise in niche marketing, looking specifically for particular types of consumer, while others are more general. All are concerned with making profit. In this final chapter, we draw together some of the main themes presented in the text and suggest some of the likely factors which will influence retailing in the future.

Retailing as big business

The traditional image of the British as being a nation of small shopkeepers is inappropriate to the current situation. British retailing is one of the largest industrial employers in the country, contributing significantly to national wealth, and offering a varied range of job types. The history of retailing this century is largely one of concentration into retailing corporations which operate from a decreasing number of very large shops and shopping centres. The grocery industry is perhaps the most affected by this with 70% of national trade being channelled through stores controlled by the top 5 firms.

The trend towards multiple trading and corporatism has been apparent since the end of the last century (see Jeffreys 1954) with attention focused primarily on capturing the best share of the domestic market. Since 1980 the combination of a flat domestic market and low profit margins has brought about major changes in trading. Whereas price was previously the cutting edge of retail marketing, the 1980s have seen the major operators attempting to trade upmarket, creating new opportunities for their services, and attempting to diversify their product lines at home and increasingly abroad. Dawson suggests that:

A major reason for the emergence of multinational retailers is simply that the national markets are not large enough to contain the market potential of the organisation or company. (Dawson 1982 p. 93)

Most of these multinationals operate in non-food retailing, for example, Laura Ashley, Marks and Spencer and Habitat, and have been restricting their attention to countries in Western Europe. However, Hamill (1988) notes that the number of direct investment transactions in the United States by British firms also rose sharply after about 1978 to stabilise at about 178 per year since. Companies such as Debenhams and Habitat-Mothercare have made relatively small investments (less than $50 million) acquiring US companies in related sectors. Conglomerate holding companies such as British American Tobacco, Thomas Tilling and Hanson Trust have also been active acquiring a range of retail organisations as part of their estimated $9 billion acquisition programme. This trend is likely to continue accompanied by the increasing permeability of the domestic market to foreign retailers.

Spatial faces of retailing

The spatial expression of retailing has been emphasised in this text because it is the visible manifestation of the industry. Spatial matters are particularly important to geographers and planners. For the former, retailing illustrates the importance of space in the functioning of the economy. For the latter, space is a commodity to be planned for and managed in accordance with statutory and legal obligations. The fact that there are many faces to retailing within a single country illustrates the need to recognise this spatial dimension. What is built in any locality reflects the frequently incompatible demands for retailing from consumers, local government officials and developers. The interplay of these actors leads to different townscapes across the country, with edge-of-town development hindered in some places and encouraged elsewhere. While planning authorities seem to be more flexible about allowing large retailing developments than before, it is likely that this tension will remain. It is still clear that contemporary trends in retailing are seen as anathema by some and a godsend by others.

Socio-demographic trends for the 1990s and beyond

Retailing in the 1990s and 21st century will have to respond to societies which are qualitatively different from our own. Three trends are particularly important: increasing urban congestion; the ageing of western populations; the real decline in the size and quality of the workforce. These pose major challenges to the current assumptions of retail managers and are likely to have great impact on retailing.

Urban congestion

By 2000 many major cities may have introduced restrictions on the use of private cars in city centres simply to stop them being choked by traffic. Schemes to encourage the use of public transport in Britain in preference to the private car have not been popular in the past, and any sort of restriction is likely to be widely resented. Furthermore, the flexibility offered by private transport cannot easily be matched by any existing form of public transport, all of which assume levels of personal mobility not likely to be met in steadily ageing populations. The implications for retailing are varied. If bans on the use of cars lead to reductions in car sales, perhaps decentralised, edge-of-town retailing will cease to be viable, except where served by efficient and accessible public transport. If only the inner city areas are affected, then retailing may see further decentralisation with entirely new forms of development focused on a wholly pedestrian city centre.

Ageing populations

A major demographic change is taking place in Britain. The population is ageing and the percentage of elderly people (women aged 60 + and men aged 65 +) is expected to rise from 18% in 1985 to 22.3% in 2025 (figures from the Government Actuary's Department). At the same time the percentage of the population of working age will fall from 61.2% in 1985 to 58% in 2025. The number of elderly people expressed as a percentage of the working population will rise from 29.4% to 38.5% over the same period (Peters 1989). This is not just a percentage rise; there will be 3.5 million more elderly people by 2025. The elderly are major consumers of national wealth and are also relatively immobile. Their concentration in favoured localities, often coastal, suggests that certain areas will be disproportionately affected by their presence. The concentration of the elderly in inner urban areas also poses problems as the centre of retail activity has changed towards the edge of town.

The crisis in the workforce

Studies by the Institute of Manpower Studies suggest that by 1995 Britain will be in the middle of a major labour shortage. Declining birthrates since the 1960s (Table 9.1) have resulted in fewer people coming into the workforce at school leaving age. This means that there are fewer people capable of generating the wealth needed to sustain the sorts of lifestyles we have come to take for granted.

The problem is not just one of numbers. The quality of the workforce is

| | **Birth Rate (per 1000 per annum)** | | | | | |
	UK	France	W. Germany	Canada	Japan	USA
1966–70	17.1	16.9	15.9	18.0	17.8	17.9
1971–75	14.1	16.0	10.8	15.9	18.6	15.3
1976–80	12.5	14.1	9.6	15.5	14.9	15.2
1981–85	12.9	14.2	9.8	15.1	12.6	15.7

Table 9.1   Changes in the Birth Rate – UK compared to some major economic competitors. 1966 – 1985.

(Source: Population Trends)

also likely to be lower as many of the new recruits will have few formal educational qualifications or none at all. Estimates of 65% of school leavers without any formal educational qualifications are common. Though GCSE and A level qualifications are not in themselves adequate skills for business, they have been accepted as indicating potential. Without these many employers will be forced to develop their own training initiatives 'in-house', increasing business costs, or participate more widely in government-sponsored training ventures organised by the Training and Enterprise Councils or the National Council for Vocational Qualifications (Thompson 1989). It is unlikely that major structural changes in secondary education, such as the introduction of GCSE, can quickly overcome what some see as a cultural indifference to education and training in Britain (Willis 1989). Without skills to take them further into technical or business training, the workforce is likely to polarise into those who are thought capable of training at reasonable cost and those who are not. The former are likely to be the traditional educationally-qualified groups from schools and higher education. The latter may include school leavers who fail to acquire any form of educational qualification in spite of the national curriculum, marginalised groups such as the disabled and women, and those with traditional skills which are no longer in demand.

Ten years of Thatcherism have changed the thrust of much of higher education away from purely theoretical and speculative work into topics which have a more commercial value. In geography, the development of spatial information technology, computer and numerical skills, allied to the traditional abilities in map analysis and survey work, has made the subject more commercially viable. Indeed, the geodemographics industry has led to the creation of a non-academic professional geography, similar in some respects to professional economics or psychology. People with educational and technical skills are in demand now and are likely to be so in the future. Those without such skills may not be unemployable, but may have increasing difficulty to get and keep work, especially as technological change is likely to lead to job-shedding as a means of cutting costs. The very jobs that they are most suited for may be those which are most expendable.

Retailing is typical of the industries which have developed this type of bipolar workforce. As Wrigley (1988) points out, there are essentially two types of worker in the business. The first is the numerically small group of career professionals who are concerned with commercial strategy, finance, advertising, personnel and store development. These are recruited from the pool of the educationally-qualified. The second, numerically much larger group, includes the sales staff, shelf fillers, till operators, cleaners, security staff and so on. Many of these are women working part-time. For these, the levels of skills required are negligible (though this may change in jobs like warehousing and security) and there is little or no career structure. They are thus highly vulnerable to job-shedding due to competition or technological change. It seems likely that there will be a sufficient pool of this type of labour for some time to come. The main problem for retailing is that it will be in increased competition with other sectors of business for its career professionals.

Geographical data, information and analysis

The concentration of retailing in large corporations, especially in the grocery trade, has produced a major demand for good quality information on the retailing behaviour of consumers. As this behaviour is mediated by the opportunities and impedences of space, devising the means of getting this information has been of interest to retailers for many years. It has also interested academics such as quantitative geographers and planners, and has led to the creation of a new type of business analyst dealing principally in commercial applications of geodemographics. The collection of articles in Wrigley (1988) illustrates the sorts of things which have been developed from these areas.

Two articles from this collection are particularly worth considering here, both of which come from the commercial sector. For Beaumont (1988) the key issue is providing business managers with information they can understand about the financial implications of alternative retail locations. He argues that in many companies there are poor lines of communication between management and researchers. The function of the former is to plan strategy based on available information and acceptable forecasts of the future. The purpose of the latter is to collect the data and turn them into information. Both areas are skilled, but the skills are different. If one side does not understand enough about the work of the other the most probable result will be misunderstanding, even chaos. The need therefore is for managers to become more conversant with the nature of research, its assumptions and limitations; for researchers to become more conversant with the needs of managers, especially their time and cost constraints; or to establish some form of liaison staff who can talk to both.

The information needs of the future may be met by the development of integrated data bases on the many types of geographically-variable consumer behaviour that are now recognised by the industry. These will have to provide information which can meet existing needs within existing time horizons, becoming a corporate resource for the company. Only if they meet this organisational requirement are they likely to be taken more seriously and play a more extensive role in strategy.

The article by Humby (1988) takes a different tack. In this he argues that academia has focused too much on the behaviour of fast-selling consumer goods and the grocery trade and has ignored many of the other areas of retailing. This has a number of key implications. First, there is the tendency to assume that all retail markets behave like grocery retailing. This is not the case, Indeed, the growth of the large multiple and the standardised product, store and shopping atmosphere associated with it has made this sector rather different from retailing in general. There are many other retailing markets in which consumer choice, fashion and lifestyle appear to play a much greater role in consumer decision processes and in which the fundamental behavioural assumptions of most academic models are invalid. Second, the thrust of academic research into studying the relationships between catch-ment market areas and retail stores is excessive. Catchment area research is relatively easy; it does not need a massive research effort and can be conducted in-house using a variety of *ad hoc* procedures. He notes:

> The majority of retailers are sitting on, or have direct access to, a vast wealth of information on these (relationships). Some is already collected in omnibus research; more importantly, there are over 15.5 million adults with credit cards in Britain. It is not diffcult to analyse the relationship between their spending patterns at particular retail chains and the location of their homes. A pressing need now is to understand how to relate the patterns displayed in the credit-using society to the non-users. (Humby 1988, p. 326)

Third, the traditional assumptions associated with grocery retailing may now be changing. As market segmentation becomes more pronounced in the field of green retailing, supermarket chains have been trying very hard to establish green images with the public. The *Green Consumer Guide* suggests that Safeway and Sainsburys are leading at the moment but with every other chain making efforts to develop their image.

What is happening in green retailing can also happen in other areas of the grocery trade, for example, bottled water and delicatessen foods; indeed, anywhere a mass market can be decomposed into niches by responding to consumer tastes. For Humby, the recognition of lifestyle retailing is the key for the future:

> The acid test . . . is lifestyle – the measurement and understanding, not of the

whole population, but of discrete lifestyle or niche segments. We must set aside much of the existing research and look to the future; redraw our priorities and look again on how we will cope with the information revolution. (Humby 1988, p. 327)

The quality of information

There may have been an explosion in the quantity of information on retailing in the last twenty years but there has been no such explosion in quality. This is most serious given the views expressed by Humby above, and generally supported by those academics and consultants busily developing geodemographic and geographical information systems.

The value of geographical information systems is that they integrate different types of information in a way which allows them to add value to what already exists. Linking together information on demographics, spatial structure and market research (all of which already exists) can provide the analyst with a database for assessing market potential and sales trends. None of the component data sets were created to provide this information, but linking them together makes it possible to obtain it. For many, this ability to add value to existing information is a sign of increasing data quality; however, without an appropriate concern for what the data really mean, many geoanalysts may be guilty of misrepresentation by extension, that is, reading more into the data than is really there.

The Population Census is one of the key data sets used in geodemographics. It provides small area information for 21 census questions which, when disaggregated and cross-classified by each other, expands to 4417 different pieces of data (O'Brien *et al.*, 1988). It is paramount that analysts realise that the classes and categories used in this expansion are socially-determined and are not cast-iron facts. They represent the thinking of OPCS and their advisors in the late 1970s and naturally steer in favour of the views of government departments and their advisors. The Census is produced to help inform government policy so it must be in reasonable accord with the social and economic categories considered appropriate by them. There is no guarantee that these are even remotely adequate for other types of information analysis. (For a discussion of these issues see, for example, Sayer 1984, and O'Brien 1990a.)

It should be stressed that analysts are already aware of some of the technical difficulties of using statutory data for uses other than for which they were collected. There are many articles in the social science literatures comparing the relative performance of different data sources for different types of analysis. Not surprisingly, different data sources yield different results, as do different types of analysis applied to the same data source. Whether these differences are sufficient to render one approach more acceptable commercially depends on what the analyst needs and how quickly.

However, one feature of data quality which is poorly understood by many quantitative analysts, including those in higher education, is the social (economic, historic) context of the data. The classes which lie at the heart of databases and spatial information systems (both the socio-economic classes and the spatial zoning systems) are largely arbitrary. Very few categories are actually fixed by nature; most represent the result of administrative or functional thinking by a group of people whose economic and social status allows them to perform this type of work. Elitist social systems and elitist thinking are intertwined and inevitably lead to a form of intellectual myopia in areas outside the direct personal experience of the group. The identification and naming of categories thus cannot be divorced from their creators, who are just as likely to be misinformed or misunderstand what they are told as anybody else. Retailers planning for their commercial future in a world of market segments should be concerned about categories which are out-of-date or wholly out-of-order.

There are many possible examples to illustrate this based on social groupings already well served by retailing. However, a group which is generally poorly served by British society, and which is inherently misrepresented because of the calumny of its categorisation, is the disabled. Disability, like death, is not discussed openly in Britain, but unlike death, which comes to us all, disability *may* come to us all. No-one is immune from having an accident or from contracting an illness which incapacitates. Disability is thus a concern for the whole population. Classes such as 'normal' and 'not-normal' (essentially meaningless but typical of much British social thinking) are commonplace; more appropriate conceptions are 'potentially disabled' and 'already disabled'. If the general managers of international conglomerates truly perceived their vulnerability, the assumptions underpinning their whole approach to work, leisure, transport, education and shopping would inevitably be different.

A number of things would change. First, the notion that disability is synonymous with immobility would be scotched. Retailing facilities would have to be made appropriate both to the wheelchair population and to those whose problems were less obvious. Second, disability would no longer be seen as a purely medical matter but something which reflects the environment the person with the problem lives in. Disability as a spatial phenomenon which can be overcome by understanding and planning is a relatively novel idea but one with considerable potential. Third, the disabled would not be considered 'dependents' because work would be available to all those who could do it. Currently, many British disabled people (many with skills gained before becoming disabled) cannot get back into the workforce in spite of efforts by government to train them (Newcastle Council for the Disabled 1988, O'Brien 1990b). In effect, the whole culture which sees people with disabilities as 'disabled people', that is, dependent non-functionaries, would be set on its head. Currently retailing views the disabled in this way. With between 10% and 15% of the British population falling into this category, it cannot be commercially sensible to continue with this view, especially as considerable numbers of people with disabilities are employable, many as skilled professionals.

The future for retailing

As Levitt noted as far back as the 1960s:

> there is no such thing as a growth industry... There are only companies organised and operated to create and capitalise on growth opportunities. (Levitt 1960, quoted in Enis and Cox 1988, p. 6)

This is sound advice for those involved in retailing. With so many retail staff employed behind the scenes, many in information-handling tasks, perhaps the industry ought to see itself more generally as in the information business rather than distribution. Understanding the motivations which lead to certain types of behaviour can provide retailing with a key to the sorts of services it should be providing by the end of the decade. The traditional mould of getting the shoppers to the shops may be broken, especially as shops for market segments cannot support the whole economy or supply all its needs. Information used creatively may lead to new initiatives which actually increase the quality of life rather than its material trappings, and so help to remove the links which still bind the majority of the population to capitalist working practices. Replacing the dark satanic mill by the shopping centre does not remove the underlying process of alienation, irrespective of how attractive new shopping centres may appear.

Business consultants seem to agree that 'creativity and innovation will be the cornerstones of tomorrow's business' (*The Times*, Feb 6th, 1989, p. 25), and that this is likely to mean a 24 hour-a-day economy with a concentration on quality and service. Peculiarly, some of the characteristics of this future – home delivery of products, catalogue shopping, leisure shopping – will merely be 21st century adaptations of the retailing systems of the late 19th and earlier 20th centuries. Whether the more audacious speculations about the development of 'a paradigm of consciousness' or the spiritual awakening which leads to a tiring with materialism actually come about remains to be seen. For the moment the stage is set for the debate about environmentalism, the quality of food, water and health-related eating. These are the public concerns at the beginning of the 1990s. How they are incorporated into a mass distribution system is yet to be seen.

References

Alderson, W. (1958) 'The analytical framework for marketing'. Reprinted as Article 2 in Enis, B. M. and Cox, K. K. (1988) *Marketing Classics*, 6th Edition, Allyn and Bacon Inc., Boston.

Alexander, D. (1970) *Retailing in England during the Industrial Revolution*, Athlone Press, London.

Ambrose, P. and Colenutt, R. (1975) *The Property Machine*, Penguin, Harmondsworth.

American Marketing Association (1948) 'Report of the Definitions Committee', *Journal of Marketing*, **12**, 202–217.

Applebaum, W. (1954) 'Marketing Geography', *American Geography: Inventory and Prospect*, Syracuse University Press, pp. 245–251.

Arts Council of Great Britain (1989) *Annual Report*, available from Arts Council, 105 Piccadilly, London.

Bacon, R. W. (1971) 'An approach to the theory of consumer shopping behaviour', *Urban Studies*, **8**, pp. 55–64.

Bacon, R. W. (1984) *Consumer Spatial Behaviour: a model of purchasing decisions over space and time*, Clarendon Press, Oxford.

Bamfield, J. (1980) 'The changing face of British retailing', *National Westminster Bank Quarterly Review*, May, pp. 33–45.

Bamfield, J. (1988) 'Competition and change in British retailing', *National Westminster Bank Quarterly Review*, February, pp. 15–29.

Bates, J. J. (1988) 'Stated preference techniques and the analysis of consumer choice', in Wrigley, N. (ed) *Store Choice, Store Location and Market Analysis*, Routledge, London, pp. 187–202.

Bayton, J. A. (1958) 'Motivation, cognition, learning – basic factors in consumer behaviour', *Journal of Marketing*, **22**, pp. 282–289.

Beaujeu-Garnier, J. and Delobez, A. (1979) *Geography of Marketing*, Longmans, London.

Beaumont, J. R. (1988) 'Store location analysis: problems and progress', in Wrigley, N. (ed) *Store Choice, Store Location and Market Analysis*, Routledge, London, pp. 87–105.

Bell, D. (1973) *The coming of Post-Industrial Society: a venture in Social Forecasting*, Basic Books, New York.

Bell, D. (1980) 'The social framework of the Information Society', in Forester T. (ed) *The Microelectronics Revolution*, Blackwell, Oxford.

Benn, T. (1980) *Arguments for Socialism*, Penguin, Harmondsworth.

Beresford, P., Cahill, K. and Masters, P. (1990) 'Britain's rich – the top 200', *Sunday Times Magazine*, April 8th, pp. 33–65.

Berry, B. J. L. (1967) *Geography of Market Centers and Retail Distribution*, Prentice-Hall, Englewood Cliffs.

Bidder, J. (1989) 'How mother-friendly is your supermarket?', *Good Housekeeping*, November, pp. 178–185.

Blakemore, M. J. and Nelson, R. (1985) 'Data compaction in NOMIS: a geographical information system for the management of employment, unemployment and population data', *University Computing*, 7, 144–147.

Bolter, D. (1984) *Turing's Man: Western Culture in the Computer Age*, Duckworth, London.

Breheny, M. J. (1988) 'Practical methods of retail location analysis: a review', in Wrigley, N. (ed) *Store Choice, Store Location and Market Analysis*, Routledge, London, pp. 39–87.

Bristol City Planning Department (1972) 'Cribbs Causeway out-of-town shopping centre enquiry: A report of the proceedings', Bristol City Council.

Bruce, A. J. and Mann, H. R. (1977) The Brent Cross Shopping Centre Impact Study: Results of the first diary study of household shopping trips, Greater London Council Research Memorandum 522, London.

Bucklin, L. P. (1963) 'Retail strategy and the classification of consumer goods', *Journal of Marketing*, 27, 51–56.

Burt, S., Dawson, J. A. and Sparks, L. (1983) 'Structure plans and retailing policies', *The Planner*, 69, 11–13.

Cadman, D. and Austin-Crowe, L. (1978) *Property Development*, Spon Ltd., London.

Cane, A. (1983) 'Britain's shopping revolution: The challenge to the cheque', *Financial Times*, December 8th.

Cannon, T. (1986) *Basic Marketing: Principles and Practice* (2nd ed), Cassell, London.

Carson, R. (1951) *The Sea Around Us*, Staples Press.

Carson, R. (1988) *Silent Spring*, Houghton Mifflin, Boston.

Cater, J. and Jones, T. (1989) *Social Geography*, Edward Arnold, London.

Charles, R. (1989) 'Canada-United States Free Trade Agreement: a Canadian's personal perspective', *National Westminster Bank Quarterly Review*, May, pp. 17–26.

Charlton, M., Openshaw, S. and Wymer, C. (1985) 'Some new classifications of census enumeration districts in Britain: A poor man's ACORN', *Journal of Economic and Social Measurement*, 13, 69–96.

Christaller, W. (1933) *Die Zentralen Orte in Suddeutschland*, translated by C. W. Baskin as *Central Places in Southern Germany* (1966), Prentice-Hall, New Jersey.

Clarke, M. (1984) Integrated dynamical models of urban structure and activities: An application to urban retail systems, Unpublished PhD Thesis, School of Geography, University of Leeds.

Cooper, J. (1979) *Class*, Eyre Methuen, London.

Couch, D. (1989) *Retailing*, Penguin, Harmondsworth.

Cozens, J. (1990) 'Spend, spend, spend', *Good Housekeeping*, 137, 100–102.

Dale, G. (1989) *The Business of Retailing*, Hutchinson, London.

Davies, R. L. (1973) Patterns and Profiles of Consumer Behaviour, Research Series 10, Department of Geography, University of Newcastle upon Tyne.

Davies, R. L. (1976) *Marketing Geography*, Retail and Planning Associates, Corbridge, Northumberland.

Davies, R. L. (1984) *Retail and Commercial Planning*, Croom Helm, London.

Davies, R. L. (1985) 'The Gateshead shopping and information service', *Environment and Planning B*, 12, 209–220.

Davies, R. L. and Rogers, D. S. (eds) (1984) *Store Location and Store Assessment Research*, John Wiley, Chichester.

Daws, L. F. and McCulloch, M. (1974) 'Shopping activity patterns: a travel diary study of Watford', Building Research Establishment Paper 31/74.

Dawson, J. A. (1979) *The Marketing Environment*, Croom Helm, London.

Dawson, J. A. (1982) *Commercial Distribution in Europe*, Croom Helm, London.

Dawson, J. A. (1983) *Shopping Centre Development*, Longman, London.

Dawson, J. A. (1988) 'Futures for the high street', *The Geographical Journal*, **154**, 1–12.

Dawson, J. A. and Lord, J. D. (eds) (1985) *Shopping Centre Development: Policies and prospects*, Croom Helm, London.

Department of Employment (1988) *Employment for the 1990s*, HMSO, London.

Department of the Environment (1972) 'Out-of-town shops and shopping centres', *Development Control Policy Note 13*, HMSO, London.

Department of the Environment (1974) 'Warehouses – wholesale, cash-and-carry etc', *Development Control Policy Note 14*, HMSO, London.

Department of the Environment (1977) 'Large new stores', *Development Control Policy Note 13*, HMSO, London.

Department of the Environment (1988a) 'Land for housing', *Planning Policy Guidance Note 3*, HMSO, London.

Department of the Environment (1988b) *Handling Geographic Information*, HMSO, London.

Department of the Environment and Welsh Office, (1988) 'Major retail development', *Planning Policy Guidance Note 6*, HMSO, London.

Dicken, P. (1986) *Global Shift: Industrial Change in a turbulent world*, Harper and Row, London.

Dicken, P. and Lloyd, P. (1981) *Modern Western Society*, Harper and Row, London.

Distributive Trades Economic Development Council (1982) *Technology: The Issues for the Distributive Trades*, National Economic Development Office, London.

Distributive Trades Economic Development Council (1988) *The Future of the High Street*, National Economic Development Office, London.

Donaldson, P. (1973) *Economics of the Real World*, Pelican, Harmondsworth.

Downs, R. M. (1970) 'The cognitive structure of an urban shopping center', *Environment and Behaviour*, **2**, 13–39.

Ehrenberg, A. S. C. (1968) 'The practical meaning and usefulness of the NBD/LSD theory of repeat buying', *Applied Statistics*, **17**, 17–32.

Ehrenberg, A. S. C. (1972) *Repeat Buying: Theory and applications*, North Holland, Amsterdam.

Ehrenberg, A. S. C. and Goodhardt, G. J. (1979) *Understanding Buyer Behaviour*, J. Walter Thompson and MRCA, New York.

Elkington, J. and Hailes, J. (1988) *The Green Consumer Guide*, Gollancz, London.

Elkington, J. and Hailes, J. (1989) *The Green Consumer's Supermarket Guide*, Gollancz, London.

Engel, J. F., Blackwell, R. D. and Kollat, D. T. (1978) *Consumer Behaviour* (3rd ed), Dryden Press, Hinsdale, Illinois.

Enis, B. M. and Cox, K. K. (1988) *Marketing Classics*, 6th Edition, Allyn and Bacon Inc., Boston.

Evans, A. W. (1972) 'A linear programming solution to the shopping problem posed by R. W. Bacon', *Urban Studies*, **9**, 221–222.

Evans, L. (1990) 'The demographic-dip: A golden opportunity for women in the labour market?', *National Westminster Bank Quarterly Review*, February, 48–69.

Flint, A. (1981) 'The market restored and open: The first year and beyond', Seminar Paper, Waldorf Hotel, 26th May.

Fothergill, S. and Gudgin, G. (1982) *Unequal Growth*, Heinemann, London.

Fotheringham, A. S. (1988) 'Market share analysis techniques: a review and illustration of current US practice', in Wrigley, N. (ed) *Store Choice, Store Location and Market Analysis*, Routledge, London, pp. 120–159.

Frobel, F., Heinrichs, J. and Kreye, O. (1980) *The New International Division of Labour*, Cambridge University Press, Cambridge.

Galbraith, J. K. (1969) *The Affluent Society*, Penguin, Harmondsworth.

Gardner, C. and Sheppard, J. (1989) *Consuming Passion: The Rise of Retail Culture*, Unwin Hyman, London.

Geist, J.F. (1983) *Arcades, The History of a Building Type*, MIT Press, Cambridge, Mass.

Gershuny, J. (1978) *After Industrial Society?: The Emerging Self-Service Economy*, Macmillan, London.

Gershuny, J. and Miles, I. D. (1983) *The New Service Economy: The Transformation of Employment in Industrial Societies*, Pinter, London.

Gibbs, A. (1981) 'An analysis of retail warehouse planning enquiries', Report U22, URPI, Reading.

Goddard, J. B. and Champion, A. G. (eds) (1983) *The Urban and Regional Transformation of Britain*, Methuen, London.

Golledge, R. G. (1967) 'Conceptualising the market decision process', *Journal of Regional Science*, 7, 239–258.

Guy, C. M. (1980) *Retail Location and Retail Planning in Britain*, Gower, Farnborough.

Guy, C. M. (1984) 'Food and grocery shopping behaviour in Cardiff,' Papers in Planning Research 86, Department of Town Planning, UWIST, Cardiff.

Guy, C. M. (1985) 'The food and grocery shopping behaviour of disadvantaged consumers: some results from the Cardiff Consumer Panel', *Transactions of the Institute of British Geographers*, 10, 181–190.

Guy, C. M. (1988) 'Information technology and retailing: the implications for analysis and forecasting', in Wrigley, N. (ed) *Store Choice, Store Location and Market Analysis*, Routledge, London, pp. 305–322.

Guy, C. M. and Wrigley, N. (1981) A long-term grocery shopping diary survey in Cardiff, Research Grant Application, Social Sciences Research Council, London.

Guy, C. M., Wrigley, N., O'Brien, L. G. and Hiscocks, G. (1983) 'The Cardiff Consumer Panel: A report on the methodology', Papers in Planning Research 68, Department of Town Planning, UWIST, Cardiff.

H.M.S.O. (1988) *1991 Census of Population*, Cm 430, HMSO, London.

Haley, R.I. (1968) 'Benefit segmentation: a decision-oriented research tool', *Journal of Marketing*, 32, 30–35.

Hamill, J. (1988) 'British acquisitions in the United States', *National Westminster Bank Quarterly Review*, August, pp. 2–17.

Hamnett, C. (1977) Urban Land Use, 16, D204. Open University, Milton Keynes.

Harris, F.W. and O'Brien, L.G. (1988) 'The changing face of the town', *Geographical Magazine*, 60, 34–37.

Harvey, D. W. (1982) *The Limits to Capital*, Blackwell, Oxford.

Hensher, D.A. and Johnson, L.W. (1981) *Applied Discrete Choice Modelling*, Croom Helm, London.

Hepworth, M. (1989) *Geography of the Information Economy*, Belhaven Press, London.

Hillier Parker May and Rowden (1986) *Shopping Centre Refurbishment*, Hillier Parker May and Rowden, London.

Hillier Parker May and Rowden (1987) *British Shopping Developments Master List*, Hillier Parker May and Rowden/British Council of Shopping Centres, London.

Hillier Parker May and Rowden (1989a) *British Shopping Developments 1988 supplement*, Hillier Parker May and Rowden/British Council of Shopping Centres, London.

Hillier Parker May and Rowden (1989b) *Retail Parks*, Hillier Parker May and Rowden, London.

Hillier Parker May and Rowden (1990) *Retail Parks*, Hillier Parker May and Rowden, London.

Humby, C. (1988) 'Store choice, store location and market analysis: some final observations on future research priorities', in Wrigley, N. (ed) *Store Choice, Store Location and Market Analysis*, Routledge, London, pp. 323–327.

Hudson, R. and Williams, A. (1986) *The United Kingdom*, Harper and Row, London.

I.C.I.D.I. (1980) *North-South: A Programme for Survival*, Pan, London.

Institute for Employment Research (1989) *Review of the Economy and Employment*, Volume 1.

Jansen, A. C. M. (1989) 'Funshopping as a geographical notion, or: The attraction of the Inner City of Amsterdam as a shopping area', *Tijdschrift voor Economische en Sociale Geografie*, **80**, 171–183.

Jeffreys, J. B. (1954) *Retail trading in Britain 1850–1950*, Cambridge University Press, Cambridge.

Johnson, G. (ed), (1987) *Business Strategy and Retailing*, John Wiley, Chichester.

Johnson, P. (1983) *A History of the Modern World from 1917 to the 1980s*, Weidenfeld and Nicholson, London.

Jones, F. E. (1978) 'Our manufacturing industry – The missing £100,000 million', *National Westminster Bank Quarterly Review*, May, 8–17.

Jones, K. and Simmons, J. (1987) *Location, Location, Location: Analysing the Retail Environment*, Methuen, Toronto.

Jones, P. (1983) 'DIY and home improvement centres: a growth area', *The Planner*, **69**, 13–15.

Katona, G. (1953) 'Rational behaviour and economic behaviour', *Psychological Review*, **60**, 307–318.

Kau Ah Keng and Ehrenberg, A. S. C. (1984) 'Patterns of store choice', *Journal of Marketing Research*, **21**, 399–409.

Kay, W. (1987) *Battle for the High Street*, Piatkus, London.

Kivell, P. T. and Shaw, G. (1980) 'The study of retail location', in J. A. Dawson, (ed), *Retail Geography*, Croom Helm, London.

Kohn, A. (1986) *No Contest: The Case against Competition*, Houghton Mifflin, Boston.

Kotler, P. (1965) 'Behavioural models for analysing buyers', *Journal of Marketing*, **29**, 37–45.

Kotler, P. (1980) *Marketing Management: Analysis, Planning and Control*, Prentice-Hall, New Jersey.

Kotler, P. and Levy, S. (1969) 'Broadening the concept of marketing', *Journal of Marketing*, **33**, 10–15.

Knox, P. and Agnew, J. (1989) *The Geography of the World Economy*, Edward Arnold, London.

Lancaster, K.J. (1971) *Consumer Demand: A New Approach*, Columbia University Press, New York.

Lavidge, R. J. and Steiner, G. A. (1961) 'A model for predictive measurements of advertising', *Journal of Marketing*, **25**, 59–62.

Lavery, I. and Andersson, P. (1989) 'A 1987 trip-based urban transportation strategy – still ignoring the needs of elderly and disabled people', Paper presented to the 5th

International Conference on Mobility and Transport for elderly and disabled persons, Stockholm, Sweden, May 23rd.

Lee, M., Jones, P. and Peach, C. (1973) 'Caerphilly Hypermarket Study', Research Report 1, Donaldsons.

Levitt, T. (1960) 'Marketing myopia', *Harvard Business Review*, **35**, 24–48 Reprinted as Article 1 in Enis, B. M. and Cox, K. K. (1988) *Marketing Classics*, 6th Edition, Allyn and Bacon Inc, Boston.

Lewis, R. (ed), (1989) *IT in Retailing: Applications of Information Technology and Corporate Models in Retailing*, Kogan Page, London.

Lipsey, R. G. (1975) *An Introduction to Positive Economics*, Weidenfeld and Nicolson, London, (4th edition).

Lierop, W. van and Nijkamp, P. (1980) 'Spatial choice and interaction models: criteria and aggregation', *Urban Studies*, **17**, 299–311.

Lomax, D. (1988) 'The Big Bang – 18 months after', *National Westminster Bank Quarterly Review*, August, pp. 18–30.

Lord, J. D. (1985) 'Revitalisation of shopping centres', in Dawson, J. A. and Lord, J. D. (eds) *Shopping Centre Development: Policies and Prospects*, Croom Helm, London, pp. 226–242.

Lyon, D. (1988) *The Information Society*, Polity Press, Cambridge.

Mackeith, M. (1985) 'The changing high street', *The Planner*, **71**, 9–12.

Mackeith, M. (1986) *The History and Conservation of Shopping Arcades*, Mansell, London.

Marsh, P. (1982) 'Will Britain buy electronic shopping?', *New Scientist*, April 29th.

Marti, J. and Zeilinger, A. (1985) 'New technology in banking and shopping', in Forester, T. (ed) *The Information Technology Revolution*, Blackwell, Oxford, pp. 350–358.

Maslow, A. H. (1968) *Toward a Psychology of Being*, 2nd edition, Van Nostrand, New Jersey.

Maslow, A. H. (1970) *Motivation and Personality*, 2nd edition, Harper and Row, New York.

Massey, D. (1984) *Spatial Divisions of Labour: Social Structure and the Geography of Production*, Macmillan, London.

McAnnaly, P. (1971) *The Economics of the Distributive Trades*, Allen and Unwin, London.

McFadden, D. (1968) 'The revealed preferences of a government bureaucracy', Technical Report W17, Institute of International Studies, University of California, Berkeley.

Miles, I. and Gershuny, J. (1986) 'The social economics of information technology', in Ferguson, M. (ed) *New Communications Technologies in the Public Interest*, Sage, London.

Mills, E. (1974) 'Recent developments in retailing and urban planning', PRAG Technical Papers TP3, Planning Research Applications Group.

Ministry of Housing and Local Government (1962) 'Town centres: approach to renewal', HMSO, London.

Mishan, E. J. (1990) 'Economic and political obstacles to environmental sanity', *National Westminster Bank Quarterly Review*, May, pp. 25–42.

Molyneux, P. (1990) 'US high yield debt and the case for a European market', *National Westminster Bank Quarterly Review*, February, pp. 2–15.

Nelson, R. L. (1958) *The Selection of Retail Locations*, Dodge, New York.

Newcastle Council for the Disabled (1988) *Employment Training and Disabled People*, available from the Dene Centre, Castles Farm Road, Newcastle, NE3 1PH.

Ody, P. (1984) 'Fashion retailing – what next?', *Retail and Distribution Management*, September/October.

Openshaw, S. (1975) *Some Theoretical and Applied Aspects of Spatial Interaction Shopping Models*, Concepts and Techniques in Modern Geography 4, GeoAbstracts, Norwich.

O'Brien, L. G. (1990a) *Generalised Linear Modelling in Geography*, Routledge, London.

O'Brien, L. G. (1990b) 'The need for a geographical contribution to the study of disability', *Local Authorities Research and Intelligence Association News*, 33, 2–4.

O'Brien, L. G. and Guy, C. M. (1985) 'Locational variability in retail grocery prices', *Environment and Planning A*, 17, 953–962.

O'Brien, L. G., Nelson, R., Dodds, P. and Blakemore, M. J. (1988) *NOMIS Reference Manuals*, (4 Volumes), National Online Manpower Information System, University of Durham, England.

Pahl, R. (1984) *Divisions of Labour*, Blackwell, Oxford.

Pahl, R., Flynn, E. and Buck, N. (1983) *Structures and Processes of Urban Life*, Longman, London.

Pankhurst, I. C. and Roe, P. E. (1978) 'An empirical study of two shopping models', *Regional Studies*, 12, 727–748.

Penny, N. J. and Broom, D. (1988) 'The Tesco approach to store location', in Wrigley, N. (ed) *Store Choice, Store Location and Market Analysis*, Routledge, London, pp. 106–119.

Peters, R. H. (1989) 'Population, pensions and public sector surpluses', *National Westminster Bank Quarterly Review*, November, pp. 22–30.

Pinch, S. and Williams, A. (1983) 'Social class change in British cities', in Goddard, J. B. and Champion, A. G. (eds) *The Urban and Regional Transformation of Britain*, Methuen, London, pp. 135–159.

Porritt, J. and Winner, D. (1988) *The Coming of the Greens*, Fontana, London.

Potter, R. B. (1982) *The Urban Retailing System: Location, Cognition and Behaviour*, Gower, Aldershot.

Purvis, M. (1986) 'Cooperative retailing in England, 1835–1850: developments beyond Rochdale', *Northern History*, 22, 198–215.

Retail Pocketbook (1989) Published by AC Nielsen Marketing Research, Headington, Oxford.

Retail and Distribution Management (1984) 'Victoria Wine Company completes Thorn/EMI installation', *Retail and Distribution Management*, 12, 33–45.

Retail and Distribution Management (1985a) 'Tradanet launched by ANA and ICL', *Retail and Distribution Management*, 13, 42–43.

Retail and Distribution Management (1985b) 'Comp-U-Card's home shopping service', *Retail and Distribution Management*, 13, 47.

Roberts, J. (1981) *Pedestrian Precincts in Britain*, Transport and Environment Studies, London.

Rosen, S. (1974) 'Hedonic prices and implicit markets: product differentiation in pure competition', *Journal of Political Economy*, 82, 34–55.

Rosenberg, L. J. and Hirschman, E. C. (1980) 'Retailing without stores', *Harvard Business Review*, 58, 103–112.

Rowley, G. (1986) *Let's Talk Shop: Relocational Trends in British Retailing*, Chas. E. Goad, Hatfield.

Rushton, G. (1969) 'Analysis of spatial behaviour by revealed space preference', *Annals of the Association of American Geographers*, 59, 391–400.

Sargent, P. (1988) 'Leisure and retail – an exciting synergy', *Leisure Management*, 8, 36–40.

Samuelson, P. and Nordhaus, W. S. (1989) *Economics*, McGraw-Hill, New York (13th edition).

Sayer, R. A. (1984) *Method in Social Science: a Realist Approach*, Hutchinson, London.

Schiller, R. (1985) 'Land use controls on UK shopping centres', in Dawson, J. A. and Lord, J. D. (eds) *Shopping Centre Development: Policies and Prospects*, Croom Helm, London, pp. 40–46.

Schiller, R. (1988) 'Retail decentralisation – a property view', *The Geographical Journal*, **154**, 17–19.

Scott, P. (1970) *Geography and Retailing*, Hutchinson, London.

Senior, M. (1979) 'From gravity modelling to entropy maximising: a pedagogic review', *Progress in Human Geography*, **3**, 179–211.

Simon, H. A. (1952) 'A behavioural model of rational choice', *Quarterly Journal of Economics*, **69**, 99–118.

Simmons, J. (1964) 'The changing pattern of retail location', University of Chicago, Department of Geography, Research Paper 92.

Smith, A. (1973) 'The future of downtown retailing', *Urban Land*, **31**, 3–10.

Sparks, L. (1986) 'The changing structure of distribution in retail companies: an example from the grocery trade', *Transactions of the Institute of British Geographers*, **11**, 147–154.

Stern, P. and Stanworth, J. (1988) 'The development of franchising in Britain', *National Westminster Bank Quarterly Review*, May, pp. 38–48.

Stone, G. P. (1954) 'City shoppers and urban identification', *American Journal of Sociology*, **60**, 36–45.

Strauss, L. (1983) *Electronic Marketing: Emerging TV and Computer Channels for Interactive Home Shopping*, Knowledge Industry Publications, White Plains, New York.

Thatcher, A. R. (1984) 'A review of the 1981 Census of Population in England and Wales', *Population Trends*, **36**, pp. 5–9.

Thompson, P. J. (1989) 'Providing a qualified society to meet the challenge', *National Westminster Bank Quarterly Review*, February, pp. 22–29.

Thorne, R. (1980) *Covent Garden Market – Its History and Restoration*, Architectural Press/GLC, London.

Thorpe, D. and Kivell, P. T. (1971) 'Woolco, Thornaby: a study of an out-of-town shopping centre', Retail Outlets Research Unit, *Research Report 3*, Manchester Business School.

Timmermans, H., Heijden, R vd. and Westervald, H. (1982) 'Perception of urban retailing environments: an empirical analysis of consumer information and usage fields', *Geoforum*, **13**, 27–39.

Townsend, A. R., Blakemore, M. J., Nelson, R. and Dodds, P. (1986) 'The National Online Manpower Information System. (NOMIS)', *Employment Gazette*, February, pp. 60–64.

U.R.P.I. (1984) '1984 list of hypermarkets and superstores', Unit for Retail Planning Information, Reading.

Uncles, M. D. and Ehrenberg, A. S. C. (1988) 'Patterns of store choice: New evidence from the USA', in Wrigley, N. (ed) *Store Choice, Store Location and Market Analysis*, Routledge, London, pp. 272–299.

Wacher, T. and Flint, A. (1980) 'How Covent Garden became a speciality shopping centre', *Chartered Surveyor*, **112**, 594–600.

Wallerstein, I. (1974) *The Modern World System*, Academic Press, New York.

Wallerstein, I. (1979) *The Capitalist World-Economy*, Cambridge University Press, Cambridge.

Wallerstein, I. (1984) *The Politics of the World-Economy: the States, the Movements and the Civilisations*, Cambridge University Press, Cambridge.

Warnes, A. and Law, C. M. (1984) 'The elderly population of Great Britain: locational trends and policy implications', *Transactions of the Institute of British Geographers*, **9**, 37–59.

Weber, M. (1948) From *Max Weber: Essays in Sociology*, translated, edited and with an introduction by H. H. Gerth and C. Wright Mills, Routledge and Kegan Paul, London (1977).

Weidenbaum, M. L. (1980) *Government Power and Business Performance*, Stanford University Press.

Weinstein, S. B. (1984) 'Smart credit cards: The answer to cashless shopping', *IEEE Spectrum*, February.

Which? Magazine. (1990) 'Is your Barclaycard for the chop?', June, p. 303, Consumers Association, London.

Wild, M. T. and Shaw, G. (1979) 'Trends in urban retailing: the British experience during the nineteenth century', *Tidjschrift voor Economische en Sociale Geografie*, **70**, 35–44.

Wilkie, W. L. (1986) *Consumer Behaviour*, Wiley, London.

Wilkinson, P. and Lomax, D. (1989) 'Lessons for banking from the 1980s and the recent past', *National Westminster Bank Quarterly Review*, May, pp. 2–16.

Williams, N. (1979) 'The definition of shopper types as an aid in the analysis of spatial consumer behaviour', *Tijdschrift voor Economische en Sociale Geografie*, **70**, 157–163.

Williams, R. (1976) *Keywords: a Vocabulary of Culture and Society*, Fontana, London.

Williams, R. (1981) *Culture*, Fontana, London.

Willis, N. (1989) 'A worker's right to train', *National Westminster Bank Quarterly Review*, February, pp. 13–21.

Wilson, A. G. (1983) 'A generalised and unified approach to the modelling of service–supply structures', Working Paper 352, School of Geography, University of Leeds.

Wilson, A. G. (1988) 'Store and shopping centre location and size: a review of British research and practice', in Wrigley, N. (ed) *Store Choice, Store Location and Market Analysis*, Routledge, London, pp. 160–186.

Wrigley, N. (1980) 'An approach to the modelling of shop choice patterns: An exploratory analysis of purchasing patterns in a British city', in Herbert, D. T. and Johnston, R. J. (eds) *Geography and the Urban Environment* Vol. 3, Wiley, Chichester, pp. 44–85.

Wrigley, N. (1985) *Categorical Data Analysis for Geographers and Environmental Scientists*, Longman, London.

Wrigley, N. (1988) 'Retail restructuring and retail analysis', in Wrigley, N. (ed) *Store Choice, Store Location and Market Analysis*, Routledge, London, pp. 3–34.

Wrigley, N. (ed). (1988) *Store Choice, Store Location and Market Analysis*, Routledge, London.

Wrigley, N. and Dunn, R. J. (1984a) 'Stochastic panel data models of urban shopping behaviour: 1 Purchasing at individual stores in a single city', *Environment and Planning A*, **16**, 629–650.

Wrigley, N. and Dunn, R. J. (1984b) 'Stochastic panel data models of urban shopping behaviour: 2 Multistore purchasing patterns and the Dirichlet model', *Environment and Planning A*, **16**, 759–778.

Wrigley, N. and Dunn, R. J. (1984c) 'Stochastic panel data models of urban shopping behaviour: 3 The interaction of store choice and brand choice', *Environment and Planning A*, **16**, 1221–1236.

Wrigley, N. and Dunn, R. J. (1985) 'Stochastic panel data models of urban shopping behaviour: 4 Incorporating independent variables into the NBD and Dirichlet models', *Environment and Planning A*, **17**, 319–331.

Index